Global Finance in the New Century

Also by Libby Assassi and Duncan Wigan

GLOBAL REGULATION: Managing Crises after the Imperial Turn (*co-editors with K. van-der-Pijl*)

Global Finance in the New Century

Beyond Deregulation

Edited by Libby Assassi, Anastasia Nesvetailova and
Duncan Wigan

First published 2007 by
PALGRAVE MACMILLAN
Houndmills, Basingstoke, Hampshire RG21 6XS and
175 Fifth Avenue, New York, N.Y. 10010
Companies and representatives throughout the world

PALGRAVE MACMILLAN is the global academic imprint of the Palgrave Macmillan division of St. Martin's Press, LLC and of Palgrave Macmillan Ltd. Macmillan® is a registered trademark in the United States, United Kingdom and other countries. Palgrave is a registered trademark in the European Union and other countries.

ISBN 13: 978–0–230–00687–4   hardback
ISBN 10: 0–230–00687–6   hardback

This book is printed on paper suitable for recycling and made from fully managed and sustained forest sources.

A catalogue record for this book is available from the British Library.

Library of Congress Cataloging-in-Publication Data

Global finance in the new century : beyond deregulation / edited by
  Libby Assassi, Anastasia Nesvetailova and Duncan Wigan.
      p. cm.
  Includes bibliographical references and index.
  ISBN-13: 978–0–230–00687–4 (cloth)
  ISBN-10: 0–230–00687–6 (cloth)
    1. Financial institutions–Deregulation. 2. Globalization–Economic
  aspects. 3. International economic relations. I. Assassi, Libby.
  II. Nesvetailova, Anastasia. III. Wigan, Duncan, 1970–

  HG173.G633 2007
  332′.042–dc22   2006047188

10 9 8 7 6 5 4 3 2 1
16 15 14 13 12 11 10 09 08 07

Printed and bound in Great Britain by
Antony Rowe Ltd, Chippenham and Eastbourne

Contents

Acknowledgements   vii

List of Figures and Tables   viii

List of Contributors   ix

Chapter 1   Global Finance in the New Century: Deregulation and
             Beyond   1
             Libby Assassi, Anastasia Nesvetailova and Duncan Wigan

Part I   The Political Economy of Precision   11

Chapter 2   Globalisation, Efficient Markets, and Arbitrage   13
             Donald Mackenzie

Chapter 3   Financial Derivatives: Bubble or Anchor?   25
             Dick Bryan and Mike Rafferty

Chapter 4   Offshore Financial Centres, Hot Money and Hedge
             Funds: A Network Analysis of International Capital
             Flows   38
             Nick Coates and Mike Rafferty

Chapter 5   Who Do Derivatives Markets Serve? Rhetoric Versus
             Reality   55
             Sasha Breger

Part II   The Popularisation of Finance   71

Chapter 6   The Quiet Panic about Financial Illiteracy   74
             Julie Froud, Adam Leaver, Karel Williams, Wei Zhang

Chapter 7   The Feminisation of Pensions? Gender, Political
             Economy and Defined Contribution Pensions   89
             Mary Condon

Chapter 8   The Alchemy of Banks: The Consumer Credit Industry
             After Deregulation   102
             Johnna Montgomerie

Chapter 9   Central Europe in the EU Financial Embrace   113
             Or Raviv

Chapter 10   Finance and Management in the Dynamics of Social
             Change: Contrasting Two Trajectories – United States
             and France   127
             Gérard Duménil and Dominique Lévy

Part III   Embedding Deregulated Finance   149

Chapter 11   Monetarism in the US: The Development of New
             Forms of Institutional Control Over Banks and
             Financial Markets   151
             Martijn Konings

Chapter 12   The Political Economy of Post-Soviet Offshorisation 166
             Kirill Haiduk

Chapter 13   Tax, Subsidies and Profits: Business and the Modern
             State   177
             Ronen Palan and Richard Murphy

Chapter 14   Financial Regulation and the War on Terror   193
             Marieke de Goede

Chapter 15   Redesigning Financial Regulation   207
             Avinash Persaud and John Nugée

Bibliography   220

Index   248

Acknowledgements

The volume is comprised of papers drawn from the international conference, 'After Deregulation: Finance in the 21st Century', held at the University of Sussex on 26–28 May 2005, and organised by the Centre for Global Political Economy (CGPE). The editors want to thank the ESRC, our colleagues at the Warwick Centre for the Study of Globalisation and Regionalisation (CSGR), and the British Academy for their generous support of the conference. The papers reflect the high quality of participation, and are selected for their original contribution to a thematically cohesive and balanced collection. All chapters have been rewritten for publication. While reserving our particular gratitude for the work of the contributors, we are extremely grateful to all the participants at the conference. Our most sincere gratitude goes to the editorial and production team at Palgrave for their hard work and cooperation in this project.

Libby Assassi, Anastasia Nesvetailova and Duncan Wigan

List of Figures and Tables

Figures

Figure 4.1   Securitisation and Cross-Border Lending   46
Figure 4.2   Hub Analysis of IPI for Top 15 Countries by Total Asset,
             2002   48
Figure 4.3   Hub Analysis of OFCs' Role in International Capital
             Flows   49
Figure 4.4   Intra-OFC Total Assets, 2002   51
Figure 10.1 The Share of Financial Incomes in the Total Income of
             Households: US and France   129
Figure 10.2 Share in the Total Income of all Households of the
             1% of Households with Larger Incomes: US,
             Total Income and its Components   130
Figure 10.3 Ratio of the Average Wage in the 99–100
             Income Fractile to the Average Wage in the 0–90
             Fractile: US and France   132
Figure 12.1 Distribution of Foreign Investment in Russia in 2003   168

Tables

Table 5.1   Wheat farms, bushels produced, 2002   62
Table 5.2   Corn farms, bushels produced, 2002   62
Table 5.3   Monthly volume for commodity futures in Chicago,
             2004   64
Table 5.4   Open interest on commodity futures, 2002–4   65
Table 6.1   Number of countries offering selected financial
             education initiatives   88
Table 6.2   Responses by socio-economic group to the question
             'If you were to put £2000 on deposit at 4% for two years,
             what interest would you expect to receive at the end of the
             two years? Would it be around ....'   88
Table 12.1   Deposit Dollarisation Ratio in selected CIS countries,
             1993–2001   168
Table 13.1   Asset life assumption in Vodafone's 2003 accounts   189
Table 13.2   US companies with nil tax bills   190
Table 13.3   Accounting conventions   191

List of Contributors

Dr Libby Assassi, Department of International Relations, University of Sussex, UK

Dr Anastasia Nesvetailova, Department of International Relations, University of Sussex, UK

Duncan Wigan, Department of International Relations, University of Sussex, UK

Professor Donald Mackenzie, School of Political and Social Studies, University of Edinburgh, UK

Dr Dick Bryan, University of Sydney, Australia

Dr Mike Rafferty, Graduate School of Business, University of Wollongong, Australia

Dr Nick Coates, University of Western Sydney, Australia and Senior Policy Officer Financial Services, Australian Consumers' Association, Australia

Sasha Breger, Graduate School of International Studies, University of Denver, USA

Dr Julie Froud, Manchester Business School, University of Manchester, UK

Dr Adam Leaver, Manchester Business School, University of Manchester, UK

Professor Karel Williams, Centre for Research on Socio-Cultural Change, University of Manchester, UK

Wei Zhang, Manchester Business School, UK

Professor Mary Condon, Osgoode Law School, York University, Canada

Johnna Montgomerie, Department of International Relations, University of Sussex, UK

Or Raviv, Department of International Relations, University of Sussex, UK

Professor Gérard Duménil, MODEM-CNRS, Université de Paris X-Nanterre, France

Dominique Lévy, CEPREMAP-ENS, Paris, France

Martijn Konings, York University, Canada

Kiryl Haiduk, International Relations and European Studies Department, Central European University, Budapest, Hungary

Professor Ronen Palan, Department of International Relations, University of Sussex, UK

Richard Murphy, Director, Tax Research LLP, UK

Dr Marieke de Goede, Faculty of Humanities, University of Amsterdam, Netherlands

John Nugée, Director, State Street Global Advisors Ltd

Professor Avinash Persaud, Intelligence Capital, London

1
Global Finance in the New Century: Deregulation and Beyond

Libby Assassi, Anastasia Nesvetailova and Duncan Wigan

Over the course of the past quarter of a century, finance has been subject to an accelerated process of change and innovation. Regulatory transformations of its institutional basis, spectacular product innovation, and burgeoning volumes of financial assets have arisen in combination with a radical restructuring of the international political economy (IPE) in the name of neoliberal globalisation. This integrated process has generated a renewed concern with the operations and consequences of a rapidly globalising financial sphere. In the context of an unprecedented and precariously indebted US economy, global finance has been reinvented as both the engine and Achilles' heel of a fragile and volatile social constellation. One key characteristic of the global financial system is now widely recognised to be its complexity and obscurity, which few are able to penetrate.

This volume seeks to unravel this complexity, examining various institutional foundations and social manifestations of financial deregulation, to identify and illuminate those mechanisms that can be accorded a degree of novelty or peculiar volition at the outset of the new century. The instability of the system and the social risks associated with it are rising rapidly to the top of the agenda of global governance. The speed with which financial crises hit the regions of Asia, Latin America and Russia was disconcerting. Heightened financial instability has been equally evident in the corporate sphere of advanced capitalist countries. Paradoxically, however, this wave of financial volatility, proximately driven by financial innovation, appears to have reinforced two diametrically opposing opinions. On the one hand, pessimists envisage recession, deflation and possibly, depression, looming over the entire world economy (Bonner and Wiggin 2005; Krugman 2000; Warburton 2000). On the other hand, optimists point to the remarkable resilience of global financial markets in the face of recent shocks associated with raw materials price volatility, political upheavals, asset bubbles, terrorism and global imbalances (Greenspan 2002, 2005a, b; IMF 2005: 1).

Only time will show which of the two camps is right. Instead of adjudicating between these opposing arguments, this volume seeks to transcend this orthodox dichotomy. By examining the inner constitution of global finance, we address the question of how financial power works in the contemporary political economy. This focus is based on the contention that at the beginning of the 21st century and in the wake of a sustained period of deregulation, finance has taken on new forms and propensities that demand specific attention. To date, critical political economy has viewed the complexities of financial innovation, regulation and related social reorganisation through a radical prism. Typically, this angle emphasises the politics within consequences, at the expense of the politics of the inner constitution of contemporary finance. We do not disavow the underlying drive to arrive at a sociopolitical evaluation of seemingly arcane and increasingly important economic processes, but assert that such an understanding lacks authority and compulsion if the mechanics of global finance are left out of the picture.

Taking the themes of financial expansion, deregulation, reintermediation, governance and instability liberally, this collection of essays reflects on the emergent character of a deregulated credit system as at once a social, cultural and a political economic entity. Themes of money and finance have become well rehearsed in IPE, political science, sociology, human geography and other social disciplines. Over the past 10 years, social scientists have sought to carve out an analysis of finance that would constitute a comprehensive alternative to the dominant Efficient Market Hypothesis (EMH) and revisionist behavioural approaches. Here, the discipline of IPE has been at the forefront of critical research in finance, focusing on the issues conventionally overlooked by orthodox finance studies, such as inequality, poverty, international imbalances and sociopolitical outcomes of the deepening 'financialisation' of capitalism in societies across the globe. Altogether, this now rich IPE literature on finance has substantially advanced our understandings of the post-Bretton Woods financial revolution. In particular, recent writings have addressed the role that international money and credit have played in reconfiguring power structures in the global economy, and the challenges that globalising financial markets present to world economic stability, national and international policy makers, economic institutions in the developed and developing world, and ordinary people in everyday life (for example, Bello *et al.* 2000; Cerny 1993; Strange 1997, 1998; Germain 1997; Helleiner 1994; Palan 2003; Scholte and Schnable 2002; Soederberg 2005).

At the same time, IPE literature has often centred on the state as its key area of investigation, implicitly separating the concepts of power and capital accumulation (Nitzan and Bichler 2000: 67–9). These studies have been chiefly concerned with either the proximate problems of international financial control and regulation, or with the implications of financial globalisation for national and regional political autonomy. Moreover, the analysis of recent crises and financial scandals benefits from a momentary illumination of the financial world, but tends to occlude a conception of finance as a social process which struggles to inscribe its politics in technique and apparatus. Thus, IPE's focus on polar outcomes of financial processes tends to implicitly reproduce the liberal conception of finance as rightly approached with an incremental problem solving logic, and leaves hidden their underlying mechanics.

This book aims to address these concerns in a two-fold manner. First, it aims to deepen our understanding of the complex processes and mechanisms of financial expansion and reorganisation which, as the essays contend, in many ways define an era of liberalised and unfettered capitalism. Second, the volume shows how these processes and mechanisms are articulated within contested and ongoing transformations in the global political economy. Recognising a theoretical and political imperative for an interdisciplinary social analysis of finance, the book brings together perspectives from political economy, finance, accountancy, law and sociology to develop a nuanced appreciation of financial deregulation and its consequences. In this, the volume engages with the complexity of finance driven processes today and fills the gap that has emerged in mainstream economic and IPE approaches to finance.

Our chosen focus on how financial power works does not reflect the often narrow, functional and technical concerns of financial economics, but in contrast, results from the conviction that the historical and political character of deregulated finance cannot be discerned without accounting for its complex operation and rapid evolution. We believe that the attempt to abstract the social in this way will not only enrich critical scholarship in the social sciences, but will add weight to the social significance of heterodox research in finance and facilitate an interdisciplinary dialogue within the academia and beyond. We therefore propose a vision of 'global finance after deregulation', wherein continued expansion and political consequences are being inscribed in its apparently technical apparatus across diverse spheres.

An anatomy of deregulation

Critically revisiting conventional views on global finance, this book rests upon an acknowledgment of financialisation as a main pillar of neoliberal globalisation (Aglietta and Breton 2001; Boyer 2000; Cerny 1993; Drucker 1986; Duménil and Levy 2001). Indeed, 'financialisation' has become one of the most prominent and contentious debates surrounding the post-Bretton Woods evolution of the world economy. On the one hand, much evidence today suggests that the overblown financial sector deprives the economic system of the funds necessary for real, long-term productive engagements. Financial markets are awash with funds, while the growth of the traditional economy of production and exchange is at its lowest point since the 'golden age' of the 1950–60s (for example, Brenner 2000, 2001). This polarity, many analysts maintain, is what defines the fragility and deep-rooted crisis tendency of global capitalism. On the other hand, economic historians object to such claims, mainly on two grounds. First, they argue that there is nothing particularly novel about the domineering position of finance today, because credit and the financial sphere have always driven capitalism at peaks of the business cycle. Accordingly, the current financial explosion eventually would lead to a reorganisation of capitalism at a new, more advanced, level of development. Second, some political economists also claim that the aggressive polarising of finance and production is conceptually invalid; that the two spheres are intrinsically linked to each other and thus cannot be separated even in principle. In this view, the ascendance of finance today simply reflects a new, informational phase of capitalist development, something that is often understood as the 'new economy'.

In the process of capital accumulation, the relationship between the real and financial economy has always been marked by the duality of interdependence and separation. On the one hand, there is a clear historic trend towards a growing integration of finance and industry (Germain 1997: 127; Guttman 1994: 41). On the other hand, this historical symbiosis is fast being superseded by evolutions in global finance. Banks and non-bank financial institutions increasingly seek fluid and adjustable alternatives, which insulate them from the constraints of industry. Disintermediation and financial innovation, particularly in derivatives and structured products, have generated a situation wherein the risks arising from the uncertainties of inflated capital markets are less easily identified and located. Indeed, it would seem that financial innovation and deregulation may have reduced the risks facing individual institutions while effecting burgeoning risk origination. The value of the global financial stock has risen from US$12 trillion in 1980 to US$138 trillion today, and is expected to grow to US$200 trillion by 2010 (McKinsey 2006: 12).

Since the early 1970s, the financial superstructure has been depicted as evolving on top of the world economy and most of its national units. Back in 1986 Peter Drucker, analysing the changed world economy, identified three fundamental characteristics of the post-Bretton Woods era. First, he argued that the primary products economy had become 'uncoupled' from the industrial economy. Second, in the industrial economy itself, production had become 'uncoupled' from employment. Third, he noted that capital movements rather than trade had become the driving force of the world economy. While the financial and real economy had not quite become uncoupled, he admitted the link between them had become loose and worse, unpredictable. The most significant transformation for Drucker was the changed relation between the symbolic economy of capital movements, exchange rates and credit flows, and the real economy of the flow of goods and services:

> ... in the world economy of today, the 'real' economy of goods and services and the 'symbol' economy of money, credit and capital are no longer bound tightly to each other; they are, indeed, moving further and further apart (Drucker 1986: 783).

Thus an emergence of the financial sphere as the flywheel of global capitalism, Drucker noted, is both the most visible and the least understood change of the post-Bretton Woods era. With financial revolution progressing further, Drucker's insights were received sympathetically across a wide audience. Most analyses highlighting the unprecedented position of the financial sphere under post-Fordism tend to associate it with the emergence of a qualitatively new system of economic organisation and production, a new 'knowledge' or 'information' economy, internet technologies, the inflated capitalisation of intangible assets, post-modern consumption, and so on:

> The physical economy is shrinking. If the industrial era was characterised by the amassing of physical capital and property, the new era prizes intangible forms of power bound up in bundles of information and intellectual assets. The fact is, physical assets, which for so long were a measure of wealth in the industrial world, are dematerializing (Rifkin 2000: 12).

Perhaps a more subtle understanding would conceive of the relationship between finance and the real economy to be one subject to continuing rearticulation, rather than intermittent bouts of disjuncture and integration. Indeed, not everyone agrees that the post-1973 explosion of financial operations is a qualitatively new feature of the capitalist system that necessarily embodies the crisis tendencies rooted in the disjuncture between finance and real economies. Mainstream economists, for instance, insist that the mathematical sophistication of modern financial theory allows asset prices to be closely matched to underlying economic fundamentals. Yet the very mathematical models used to price financial derivatives introduce a further element of risk. These models, typically derived from the physical sciences, are based on the characteristics of the probability distributions of random movements. In reality, however, the cumulative outcome of the financial 'beauty contest'[1] are massive concentrations of extreme price swings. The mathematical models tend to price events at the extremes incorrectly. Moreover, ignoring the historical developments in economics, a firm and prior belief in the power of mathematics, and the tendency to stay away from controversial social issues, isolate the social fabric and resonance of financial markets from modern financial economics (Eatwell and Taylor 2000: 103; Saber 1999: 15–16).

This obfuscation of the social is further grounded in a discourse and culture of risk (Green 2000). On the back of a series of theoretical innovations proximately originating in Markowitz's portfolio theory (1952) and culminating in a string of Nobel laureates recently awarded to financial economists, risk discourse and practices have expunged the social basis and historical ramifications of finance from the picture. The audience, impotent in the face of the mathematical density and institutional complexity of contemporary financial markets, consequently must passively accept the claims to parsimony embedded in financial theory. Risk and risk management should be understood as a political technology, and an appreciation of the power of the markets must incorporate this discursive foreclosure (de Goede 2004). It may also be that the fabrication of finance as risk is propelling a profound transformation of ownership and money itself.

The centrality of this risk discourse has been compounded through the experience of recent speculative asset bubbles. Intriguingly, some argue that speculative bubbles are really not so bad (Eatwell 2004). Investor euphoria and booms tend to coincide with periods of innovation that make society better off. In such a view, the dotcom bubble was more of an example of messy Schumpeterian creative destruction exploring a new technology than a structural problem (*The Economist* 16 May 2002: 18). The potential of e-commerce has been explored faster and more thoroughly thanks to the American open market system; hence the bubble represented a fast-forwarding of experimentation.

Keynes (1936) himself made the crucial distinction between speculation – for the activity of forecasting the psychology of the market – and enterprise – for the activity of forecasting the prospective yield of assets over their whole life. Investment in securities by 'those who deal on the stock exchange' and the 'professional investor' embodies the private goal to out-guess the market. By contrast, enterprise investment by the 'professional entrepreneur' involves the purchase of physical equipment or construction of infrastructure after forecasting 'the prospective yield of assets over their whole life' and thereby meeting the Keynesian 'social object' of 'defeating the dark forces of time and ignorance which envelop our future' (in Froud *et al.* 2001: 70). In the famous passage, Keynes linked this distinction to the performance of investment and the real economy:

> Speculators may do no harm as bubbles on a steady stream of enterprise. But the position is serious when enterprise becomes the bubble on a whirlpool of speculation. When the capital development of a country becomes a by-product of the activities of the casino, the job is likely to be ill-done; this is a scarcely avoidable outcome of our having successfully organised 'liquid' investment markets. It is usually agreed that

casinos should, in the public interest, be inaccessible and expensive (Keynes 1936: 376).

On the one hand, it is tempting to view recent outbreaks of financial instability as a prelude to a global financial crash that would make 1929 look like a footnote in history. On the other hand, circumstances appear radically different this time around. The financial instruments issued by firms are held today by governments, households and a broad array of financial institutions. Consumer, corporate, and governmental debts are intimately intertwined, permitting the simultaneous regulation of both consumption and production magnitudes through speculative and fictitious financing. The network of these liabilities can complicate cash flows and offer routes that can dampen and amplify the effect of the debt structure on the performance of the economy (Minsky 1991). While this volume observes the speculative tendency of today's finance, it must be acknowledged that this is more of a reorientation than a repolarisation.

On a global scale, it is also much easier to deploy strategies of temporal, geographical and sectoral reorganisation under the umbrella of financial markets. Innovation within the financial system appears to have been a necessary prerequisite to overcoming the general rigidities as well as the distinctive temporal, geographical, and even geopolitical crisis into which Fordism had fallen by the late 1960s (Harvey 1990: 189, 195–6).

Overall, there has been a sea change in the organisation and operation of capitalism since 1973, even though the underlying logic of capitalist accumulation and its crisis tendencies remain the same. Bello *et al.* (2000: 4) identify several core characteristics of the new financial capitalism:

- Having become overexposed in the developing world in the 1970s and early 1980s, the commercial banks pulled back from international lending; other major players emerged as key conduits for cross-border flows of capital.
- 'Securitisation', or the transfer of capital via the sale of stocks and bonds, eclipsed the role of banks and conventional lending for raising funds.
- There was an explosion of both old and new activities and instruments, such as arbitrage, leverage and derivative trading techniques.
- Many of these transactions are difficult to monitor because they are executed 'over the counter': not *via* the floor of an exchange but among a few parties by telephone and computers, often as 'off-balance sheet' transactions.

There is no doubt that this sea change brings with it new and more acute dangers of financial, economic, and sociopolitical crises. Innovations continue to proliferate, most recently in the form of credit derivatives, and political economic transformations are likely to become even more significant. Indeed, though well established, the IT revolution is not over yet. Capitalising on continual technological deepening and popularisation of capital market intermediation, the finance sector seems positioned for a sustained phase of innovation-driven expansion.

At the same time, this phase does in no way guarantee that the emergent role of finance in the global political economy will provide any basis of cohesion or progress. The late 1990s saw the emergence and burst of a huge technology and financial bubble. The drivers of such bubbles are the emergence of new and potentially transforming technology, a climate of relatively easy credit conditions, investor euphoria and consumer optimism, an efficient credit supply mechanism, and the 'suspension of normal valuation and other assessment criteria'. At present, investors, companies and economies are struggling with the aftermath of what might have been the biggest of such bubbles. The 2001 collapse of the dotcom bubble, and the corporate scandals that coincided with it, show that more information does not ensure better knowledge, transparency or efficiency.

Indeed, today's financial system is saturated with information of ostensibly unprecedented precision and scope. This has been appreciated and endorsed by mainstream financial elites as the key foundation of perfecting markets, and as the basis for optimal risk allocation. However to us, the paradox of privatised finance and perfecting markets is that the very innovations that herald market completion, generate novel and acute threats to systemic stability. While for *the individual* market participant derivatives and structured finance have added the semblance of security to their market profiles, these innovations have rendered *the system* increasingly opaque. At the aggregate level, they accentuate the threat of systemic instability and contagion. Furthermore, it appears that the recent series of regulatory experiments targeting systemic risk fail to account for the intersubjective and regulatory construction of market homogeneity at junctures when the system most requires a diversity of trades and policy responses (see Persaud and Nugée, Chapter 15).

The question, for us, is whether today's finance can resolve this danger through a continued process of institutional and product innovation. The fluidity and flexibility of financial structures and the disproportionately important role of the social context in the operation of finance, means that the design and position of financial systems reflect conditions specific to each capitalist entity. In this respect, the on-going shifts in the architecture of global financial governance suggest that in the light of recent crises, policy makers have significantly adjusted their perceptions about the operation of today's finance, partially incorporating lessons of capital market failures, break-downs in liquidity, and the ambiguity of accounting into the new macro-prudential regulatory framework. Securitisation and structured finance, as well as the continued emergence of new derivative and retail products, may help explain why the global financial system has been able to absorb individual shocks, most recently in the guise of the ratings down-grades of General Motors or the implosion of Parmalat.

At the same time however, financial innovation continues to drive much of the global financial system beyond the gaze and expertise of existing regulatory bodies. As the history of financial cycles and bubbles suggests, when faced with distress or a shock, these young industries may well prove to be the amplifiers of financial contagion and systemic crisis. While there is little policy consensus on the sustainability of current financial stability, our point is that the process of financial innovation, accelerated by deregulation and liberalisation policies, provides finance with a 'security blanket'. It does so by constructing new opportunities for credit expansion, and effectively, privatising systemic risk. These developments are enmeshed in substantive social reorganisations and regulatory transformations which, as yet, have not been tested. As depicted by earlier studies, the process of financial innovation contains the danger of systemic risk, yet it provides market participants, policy makers and increasingly, individual consumers, with tools to ostensibly navigate an increasingly opaque, complex, and fragile financial configuration. It should be noted that this round of financial innovation may be just beginning. This volume attempts to grasp a nascent transformation.

The structure of the book reflects the above concerns. Part I addresses the most technologically developed and mathematically sophisticated aspects of contemporary finance. While necessarily incomplete, it constitutes an attempt to outline and repoliticise aspects of the 'new international financial architecture' which we accord a key and novel volitional force. Crucially, this political architecture is not identified merely in terms of states and webs of governance, but within the markets and products themselves. The four chapters here represent the shared contention that the political economy of finance must invert its default method of conceptualising 'from the outside in.'

Part II emphasises the often implicit social basis of a broad process of financialisation. It shows that the promise of efficiency and parsimony embodied in markets and products appears shallow when confronted with the reality on the ground. The expansion and evolution of finance rest upon, and reformulate, a fragile social constellation, which ultimately may not be sufficiently cohesive or robust to sustain the process.

The final part elaborates upon the tension between regulatory efforts and policies, and the institutional reproduction of financial dynamics. This reproduction, identified across temporally and functionally diverse settings, is counterpoised with a dominant risk-based approach in emergent forms of global financial governance. As Part III of the volume contends, current regulatory initiatives and revisions are still unable to grasp the inner mechanisms driving financial innovation, and are likely to fail to resolve the contradictions of globalising finance. In elucidating the political economy of financial precision, popularisation, regulation and institutionalisation, this volume strikes a blow against the politics of contemporary finance and its sociology of exploitation. The book is constructed so that each part is preceded by a more detailed introduction.

Notes

1   The metaphor belongs to Keynes. He believed that investment is like a newspaper competition in which readers had to pick out the six prettiest faces from a hundred photographs. The crucial point was that the contestant had to choose those faces that he thought the other competitors would find prettiest rather than the ones he would find most attractive. Investing was similarly, in his view, about forecasting how others would behave (Ben-Ami 2001: 43).

Part I
The Political Economy of Precision

A prolonged period of financial innovation and deepening has generated an historically novel international financial architecture to navigate, and add a semblance of stability to, the socio-political and geographic discontinuities of a burgeoning financial system. Highly mathematised and sophisticated techniques of financial engineering, a correspondingly arcane discourse and the very complexity of today's financial flows have led to a situation wherein critical political economy can seem locked out. Complexity and obscurity contribute to the difficulty of reimagining the inherent politics of contemporary finance. By collectively reorientating the critical gaze to the inner workings of global finance the chapters in this section constitute a basis upon which this reimagining may occur. The identification and elucidation of the new International financial architecture depart from this point.

Donald Mackenzie in 'Globalisation, Efficient Markets, and Arbitrage' opens the volume by breaking down the barriers to social enquiry embodied in the 'Efficient Market Hypothesis'. These barriers are based upon the constructed efficacy of modern financial theory and its enforcement through arbitrage. If arbitrage and its generative grammar can be revealed as contingent and contested then, 'the Parsonian separation between economics and sociology' can be redressed. Drawing on the case of Long-Term Capital Management (LTCM), Mackenzie shows that arbitrage, far from always being a risk free exercise conducted by atomistic economic agents, is embedded in a 'Granovetterian' sociology which propelled 'arbitrage flight' and unravelled a 'superportfolio' imitating LTCM's positions in the wider market. Crucially, Mackenzie concludes that the capacity to insulate 'the economic' from 'the social' is limited, and the dynamics of globalisation cannot be understood without acknowledgement of its 'micro social' character.

Dick Bryan and Mike Rafferty apply a wider lens to investigate the historic character of a 'system of derivatives'. In 'Financial Derivatives: Bubble or Anchor?' the authors assert that the IPE of financial derivatives must transcend a one-dimensional emphasis on speculation, bubbles and crashes to scrutinise instead their systemic function in 'anchoring the global financial system'. Derivatives lock temporary stability into financial markets and provide some systematic link between the spheres of production and finance. Through a two-fold process of 'binding' and 'blending', the system of derivatives renders 'any financial asset, in any form, and across time and space, commensurable with any other asset in any form at any place and over time.' This process of commensuration results in heightened competition between different forms of capital, with the consequence that labour in close parallel to the Gold Standard, 'provides the primary flexibility that permits stability in asset values'.

Third, 'Offshore Financial Centres, Hot Money and Hedge Funds: A Network Analysis of International Capital Flows' presents the first geographical network analysis of the IMF's Co-ordinated Portfolio Investment Survey. Nick Coates and Mike Rafferty redress the inadequacies of existing categories of national economic analysis in reconceptualising the nature and cartography of portfolio investment, its relationship with Offshore Financial Centres (OFCs), and their novel role in contemporary finance. While the activities of hedge funds and the role of the offshore in contemporary crises have attracted significant attention, this scrutiny has so far been hampered by data limitations. The paper explains the continuing significance of OFCs despite pressures towards regulatory harmonisation. OFCs are both 'critical mediation points acting as hubs for hybrid securities issues' and places where portfolio investment flows are 'funnelled and recycled into all sorts of capital flow.' The chapter breaks down these flows to map them on a bilateral basis, revealing the continued predominance of the main global financial centres and novel role of OFCs as sites for the production of securities themselves.

To identify 'who derivatives markets serve' Sasha Breger investigates the seedbed of a 'system of derivatives' in US agricultural futures markets. The argument that a private system of risk management, 'is a boon for the economy insofar as risks can be diversified, diffused, and better matched to those best able to bear them' is gauged against the technical and sociopolitical obstacles to farmers benefiting from derivatives. Disaggregating farms by size and output Breger shows, the standard wheat and corn futures contract size, the absence of liquidity in the mini-futures market, and small farmers' lack of the 'informational capabilities necessary to navigate futures markets' mitigate against the fulfilment of the promise of private risk management. In so doing, the chapter demonstrates that governments cannot abrogate responsibility for risk management, and iterates that the political economy of contemporary finance is apparent in its mechanics and operations.

2
Globalisation, Efficient Markets, and Arbitrage

Donald Mackenzie

It is not on every bookstall, but the Bank of England's *Financial Stability Review* is useful reading for students of global finance.[1] Every six months, the Bank's experts calmly and intelligently interrogate, from the viewpoint of financial stability, the current 'conjuncture and outlook' internationally and domestically. The mix of elements they invoke, changes. The December 2005 issue, for example, cites items such as the foreign exchange reserves of China and South Korea (p. 20), recent hurricanes in the US (p. 22), forthcoming elections in Latin America (p. 25), and overseas ownership of Turkish government bonds (p. 95). It includes warnings not to let the apparent calm in the financial markets feed over-optimism and complacency, noting that 'Risk transfer markets have made the ultimate destination of ... risks more opaque' (p. 20). There is even an acknowledgement of the need to understand markets 'as something more than the positions of atomistic agents' (p. 77).

What each issue of *Financial Stability Review* always contains is arrays of apparently abstruse data from the global markets, especially the markets for derivatives. (A financial derivative is a contract or security the value of which depends on the price of another 'underlying' asset or on the level of an index or interest rate.) My favourite graph from the *Review* – it appears regularly – gives the history of loans by banks that report to the Bank for International Settlements to the non-bank private sector in the Cayman Islands. The most recent total (Bank of England December 2004: 57 chart 2.22) was nearly US$350 billion. The recipients of most of this apparent largesse are not the long-standing residents of George Town, West Bay, Bodden Town, Little Cayman or Cayman Brac. The Caribbean UK Crown colony is the legal domicile of choice of many of the world's hedge funds, and the borrowing (typically collateralised by securities such as G7 government bonds) reflects the exigencies of the funds' financial strategies – which is why the Bank of England monitors it.

To read the *Financial Stability Review* is to enter a world of 'zero-coupon yields', 'credit default swaps', 'ten-year government bond yield implied volatility', 'banks' Tier 1 capital ratios', 'corporate income gearing', 'Euro-denominated investment-grade credit spreads', and the like. It is a daunting world that only a limited number of social scientists outside of financial economics have done more than peep into. Yet if we want to understand global finance we have no choice but to enter that world.

This chapter suggests one way into *Financial Stability Review*'s world: the study of arbitrage. Arbitrage is trading that exploits price discrepancies. There is a sense in which arbitrage is as old as markets: a merchant who buys goods cheap in one place, and sells the same goods dear in another, is in a sense an arbitrageur. By linking markets, arbitrage has always been an engine of globalisation. That the yen, the pound sterling, or particular grades of standardised, easily transportable commodities such as gold or oil have at any given moment essentially a unique global dollar wholesale price is, at root, a matter enforced by arbitrage. Yet arbitrage has attracted only very limited sociological attention: see, in particular, Beunza and Stark (2004) and Miyazaki (2003).

Arbitrage is one of the main activities of Grand Cayman's hedge funds – and, indeed, of many of the banks which lend to them. To be sure, a hedge fund would not prosper if it relied on classic forms of arbitrage such as exploitation of discrepancies in currencies' mutual exchange rates (Cetina *et al.* 2002b), or differences between the price of gold in New York and in Saudi Arabia. These discrepancies are now small – that is part of what globalisation means – and they do not yield substantial arbitrage profits. But the vanishing opportunities in these 'spot' markets (markets for immediate or near-immediate delivery) have been replaced by new opportunities in the burgeoning markets for financial derivatives, the markets that provide *Financial Stability Review* with much of its data. By June 2005, derivatives contracts totalling almost US$329 trillion were outstanding worldwide, a sum equivalent to around $51,000 for every human being on earth.[2]

If arbitrage in spot markets enforces globalisation in the sense of the tendency to globally uniform wholesale prices, so arbitrage in derivatives markets tends to enforce *theoretical* pricing. Arbitrage is *the* key mechanism in financial economics: it is the mechanism most often invoked to argue that patterns of empirical prices must correspond to theoretical models, and also the main grounds for arguing that financial markets can be 'efficient' even in the presence of investor irrationality. If economics does not simply describe pre-existing markets, but *performs* those markets (the thesis of Callon 1998), then arbitrage is crucial terrain in which to investigate performativity.

Consider the theory of the pricing of derivatives. The area's 'stem papers' were by Fischer Black, Myron Scholes, and Robert C. Merton (Black and Scholes 1973; Merton 1973), work that in 1997 won Nobel Prizes for Scholes and Merton (Black died in 1995). The problem they solved was the pricing of options: derivatives that give their holder the right, but do not oblige him or her, to buy ('call') – or, in an alternative form of the contract, to sell ('put') – a given asset at a given price, at (or up to) a given expiry date. Assuming a 'perfect market' (frictionless trading, and so on), Black, Scholes and Merton showed that an option on an asset such as stock could be replicated exactly by a continuously-adjusted portfolio of the asset and cash, so long as the returns on the asset followed the by-then-standard model of a log-normal random walk in continuous time, in which changes in the logarithms of prices follow the normal distribution. If the price of the option diverges from the cost of the replicating portfolio, arbitrageurs will buy the cheaper of the two and short sell (borrow, sell, and later repurchase and return) the dearer, and they will continue to do so until equality is restored.

More generally, their analyses suggested a methodology for the rational pricing and hedging of derivatives in general: identify the replicating portfolio of more basic assets (if it exists), and use its cost to work out the arbitrage-imposed price of the derivative, and (if desired) to hedge its risks. The resultant theoretical work is critical to the global markets: one could not plausibly trade US$329 trillion of derivatives without the guide to pricing and hedging that the theory provides.

Arbitrage is also crucial to the justification of the overall notion of 'market efficiency'. The hypothesis that the financial markets are 'efficient' – that prices in them 'always "fully reflect" available information' (Fama 1970: 383) – forms the central divide in social science approaches to markets, for example, separating orthodox economics (which adheres to it) from psychologically-based 'behavioural finance', which sees market participants as less than entirely rational and subject to systematic biases, normally psychological in their nature. The theoretical impact of the efficient market hypothesis goes far beyond economics, stretching for example, into human geography (Clark 2000: 4). Its proponents see it as the best-established in economics, indeed in the entire social sciences.

The efficient market hypothesis has had practical as well as theoretical effects. For example, derivatives trading had often been the object of suspicion – even of legal bans – because it looked dangerously like gambling on price movements. The argument that derivatives could contribute to market efficiency was key to the gradual removal in the 1970s and 1980s of legal and regulatory constraints (MacKenzie and Millo 2003).

What might make financial markets efficient? If all investors were taken to be rational and well-informed, it would be difficult to explain high volumes of trading. If prices already incorporate all publicly available information, why should rational investors trade once they have diversified their portfolios satisfactorily and made any sales needed to raise cash? 'Noise trading', said options theorist Fischer Black (1986: 531), 'provides the essential missing ingredient. Noise trading is trading on noise as if it were information. People who trade on noise are willing to trade even though from an objective point of view they would be better off not trading. Perhaps they think the noise they are trading on is information. Or perhaps they just like to trade'.

Invocation of arbitrage, however, allows one to defend the hypothesis of market efficiency even while conceding the existence of noise trading and other departures from rationality:

> Neoclassical finance is a theory of sharks [arbitrageurs] and not a theory of rational homo economicus... In liquid securities markets... profit opportunities bring about infinite discrepancies between demand and supply. Well financed arbitrageurs spot these opportunities, pile on, and by their actions they close aberrant price differentials.... Rational finance has stripped the assumptions [about the behaviour of investors] down to only those required to support efficient markets and the absence of arbitrage, and has worked very hard to rid the field of its sensitivity to the psychological vagaries of investors (Ross 2001: 4).

There is a sense, then, in which arbitrageurs are the border guards, in economic practice, of one of the social sciences' crucial boundaries: the boundary between 'the economic' and 'the social'. Arbitrage is the main mechanism posited as preventing 'social' or 'psychological' phenomena, like fads and fashions or investors' excessive enthusiasms and fears, shaping 'economic' phenomena like patterns of prices in financial markets. To the extent that arbitrage can do this, it justifies not just the efficient market hypothesis but also the Parsonian notion of 'the economy' as a differentiated subsystem (Parsons and Smelser 1956), and thus the Parsonian separation of economics and sociology.

Long-Term Capital Management[3]

A parameter that *Financial Stability Review* regularly monitors is 'implied volatility'. It is an entirely theoretical term, calculated by running an option pricing model such as Black-Scholes 'backwards' to discover the volatility (extent of price fluctuations) of the underlying asset consistent with the price of options on the asset. The implied volatilities of major stock market indices, for example, are a good guide to the markets' nervousness: in normal, stable conditions, implied volatility is below 20%, while 30% suggests major uncertainty, and 40% serious crisis. Amongst *Financial Stability Review*'s charts is the six-month implied volatility of the single most important stockmarket index, the S&P 500, from 1988 to 2003 (Bank of England 2004: 19, chart 9). The graph begins in the aftermath of the 1987 stockmarket crash at around 30%, dips, spikes upward with the 1991 Gulf War and early 1990s recession, dips again, then spikes upward several times during the crises of the late 1990s and early 2000s. The graph's peak, at nearly 40%, was in the autumn of 1998, in a crisis that began in Russia but then flowed into the heartlands of the Western economy. At its centre was the hedge fund Long-Term Capital Management (LTCM). In the light of the above discussion of arbitrage, it is of some interest that LTCM was probably the most large scale of all the world's arbitrageurs.

LTCM was a hedge fund legally domiciled in the Cayman Islands but managed from offices in Greenwich, Connecticut, in London and in Tokyo. It was set up in 1993 by John Meriwether, previously head of Salomon Brothers' famously successful bond arbitrage desk. Meriwether recruited to LTCM an impressive team of experienced traders and specialists in mathematical finance: amongst the partners who ran LTCM were options theorists Merton and Scholes. LTCM largely avoided risky 'emerging markets', preferring well-established ones such as those in government bonds of the leading industrial nations, in options and other derivatives, and in certain very restricted categories of stock. It eschewed speculation based upon intuitive hunches, seeking price discrepancies around which to base arbitrage strategies, and generally it constructed its positions so as to be insulated from overall market movements and interest rate changes.

Using theoretical reasoning, extensive practical experience, and databases of prices, LTCM would search for assets the prices of which ought to be closely related, which should over the long run converge (and in some cases *had* to do so), but which for contingent reasons had diverged: perhaps one was temporarily somewhat easier to trade than the other, or perhaps institutions had a particular need for one rather than the other. The fund would then buy the underpriced asset, and borrow and sell the overpriced asset (or take positions equivalent to these by use of derivatives). The close relation between the assets would mean that overall market changes would affect the prices of each nearly equally, and eventual convergence between their prices would create a small but very low-risk profit for LTCM. By 'levering' its own capital – performing arbitrage using borrowed funds – LTCM could turn this small profit into a larger one; this also increased risk, but only to modest levels. The partnership knew perfectly well that over the short and medium-term prices might diverge further, but the probabilities and the consequences of them doing so were carefully calculated by a statistical 'value-at-risk' model, which measures the potential losses from adverse market movements (by the late 1990s such models were used by most of the sophisticated institutional participants in the financial markets).

Pace standard accounts of LTCM, however, the firm did not simply assume that past price patterns would continue into the future, nor did it display an uncritical attitude to its risk model. Observed volatilities and correlations were increased by explicitly judgement-based 'safety factors' to take account of possible changes in markets and of possible deficiencies in the model. A consequence of this conservatism was that LTCM's risk model predicted risk levels that were substantially higher than those actually experienced (until the 1998 crisis). The model predicted an annual volatility of net asset value of 14.5% while the actual volatility was 11%, and both figures were considerably less than the 20% volatility that investors in LTCM had been warned to expect. LTCM also 'stress-tested' its trading positions to gauge the effect on them of extreme events not captured by standard statistical models or by recent historical experience, events such as the failure of European economic and monetary union or stock exchanges crashing by a third in a day.

Was what LTCM did 'arbitrage'? It certainly described its activities as such, and in so doing it was simply adopting the standard financial market usage of the term. However, LTCM needed to deploy some of its own capital as a foundation for borrowing, and its need to apply a 'value-at-risk' model makes clear that its trading involved risk (albeit apparently modest risk), when in orthodox finance theory arbitrage is defined as being profitable trading that demands no net capital and is entirely free from risk. An economist might therefore respond that a case study of LTCM's risky trading has no bearing on our understanding of arbitrage as a riskless theoretical mechanism.

However, amongst LTCM's major positions (and one of the two most serious sources of loss) was a close real-world counterpart of the arbitrage that imposes Black-Scholes option pricing, the central theorem of the economics of derivatives. This position, taken on in 1997, responded to a price discrepancy developing in the market for stock index options with long expirations. As the name suggests, an index option is one in which the underlying 'asset' is the level of a broad stockmarket index. Increasingly, banks and insurers in Europe and the US were selling investors products with returns linked to gains in equity indices but also a guaranteed 'floor' to losses. Long expiry options were attractive to the vendors of such products as a means of hedging their risk, but such options were in short supply.

By 1997, the demand for long expiry options had pushed the volatilities implied by their prices to levels that seemed to bear little relation to the volatilities of the underlying indices. Five-year options on the S&P 500 index, for example, were selling at implied volatilities of 22% per annum and higher, when the volatility of the index itself had for several years fluctuated between 10% and 13%, and the implied volatilities of shorter-term options were also at that point less than 20% per annum (Perold 1999: A7–A8). LTCM therefore sold large quantities of five-year index options, while hedging the risks involved with index futures and sometimes short expiry options. In effect, then, LTCM responded to the discrepancy in prices by selling the options and 'buying' and adjusting the replicating portfolio. Complications such as the use of short expiry options aside, LTCM was conducting the arbitrage that option theory posits.

The event that triggered LTCM's crisis was the decision of the Russian government on 17 August 1998 to default on rouble-denominated bonds and in effect to devalue the rouble while permitting Russian banks temporarily not to honour foreign exchange forward contracts. LTCM had only a minor exposure to Russia, but the precise form of Russia's actions caused significant losses to other hedge funds and western banks. A 'flight-to-quality' took place, as a host of institutions sought to liquidate investments that were seen as difficult to sell and potentially higher risk, and to replace them with lower risk, more liquid alternatives. Because LTCM's arbitrage generally involved holding the former, and short selling the latter, the result was a substantial market movement against the fund.

Crucially, however, the 'flight-to-quality' was amplified, overlain, and in some instances contradicted by a much more specific process. LTCM's very success had encouraged imitation: other hedge funds and leading banks had either taken up similar arbitrage trading or devoted more capital to it. In aggregate, this body of arbitrageurs held positions broadly similar to those of LTCM, but some of them had greater exposure to Russia than LTCM had. To cover losses incurred there, they had to liquidate other positions similar to LTCM's. As the prices of these moved against the arbitrageurs, they found themselves having to liquidate further positions, thus further worsening price pressures, and so on. What one might call the arbitrage 'superportfolio' (the aggregate of arbitrage positions similar to LTCM's) began to unravel. For example, falls in the prices of assets held by holders of the superportfolio did not lead to an equilibrating reduction in attempts to sell (as it would in most situations of economic exchange), but to a destabilising increase in those attempts.

Widespread efforts to liquidate broadly similar positions in roughly the same set of markets, in a situation in which those who might otherwise have bought such assets were also trying to sell, intensified the adverse market movements that were the initial problem. Crucially, these various processes unravelling the arbitrage superportfolio led to greatly enhanced correlations between what historically had been only loosely related markets, across which risk had seemed to be reduced by diversification.

LTCM's loss in August 1998 was a -10.5σ event on the firm's risk model, and a -14σ event in terms of the actual previous price movements: both have probabilities that are vanishingly small. As 'spreads' (the difference between prices of related assets) widened, and thus arbitrage opportunities grew more attractive, arbitrageurs did not move into the market, narrowing spreads and restoring 'normality'. Instead, potential arbitrageurs continued to flee, widening spreads and intensifying the problems of those who remained, such as LTCM.

LTCM was constructed so robustly that these problems, though they caused major losses, were not fatal. In September 1998 though, LTCM's difficulties became public. On 2 September, Meriwether sent a private fax to LTCM's investors describing the fund's August results and seeking to raise further capital to exploit what (quite reasonably) he described as attractive arbitrage opportunities. The fax was posted almost immediately on the Internet and seems to have been read as evidence of desperation. The nervousness of the markets crystallised as fear of LTCM's failure. Almost no one could be persuaded to buy, at any reasonable price, an asset that LTCM was known or believed to hold, because of the concern that the markets were about to be saturated by a fire sale of the fund's positions. In addition, LTCM's counterparties – the banks and other institutions that had taken the other side of its trades – protected themselves as much as possible against LTCM's failure by a mechanism that seems to have sealed the fund's fate. LTCM had constructed its trades so that solid collateral, typically government bonds, moved backwards and forwards between it and its counterparties as market prices moved in favour of one or the other. Under normal circumstances, when market prices were unequivocal, it was an eminently sensible way of controlling risk. But in the fear-chilled, illiquid markets of September 1998, prices lost their character as external facts. LTCM's counterparties marked against LTCM: that is, they chose prices that were prices that were predicated on LTCM's failure. That minimised the consequences for their balance sheets of LTCM's failure by getting hold of as much of the firm's collateral as possible, but made that failure inevitable by draining the firm of its remaining capital.

LTCM's failure thus became a 'self-fulfilling prophecy', in the sense of the phrase's coiner, social theorist and sociologist of science Robert K. Merton, father of the finance theorist. The process was a little more complicated than his simple 'sociological parable', a run on a bank, in which investors fear that a bank will fail, seek to withdraw their deposits, and in so doing cause the bank to fail (Merton 1949). The structure of the process was, however, identical.

Conclusion

How does the case of LTCM bear upon our understanding of arbitrage? Three key points emerge. First, arbitrage has a 'Granovetterian' sociology (see Granovetter 1985): it is an activity conducted not by anonymous, atomistic economic agents, but by people who are often personally known to each other. Second, included in the possible forms of interaction amongst these people is imitation. Third, for this and other reasons the capacity of arbitrage to insulate 'the economic' from 'the social' is limited: indeed, the interweaving of the economic and the social is too intimate to be captured even by notions of imperfect insulation.

Arbitrageurs often know each other and are affected by each other. That they in that sense form a 'community' (a term some of them use to describe themselves) does not imply harmony. For example, one interviewee at LTCM suggested that it had generated resentment amongst Wall Street investment banks (for instance by pressing hard to reduce 'haircuts')[4] and that others 'were, I think, jealous of the money we made'. Resentment and jealousy, however, are indicative that those involved were not atomistic individuals, but mutually aware and mutually susceptible. Positive forms of this awareness and susceptibility were also evident: I was struck, especially during the process of getting interviewees' permission for quotation in MacKenzie (2003), how concerned they often were not to give offence to each other.

These issues of mutual susceptibility are not matters incidental to the 'real business' of arbitrage, because that real business depends upon mundane forms of social interaction with personally-known others. To perform its arbitrages, Meriwether's group at Salomon and LTCM had to borrow money (*via* what participants call 'repo', in which the borrowed money is used to buy securities that are pledged as collateral for the loan, a process that for example, probably comprises a good part of the lending to the Cayman Islands) and also had to borrow bonds (for short sale). Others of its trades, for example, an arbitrage involving the stock of the two legally distinct corporations making up the Royal Dutch/Shell group, were implemented by arranging 'total return swaps' with banks. All these were wholly legitimate activities, but getting the best possible repo, bond borrowing and swap terms was critical to the profitability of arbitrage exploiting small price discrepancies. It could be done better amongst personally-known people, rather than by anonymous commercial interaction. In the 1970s and 1980s, for example, the Salomon group invested considerable amounts of time in building relations with the then relatively lowly employees in charge of repo.

The emphasis in the commentary on LTCM on its use of mathematical models has diverted attention from the extent to which its arbitrage activities (and also those of its predecessor group at Salomon) rested upon a Granovetterian, institutional understanding of the embedded nature of markets. Meriwether's reputation as a trader in the US bond market rested less on mathematical sophistication than on his understanding of matters like who held which bonds and why. As Salomon's arbitrage activities began to expand overseas, Meriwether realised that it would not be enough simply to send Americans, however sophisticated mathematically, into overseas markets. Typically, Salomon would seek to recruit people brought up overseas, train them in New York, and then send them back to the markets in the countries in which they were raised. (The head of Salomon's trading activities in Japan, the legendarily-successful Shigeru Miyojin, for example, is an instance.) The price discrepancies that were of interest to arbitrage would typically be the result of complicated tax and regulatory issues that an outsider would find hard to comprehend in sufficient depth.

The Granovetterian sociology of market embedding is thus evident in the normal practice of arbitrage. In the case of LTCM, however, that embedding took the form of imitation. The underlying general point is well-known to economic sociology: White (1981 and 2001) and Fligstein (1996 and 2001). Firms do not choose courses of action in isolation: they monitor each other, and make inferences about the uncertain situation they face by noting the success or failure of others' strategies. When this leads to diversity – to firms selecting different strategies and coming to occupy different 'niches' – a stable market structure can result. But if firms imitate, each choosing the same strategy, disastrous 'crowding' (*q.v.* White 2001: 139–44) occurs. That is what took place in global arbitrage in the 1990s.

Imitation led to extreme price movements and to disaster because of a third feature of the sociology of arbitrage: the possibility of 'arbitrage flight', the risk that arbitrage positions that, if held for long enough, have to be profitable may nevertheless have to be abandoned (see Shleifer and Vishny 1997). This possibility was expressed to me, separately, by two partners in LTCM who used the same analogy. Suppose they had been vouchsafed a little peek into the future: that they knew with certainty that at a particular point in time the stock price of company X would be zero. (These conversations took place during the dot.com bubble.) Could they, they asked, make money with certainty from this knowledge? Their question was rhetorical: they knew the answer was no. Of course, they could sell the stock short. *If* they could hold their position until the price became zero, they could indeed profit handsomely. But an unpredicted rise in price in the interim could still exhaust their capital and thus force them to liquidate at a loss. That was in essence what happened to LTCM. Many of the positions in its 1998 portfolio have gone on to converge profitably precisely as expected, but it was driven to the brink of bankruptcy before that took place.

The consequence of this third feature of arbitrage, when conjoined with the second feature (imitation), is that arbitrage's capacity to insulate 'the economic' from 'the social' is limited. (Were it not for the risk of imitation-induced correlation, the dangers posed by arbitrage flight could be reduced greatly by holding a large portfolio of diverse arbitrage positions.) This constitutes, for example, a limit on the performativity of economics: under some circumstances, arbitrage may be unable to eliminate what economic theory regards as pricing discrepancies. Ultimately, the metaphor of 'insulation', the Parsonian view of the economy as a differentiated subsystem (Parsons and Smelser 1956), is itself inadequate. The financial markets are not an imperfectly insulated sphere of economic rationality, but a sphere in which the 'economic' and the 'social' interweave seamlessly. In respect to arbitrage, the key risks may be 'social' risks from patterns of interaction within the financial markets, rather than shocks from the 'real economy' or from events outside the markets. That, at least, is what seems to be suggested by the contrast between 17 August 1998 (the Russian default, a relatively minor economic event, triggered a disastrous unravelling of a global superportfolio) and 11 September 2001. That far more dramatic external shock failed to trigger dangerous internal social processes: the flight of arbitrage capital after 1998 meant that by 2001 there was no equivalent superportfolio.

The interweaving of the 'economic' and the 'social' is not simply a matter of analytical interest. It affects the technical practices of risk management, because imitation of the kind evident in 1998 can undermine the protection flowing from the basic precept of such management: diversification. The most important way in which LTCM's successor, JWM Partners, has altered its predecessor's risk model to take account of the lessons of 1998 is that all the fund's positions, however well diversified geographically and unrelated in asset type, are now assumed to have correlations of 1.0 'to the worst event'. In an extreme crisis, it is assumed that diversification may fail completely: all the fund's positions may move in lock-step and adversely, even those positions in which the fund holds assets that should rise in relative value in a crisis.

How does the sociology of arbitrage bear upon the efficient market hypothesis? It suggests a nuanced response: that the hypothesis may be neither wholly correct (as its more enthusiastic adherents sometimes seem to suggest) nor wholly mistaken, and that a variety of factors – institutional, technological, political, even cultural – may impact upon the extent of its correctness. One can imagine, for example, that the result of broadening the empirical sociology of arbitrage beyond the single case discussed here might be a continuum of types of arbitrage. At one end might be cases (such as arbitrage of discrepancies in currency spot rates) in which arbitrage in practice comes close to resembling its theoretical definition as free of risk and demanding no capital. At the other end might be cases where arbitrage is so risky, and so demanding of capital, that it is effectively impossible. Trying to make arbitrage profits by short selling stock that is subject to an apparent 'bubble' might be an instance. Even if one knows with certainty that it *is* a 'bubble' and that it will be corrected (and certainty in this respect is seldom realistic), the chance of bankruptcy before the correction happens is too high. Most forms of arbitrage – arbitrage of discrepancies in option prices, for example – might then fall between the two extremes.

If that continuum were found to be as hypothesised, it would suggest that there will be features of financial markets (such as relations between the prices of similar assets) where efficiency will prevail, and features where it will not: prolonged, dangerous 'bubbles' in entire sectors will be possible. As Paul Samuelson, one of the founders of efficient market theory, suggests, markets may be efficient in a 'micro' sense, because discrepancies in relative value can be arbitraged away, but not in a 'macro' sense, because 'bubbles' that affect the prices of all similar assets cannot be arbitraged (Samuelson 2001).

Finally, what of globalisation? One way of expressing the forms currently taken by the inextricable interweaving of the 'economic' and the 'social' is *via* Knorr Cetina and Bruegger's notion of 'global microstructure'. The financial markets are now global in their reach, but interaction within them still takes the form of 'patterns of relatedness and coordination that are ... microsocial in character and that assemble and link global domains' (Knorr Cetina and Bruegger 2002a: 907). In a sense, it was globalisation that undid LTCM. Of course, no one was more aware than LTCM's principals of globalisation *as a general process* (they had surfed globalisation's wave, so to speak), but what caught them unawares were the consequences of the global microstructure created by imitative arbitrage. What happened in August and September 1998 was not simply that international markets fell in concert (that would have had little effect on LTCM), but that very particular phenomena, which at the level of economic 'fundamentals' were quite unrelated, suddenly started to move in close to lock-step: 'swap spreads', the precise shape of government bond 'yield curves', the behaviour of equity pairs such as Royal Dutch/Shell, and so on. LTCM's wide diversification, both internationally and across asset classes, which it had thought kept aggregate risk at acceptably modest levels, failed to do so, because of the effects of a global microstructure.

After September 1998, the linkages created by this particular microstructure dissipated as arbitrage capital withdrew from the markets. Such linkages are probably returning, albeit most likely in different forms, for example, *via* the flood of capital into hedge funds after the evaporation in 2000–1 of the dot.com boom. That fluctuation of linkage may be precisely the point. Globalisation is not a once-and-for-all event, not a unidirectional process, not something that can be stopped, but a composite of a myriad microstructures, often contradictory, waxing and waning.

Notes

1. The author's work in social studies of finance is being supported by a professorial fellowship awarded by the UK Economic and Social Research Council (RES-051-27-0062) and earlier was supported by DIRC, the Interdisciplinary Research Collaboration on the Dependability of Computer-Based Systems (UK Engineering and Physical Sciences Research Council grant GR/N13999). This chapter draws upon MacKenzie (2000, 2003, 2005a&b, and forthcoming).
2. Data from the Bank for International Settlements http://www.bis.org, accessed 3 January 2006.
3. This section draws on an earlier treatment of LTCM (MacKenzie 2000), but that treatment is in some respects in error: see MacKenzie (2003) for a fuller discussion than possible here, and for details of sources.
4. In a 'repo', discussed below, the 'haircut' is the amount by which the money lent is less than the market value of the securities.

3
Financial Derivatives: Bubble or Anchor?

Dick Bryan and Mike Rafferty

A discussion of financial derivatives is now starting to emerge within international political economy (IPE). The widely held view here is noticeably radical – more so than many other dominant positions within IPE. This view involves financial markets being seen as casinos and a source of instability and derivatives in particular being widely condemned as tools of gambling, and catalysts of speculative bubbles and crashes. Accordingly, they are said to undermine the 'real economy' and national policy sovereignty.

There is substance to these critiques, and there is a growing list of notable cases of financial disasters associated with derivatives. But this is a somewhat one dimensional interpretation. To describe them as tools of speculation and as destabilising may be true, but it is not enough. It is important to understand more about what derivatives do, why financial derivatives came into widespread use so rapidly from the early 1980s, and what role they are now playing in global capital accumulation.

The problem in posing these questions is that we immediately hit a number of obstacles. Not only is there need to move beyond the radical view of derivatives as tools of speculation; there is also a widespread approach, in economics as well as IPE, which juxtaposes finance and the 'real' economy. In this conception, any role of finance that is not passive, simply facilitating investment and production, is characterised as distortionary. Accordingly, in engaging the question of the role of derivatives in accumulation, it is important to frame the question in such a way that pejorative conceptions based around speculation and distortion are not seen to pre-judge the analysis.

The proposition developed in this paper is that, as well as being central to speculative bubbles, derivatives are performing a role in anchoring the global financial system. In making this claim, there is no suggestion that derivatives have replaced central banks or international money institutions on the one hand, nor the hegemonic status of the US dollar on the other. On the contrary, both the role of regulatory institutions and the viability of the dollar are predicated on derivatives playing this anchoring role. In a world of unpredictable and sometimes volatile financial markets, derivatives provide a material basis to finance. Not only do they provide a means to lock in temporary stability into financial markets but, more importantly, they provide some systematic link between the spheres of production and finance.

In developing this argument, there is no real need to elaborate the popular connection of derivatives to speculation.[1] Our alternative (or additional) perspective is the focus here. It can be developed by presenting a comparison of the way in which gold anchored the global financial system in the late 19th century and derivatives anchor global finance in the 21st century. The argument, in short, is that both gold and derivatives in their respective epochs have been used as a discipline on labour, and it is labour market flexibility which, in both periods, has provided a material basis to international finance.

The proposition

This is, to be sure, not a conventional sort of argument, so here we start with a simple analogy with the measurement of time, albeit one that does not yet feature the labour issue. In the 19th century, money and time were measured in terms of fixed point anchors. Money was measured by one unit (gold) and all national moneys adjusted to ensure their value with respect to gold. Time was measured at one point (Greenwich) and all other positions on the globe determined their time by reference to Greenwich. In the 21st century, time at different locations is measured not by reference to a fixed point, but by global positioning system (GPS) technology, in which multiple satellites compute their relative positions and, *via* their interactive calculations, can specify the exact time at all individual positions. These satellites can be thought of as a floating anchor for time measurement. Like GPS satellites, derivatives make up multiple (indeed thousands) of different means to 'compute' the *relative values* of a vast range of different financial assets, including currencies, and thereby specify the value of each of them. Hence the system of derivatives may be posed, by analogy, as a floating anchor.

Notice here that the focus is on the 'system of derivatives' as expressing more than the sum of individual derivative contracts. To pose this notion of a system, we need to think of derivatives outside the conventional approach, based in risk management. In that conception, with a focus on the strategies of the individual trader, derivatives are posed as a way in which traders (on behalf of others or themselves) shift risks about price movements of a particular asset without having to trade the asset itself. This framework can explain how corporations will use derivative trading to hedge exposure to unwanted price movements. And, of course, the converse of hedging is speculation: corporations (and individuals) can take on exposure to price movements as well as lay it off, and derivatives provide a cheap means to leverage speculative exposure to price movements. Hence the assertion that derivatives promote speculation is the counter to the conventional wisdom that derivatives are part of efficient risk management.

But this way of framing derivatives is focused on individual trades: whether any particular derivative transaction is about laying off or taking on risk. Insofar as it is impossible for an observer to really know (one would need an intimate knowledge of the existing risk profile of a trader to know whether any individual transaction increases or decreases exposure to asset price movements) there is something also rhetorical about the juxtaposition.

But as a system of derivatives, we are observing something about the aggregate of transactions rather than the risk impacts of individual transactions. As a system, these multiple trillion dollars a day of derivative transactions serve to give perpetual measure of the value of each asset compared with the value of all other assets at any place and across time. This is the analogy with the vast number of computations that occur between satellites in the operation of GPS. We will get to how derivatives perform this valuation shortly.

How, then, do we see this proposition linking to labour? The argument contends that the Gold Standard of the late 19th century relied on wage flexibility in response to changing national price levels associated with the net inflow or outflow of gold in trade surplus or deficit countries respectively. Once wages became more inflexible in the 20th century, gold could no longer anchor the financial system.

The 21st century has parallels here, though it is not identical. The critical parallel is that labour, through financial derivatives, provides a basis for financial stability. In essence, the argument here is that derivative markets are performative in the sense associated with Callon (1998): they are not only part of the price formation of financial assets (including national currencies), they drive the behaviour (management) of those assets as those who control them seek to achieve rates of return that will be validated in derivative markets. Here, too, labour is central as the means by which rates of return on financial assets can be managed.

To build this argument, we consider a brief and, of course, partial history of global financial regimes, starting with the Gold Standard.

The Gold Standard

The growth in international transactions in the late 19th century occurred with a stable global currency and hence rigid exchange rates between nations: the classical Gold Standard. Significantly, this stability in exchange rates came not because nation states actively managed currency values (there were virtually no central banks as such), but because the state's role was restricted merely to the provision of a dependable physical currency. On this basis, nations used gold as their currency base and trade imbalances between nations could be settled in gold transfers. Indeed, the need for convertibility of national money units into gold ensured that nation states would not meddle with money too much for fear of creating domestic price instability.

Accordingly, under the Gold Standard, high levels of international capital mobility – in some terms proportionately even higher than they are today – were directly compatible with stable exchange rates (and hence a stable global financial system) because national economic policy subordinated domestic agendas to the stability of the national monetary unit *vis-à-vis* gold. Perhaps 'subordinated' is the wrong term, for it suggests a conscious policy stance. As Eichengreen (1998) emphasises, in the major trading and capital exporting countries, there was simply no significant political aspiration or institutional basis for using state policy to pursue social agendas that might result in price instability. Labour did not have the vote, union membership was low, unemployment was not an issue for states and the state ran minimal social and military expenditures (Eichengreen and Iversen (1999). Moreover, with capital internationally mobile, labour was treated politically as the one component of production costs that was largely national.[2] Wages, employment rates and working class living standards were made flexible on a national scale, and were readily changed to ensure domestic price and hence exchange rate stability.

The Gold Standard was, therefore, not compatible with the rise of the labour movement, and its demands for social expenditure and policies to avert unemployment (deCecco 1984) – a reality that became stark with the growing social expectations of state expenditure after World War I.[3]

In monetary policy terms, the nation state could not reconcile the domestic demands on finance with the global requirements of currency convertibility to gold. The rise of national central banks in the early 20th century was associated with growing state management of the domestic monetary system. Gold was progressively withdrawn from circulation as national money and held as reserves by the central bank. National monetary liquidity thereby became a central bank policy issue (and subject to policy conjecture) rather than an automatic (that is, market-driven) product of international gold flows. Policy conjecture generated scope for speculative positions on exchange rate adjustments because there were not automatic, predictable, market-driven adjustments. Global financial markets became increasingly volatile, and nation states sought, through a variety of mechanisms, to insulate themselves from that volatility (Nurkse 1944).

The question of whether labour market flexibility should underpin the global financial system became central to Keynes' critique of Churchill's desire for Britain to return to the Gold Standard in 1925. Keynes argued, in essence, that the defence of social standards of living was incompatible with the 'economic juggernaut' that was the Gold Standard:

> We stand midway between two theories of economic society. The one theory maintains that wages should be fixed by reference to what is 'fair' and 'reasonable' as between classes. The other theory – the theory of the economic juggernaut – is that wages should be settled by economic pressure, otherwise called 'hard facts', and that our vast machine should crash along, with regard only to its equilibrium as a whole, and without attention to the chance consequences of the journey to individual groups. The gold standard, with its dependence on pure chance, its faith in the 'automatic adjustments', and its general regardlessness of social detail, is an essential emblem and idol of those who sit in the top tier of the machine (Keynes 1925: 218).

The rise of the national economy as a discrete object of national policy, to provide social supports and infrastructure, gradually became incompatible with privileging the stability and scale of the global financial system. Over the next two decades, the Gold Standard steadily unravelled and capital controls (restrictions on the cross-border movement of credit and investment) were increasingly introduced by nation states to provide national insulation from the vicissitudes of globally-volatile markets.

The Bretton Woods Agreement

With the reconstitution of the global financial system at the end of World War II, the new goal was economic certainty and stability and the asserted agenda was nation-centred accumulation, with open international trade gradually being reestablished. This regime allowed for the privileging of social programmes, 'fair' wages and full employment, funded by high (and managed) levels of economic growth. In simple terms, we can associate this with the rise of 'Keynesianism'.[4]

The Bretton Woods Agreement, negotiated principally between Britain and the United States, set the terms for the post-war international financial system which operated from 1944 to 1971. As with the Gold Standard, exchange rates would be stable. The global anchor for the global financial system was nominally still gold, albeit now in a symbolic, 'demonetised' function. The Bretton Woods Agreement saw the US dollar as the global trading currency, with the dollar convertible to gold at a fixed rate of US\$35 per ounce. Other national currencies fixed to the US dollar. Within this dollar/gold anchor, the strength of the global financial system lay more in the power of the US economy and the US state within the global economy than in the gold held in the vaults at Fort Knox.

Global financial stability would come not so much because the international flow of money to settle international debts guaranteed stability, but because nation states would target stability as a national policy objective. In the face of external imbalance, the state could invoke fiscal and monetary policies to adjust international financial flows in support of 'its' exchange rate. If the imbalance became irretrievable, the state (except perhaps the US state) could announce an adjusted currency value, but such an announcement reflected badly on national policy makers.

Hence, in this regime, wages were not to be subordinated to the agenda of currency stability: instead, international capital flows were to be the swing mechanism of national economic adjustment (Helleiner 1994). Keynes had urged that, '...control over capital movements, both inward and outward, should be a permanent feature of the postwar system' (Keynes 1943: 185).

There is significant debate about the contradictions that lay within the Bretton Woods Agreement and its capacity to provide a long-term anchor to the global financial system. In essence, its viability rested on two premises that were problematic. The first was the capacity of the US dollar to maintain its status of being as 'good as gold'. It could not. This has been attributed both to inappropriate state economic policy within the US that generated inflation (especially associated with the funding of the Vietnam War) and/or to inherent problems of national currencies having to serve both nation-specific and global requirements.

The second premise, more critical for our analysis, was whether national capital controls would effectively manage the cross-border flows of capital, and subordinate them to the requirements of national economic management. They did not. The constraints on capital movement were being challenged from the outset – indeed, the Agreement itself reflected the challenge.[5] Steadily during the 1950s and especially the 1960s virtually all central banks undertook regulatory reforms that enabled the growth of international financial and investment flows and saw the opening up of global wholesale (merchant) banking, associated particularly with the development of multinational firms and Eurofinance markets in the 1950s (Eichengreen and Sussman 2000: 31).

The particular ways in which these historical developments served to undermine and ultimately lead to the demise of the Bretton Woods Agreement in 1971 need not detain us here.[6] Suffice to say that capital controls were no longer securing stable international finance, and the policy pressure started to move towards wages. The manifestation of concurrent inflation and unemployment along with volatile exchange rates in the early 1970s saw a widespread shift in policy away from the national controls that were the hallmark of post-war 'Keynesianism', and towards a greater mobility of capital and a policy regime now often characterised as 'neoliberalism'.

The shift to floating exchange rates

A new financial regime did not emerge, fully developed, from the crisis of the Bretton Woods Agreement. The new regime that would eventually develop was not an invention of the regulatory authorities awaiting its time, or even of inspired market processes, but had to evolve out of market and nation state practices, to meet the needs of those who use these markets. Accordingly, the decade and some after 1971 lacked financial stability and a clear global financial framework.

The global financial system that emerged in the 1980s was clearly predicated on the ideological vision of a free international flow of finance and floating exchange rates. It is an era that has involved huge growth in international capital flows and financial transactions. These have been widely described and evaluated. But, for our study, one critical issue warrants focus: what became the anchor of the global financial system? In the 19th century globalisation, the anchor was gold, but the current era has no explicit equivalent.

It is important to pause before giving an answer, for the question needs clarification. For the neoclassical economists who provided the theoretical arguments for floating exchange rates and free capital mobility, the question would appear nonsensical. There is no need for an anchor (indeed, the objective was precisely to detach from anchors): the free market, they argued, would provide its own stability and, what's more, it would gravitate to efficiency in resource allocation at the same time. Theories of purchasing power parity, the efficient markets hypothesis and arguments about how speculators add liquidity to markets and help them move rapidly to equilibrium were the heavy artillery in an armoury of analytical techniques to explain that a formal anchor like gold was redundant. The market does not need anchors.

Harry Johnson (1969: 208), probably the leading international monetary theorist of the 1960s and 1970s, was emphatic:

A freely flexible exchange rate would tend to remain constant so long as underlying economic conditions (including government policies) remain constant; random deviations from the equilibrium level would be limited by the activities of private speculators.

The role of labour in this new regime was integral, for the operation of these free market forces in financial markets required critically that they operate also in labour markets. The so-called Volcker shock of 1979–82 was vital to the on-going global hegemony of the US dollar and the stability of global finance generally. It is usually posed as a monetary intervention, but it was just as much a labour market one. Nixon, in terminating the role of the US dollar in the Bretton Woods system had sacrificed the global role of the dollar for domestic agendas. But Paul Volcker, as Chairman of the US Federal Reserve, sought to reverse that effect. He introduced an era of fiscal and monetary austerity (interest rate hikes, and inflation targeting), which asserted anti-inflationary policy above all other national economic policy agendas. Part of this also was an assault on organised labour, to ensure that labour costs would cease to be a source of future inflation. Indeed Volcker later contended that 'the most important single action of the administration in helping the anti-inflation fight was defeating the air traffic controllers strike' (cited in Panitch and Gindin 2004, but see also Volcker 2000).[7]

The intention (and the effect) was to sacrifice domestic growth and living standards so that a stable (that is, non-inflationary) US dollar could be asserted as the hegemonic unit of account in global money markets (Volcker and Gyohten 1992). Indeed, Volcker himself contended that the Federal Reserve's anti-inflation policy took on a 'role in stabilising expectations [that] was once the function of the gold standard, the doctrine of annual balanced budget, and fixed exchange rates' (quoted in Johnson 1998: 178).[8]

Of course, it was not usually explained to labour in those terms; nor was it rationalised by economists in those terms.[9] It has almost without exception been explained by appeal to nationalism: that *we* as a nation cannot live beyond *our* means by running fiscal deficits or importing more than *we* export; that *we* need labour market flexibility to ensure that *our* industries remain competitive and *our* economy competitive. But the result was the same: in the name of 'national competitiveness', a range of attempts were made to force labour to become the swing mechanism of national economic adjustment.[10]

The need for derivatives as anchor

Returning to Harry Johnson's statement above, we should note the embedded caveat. It suggests that the stability that was assumed to follow from market forces would not see markets gravitate towards random points of stability, but to prices that reflect 'fundamental value'. Hence as the 'fundamentals' changed, so too would the price (exchange rate). The concept of fundamental value is clear (although how it is measured is not). It implies that prices will reflect 'real' values: the value of a corporation's shares would be a direct reflection of the profitability of the corporate asset base; a nation's exchange rate would be a direct reflection of its productivity and balance of payments, and so on. Hence Johnson can be seen to be arguing that the great benefit of floating exchange rates is that they will systematically gravitate towards fundamental value.

In this sense, there was a latent anchor in the free market vision: that prices in financial markets would be a reflection of the 'real' economy. Exchange rates, therefore, would shift to reflect changes in the relative performance of national economies, and short-term deviations from this trend would be self-rectifying. This was, of course, directly compatible with the then-dominant theory of monetarism: that money should be neutral with respect to production.

The problem was that this confidently asserted theory did not work in practice. A raft of evidence over the past 25 years has shown that there is no foundation to the proposition that the prices of financial assets including exchange rates, have systematically gravitated towards 'fundamental value'.[11] The latent anchor within the argument for free markets was not working.

Herein lies the importance of financial derivatives as the 'new' anchor of global finance.[12] Beyond the discourse of hedging and speculation, derivatives in aggregate play an additional role of commensurating the value of different forms of financial assets. All the trading in derivative markets – the 'system of derivatives' we referred to earlier – serves to give a relative valuation to all sorts of financial assets, in all places and across time.

We can break this commensuration role down into two dimensions: binding and blending to explain their role in financial market commensuration:

1. *Binding:* derivatives, through options and futures, establish pricing relationships that 'bind' the future to the present or one place to another.
2. *Blending:* derivatives, especially through swaps, establish pricing relationships that readily convert between ('commensurate') different forms of assets.

In the binding role, derivatives compensate somewhat for the absence of fixed exchange rates, and stable asset prices. While current prices may be volatile, futures and options contracts permit the 'locking in' of future prices – indeed they permit degrees of locking in according to desired levels of certainty and flexibility. This does not of itself, however, draw prices towards 'fundamentals', it merely adds stability, and permits transactions 'as if' exchange rates were stable over short periods.

Similarly in their blending role derivatives do not move prices to stable equilibria – they are not an alternative means of establishing the so-called 'fundamentals' of global purchasing power (or interest rate) parity. Indeed they are predicated on the notion that there are no 'fundamentals' – all asset values have particular temporal and spatial determination, and prices are forever changing, and in unsystematic ways. It is not possible to reduce one locality to another, one time period to another or one form of capital to another; but their values can be, and are, mediated on a daily basis.

In the blending function derivatives take the attributes of a range of different asset types and put them together in the one product. There are thousands of derivative products that can combine a range of asset attributes into one product – they may combine the Nasdaq index in the US with interest rates in Japanese yen; the LIBOR with an oil price index; the price of Singapore dollar bonds in 3 months with house prices in New York. With enough of these individual packages of links, every asset form can be linked to every other asset form (and in the sense that the GPS satellites are all linked to each other). The effect of these in aggregate, as a *system of derivatives*, is to make any financial asset, in any form, and across time and space, commensurable with any other asset in any form at any place and over time: their relative values can be measured on an ongoing basis. While managing volatility may be the immediate cause of derivative growth, it is this process of commensuration which gives financial derivatives their anchoring role.

Derivatives in this sense are performative: they are not merely a reflection of what is; they systematically generate change.

Materially, in the uses to which financial assets are put, the consequence of commensuration is profound; for closely associated with commensuration is competition. In the process of commensuration, derivatives are not just reconciling relative prices, they are giving signals to the owners of assets about the relative performance of their assets. If all assets can be measured relative to the market, all corporations can be perpetually aware of how each of their assets is performing. Assets under performing relative to the market will be 'restructured' to lift their performance (which could mean being revalued, sold or made to operate more profitably). Derivatives, therefore, require financial assets to adhere to competitive norms.

Concretely, capital cannot exert an impact on the pricing of assets for markets do, in their own clumsy ways, make these determinations with some eye to future value. But it can exert influence over the income-generating capacity of some assets: those that involve the production of goods and services. Under-performing assets need to be made more profitable, or revalued. Accordingly, a focus on labour emerges, for labour – its wage relative to its productivity – is the one area where capital exerts individual discretion in the determination of asset performance and hence asset values. And this is why, with derivatives at the centre of global finance, the determination of wages and working conditions must be the domain of individual capitals, not nation states, for the primary objective is the pursuit of globally competitive financial asset prices, and in this, labour's contribution is central.

Hence, the role of labour flexibility in the era of neoliberalism is not simply to shift income from labour to capital (nor also just the associated ideological and political shifts). Indeed, that shift requires only the generalised oppression of labour, not flexibility *per se*, and it is not evident that all wages in all jobs are falling. The particularity of flexibility is that it ties wages to profit rates: it permits wages to be responsive to the needs of individual capitals to sustain asset values, and to respond to those needs quickly. Labour provides the primary flexibility that permits stability in asset values. In the process, labour is seen as integral to the system of global financial stability generally.

Clearly, there are parallels between the current era and the Gold Standard, insofar as both are periods characterised by 'globalisation' and in both, labour flexibility has been integral to stability.

But the differences should also be noted. Under the Gold Standard, labour's role as the swing mechanism was, in effect, automatic. With all countries using gold as both domestic monetary anchor and trading currency, exchange rate stability was implicit. Moreover, there were automatic domestic price adjustment mechanisms under that regime that came from cross-national gold flows to settle trade balances. Trade deficits led to an outflow of gold and falling domestic prices. Falling nominal and, *via* domestic contraction, falling real wages were the direct consequence.

Today, neither exchange rates nor wages adjust as precisely as under the classical Gold Standard. Today, exchange rate stability is by no means guaranteed, despite the anticipation of the advocates of 'deregulation', and exchange rates are sometimes quite volatile. So in contrast with the Gold Standard, exchange rates are not a systematic mechanism of national economic adjustment: countries retain current account surpluses and deficits for long periods without the exchange rate moving systematically to secure 'balance'. What constitutes acceptably stable exchange rates is therefore a more fluid notion than applied under the Gold Standard.[13]

Similarly, labour's role as the swing mechanism of national adjustment is neither as automatic nor as nation-wide as under the Gold Standard. For the latter we saw automatic wage adjustment as a more or less direct corollary of the impact of international gold flows on the national price level. Today, at least in the advanced capitalist countries, an adult electoral franchise, trade unions, wage norms and state legislation on employment conditions continue to mediate the connection between labour's living standards and the conditions of stable global capital flows (Obstfeld and Rogoff 1995: 79). Wage adjustments are not automatic.

Nonetheless, from the 1980s, there has been a universal trend for wages to be tied more closely to workplace productivity, at the same time as workplaces themselves are adjusting to engage in productivity competitiveness on a global scale. And while under the Gold Standard, adjustments were simply nation-wide, in the current era labour adjustments are also related to each particular capital's profitability.

Conclusion

There is no doubting that derivatives are associated with financial bubbles and speculation. Many criticisms of 'globalisation' and reliance on market forces have been quick to make this association.

In this paper we have developed an argument that derivatives are also an anchor to the global financial system insofar as they mediate between labour and prices in financial markets. Ours is not a suggestion that derivatives create stability – on the contrary, when the bubble and anchor roles are seen in combination, we see a most fragile kind of anchor.

But perhaps the most important point of our analysis is to identify how integral derivatives are to global capital accumulation through their anchoring function. To confront derivatives is to confront capitalism itself – its order, its system of calculation and its now-globalised relation with labour. Accordingly, there are dangers that can be seen to follow from the preoccupation with bubbles. To the extent that this concern leads to the advocacy of policies to close down the 'casino' of financial derivatives markets as a proposed antidote to financial market volatility, it is basically misconceived. The consequence is going to be not a return to Bretton Woods-like financial stability and productive growth but, more likely, its opposite.

Notes

1. Notable contributions include Kelly (1999) and LiPuma and Lee (2004).
2. Labour was indeed quite mobile in some periods of the 19th century and the evolution of the modern state can in part be associated with the need to deal with the effects of the emergence of surplus populations, including the threat of its mobility (Cowen and Shenton 1999). We are depicting labour as 'national' in our analysis, because labour was treated 'as if' it were national.
3. This is not to idealise the 'adjustment mechanism' under the Gold Standard. The price of labour, to paraphrase Keynes, was often 'sticky' downwards. As historians often remind us, attempts to make it less sticky in the nineteenth century varied, but often involved force (Thompson 1963).
4. See Radice (1998) for an excellent summary of Keynes' privileging of national over global agendas, especially in relation to money.
5. See Helleiner (1994: esp. 44–50) for a summary of the objections of New York bankers to capital controls and the pressures they brought to the Bretton Woods negotiations, including the effective influence they exerted over the US negotiator at Bretton Woods, Harry Dexter White.
6. See Bryan and Rafferty (2006) Ch. 6 for an explanation.
7. Further, Panitch and Gindin (2004) note that, on the insistence of Congress, Volcker himself represented the US state in Chrysler's bankruptcy proceedings and that it was he who negotiated with the United Auto Workers, then America's most powerful union, to secure the wage cuts and out-sourcing that the state required before granting Chrysler a bail-out loan.
8. In an interview with the American broadcasting network PBS in September 2000, Paul Volcker (2000) also said that, as Governor of the Federal Reserve, his actions were geared toward America's international responsibilities:

...[I]f we weren't strong economically, we weren't going to be able to carry out what I saw as reasonable responsibilities in the world...and if anybody was going to deal with this it was going to have to be the Federal Reserve.... One of the major factors in turning the tide on the inflationary situation was the (air traffic) controllers' strike, because here, for the first time, it wasn't really a fight about wages; it was a fight about working conditions. It was directly a wage problem, but the controllers were government employees, and the government didn't back down. And he (Reagan) stood there and said, "If you're going to go on strike, you're going to lose your job, and we'll make out without you".

That had a profound effect on the aggressiveness of labor at that time, in the midst of this inflationary problem and other economic problems. I am told that the administration pretty much took off the shelf plans that had been developed in the Carter administration, but whether the Carter administration ever would of done it is the open question. That was something of a watershed.

9. Krugman (1999) recently observed however that the US Federal Reserve a decade or so later has become more and more explicit about the role of the state in disciplining labour. He cited a speech that Fed Chairman Greenspan gave to a business lunch in 1999, where he warned that "...labor market conditions can become so tight that the rise in nominal wages will start increasingly outpacing the gains in labor productivity". Krugman interpreted this to mean that:
[W]orkers who know that jobs are plentiful will get big raises. And that, Greenspan implied, would be a very bad thing. A market economy... requires that a certain number of people who want to work be unable to find jobs so that their example will discipline the wage demands of those who are already employed. Greenspan, to his credit, tells the truth about what he does, but until now, he has done it in a way that only the cognoscenti can understand. Well, now he has said it clearly. But is America ready to hear it?

10. We have made the argument that 'national competitiveness' was used to subordinate labour to capital on a global scale elsewhere in greater detail. See Bryan (1995: Chs. 2 and 3) and, in the context of Australia, Bryan and Rafferty (1999: Chs. 3 and 4).

11. See Bryan and Rafferty (2006: Ch. 6) for a review of this literature.

12. While commodity derivatives for cotton, grains, and so on have a many thousand year history, financial derivatives only really came to prominence in the 1980s. They developed somewhat along with the growth of Eurofinance markets, as corporations and banks sought to hedge differences between the official and Euro exchange rate and interest rate. But their prominence dates from the early 1980s with the growth of financial futures and options and, especially from the 1990s, with the growth of swaps.

13. Indeed, current exchange rates are not as volatile as might appear. Standard data on volatility refer to spot prices. Exchange rate derivatives exist precisely to hedge against such volatility.

4

Offshore Financial Centres, Hot Money and Hedge Funds: A Network Analysis of International Capital Flows

Nick Coates and Mike Rafferty

1   Introduction[1]

It is now widely recognised that the increased global scale and scope of capitalist production and circulation has challenged existing categories of national economic analysis (Bryan 1995).[2] But these processes are also posing problems even for understanding the corporation as a distinct economic entity (Walker 1989).[3] Nowhere is this evidenced more starkly than in the globalisation of finance. But perhaps because of a residual disdain for the speculative, unproductive and anarchic aspects of finance, there has been a tendency for analysis to treat these as peripheral and even pathological outgrowths of contemporary globalisation. By attaching labels such as hot money, tax havens or speculative capital to these developments, there has been a tendency to shut down analysis before it even begins. There are, however, welcome signs that this is changing (see for instance Harvey 2001; Warnock and Cleaver 2002; Flandreau and Jobst 2005; Bryan and Rafferty 2006; and of course this volume). Indeed, Clark (2005) has gone so far as to suggest that: 'the global finance industry is an essential lens through which to study contemporary capitalism...'

The growth of offshore financial centres (OFCs) and hedge funds has been very challenging for researchers and policy makers. Until recently, however, researchers have been hampered from undertaking comprehensive quantitative work because of well-known data limitations. But with problems of international financial stability and prudential control becoming more acute in policy and regulatory circles, efforts have been undertaken to produce data better suited to the task of informing such policy questions.

In particular a series of events in international financial markets over the last decade, including exchange rate realignments in the European

Monetary System in 1992 following speculative attacks by global hedge funds, turbulence in world bond markets in 1994, and the Asian financial crisis of 1997, all raised issues about the potentially destabilising propensities of hedge funds and OFCs.[4] The demise of the world's largest hedge fund LTCM in late 1998, in the aftermath of the Russian financial crisis and its coordinated rescue by the US Federal Reserve, and the recent collapse of two more hedge funds, Bayou Management and Wood River Capital Management in mid to late 2005, has only underscored for many the fact that many international financial transactions may be undermining prudential regulatory scope, and even perhaps compromising the efficiency of financial markets.[5]

This paper examines the current patterns of one form of global finance, namely cross-border portfolio investment flows. It makes use of a new data set, the Coordinated Portfolio Investment Survey (hereafter CPIS), which permits better geographic analysis of those capital flows. The CPIS data provides a bilateral record of portfolio flows rather than simply a record of domestic to 'rest-of-the-world' transactions that had previously been obtained. While International Portfolio Investment (IPI) is an evolving concept that has had to be consistently revised as financial markets have integrated and innovations in financial instruments occured, the CPIS data provides us with the first opportunity to present portfolio investment flows as geographical networks, an opportunity not hitherto available to researchers depending on standard Balance of Payments accounting data. This paper uses network analysis as a way of presenting that geographical data, and provides an introductory analysis of several important features of that geographic capital flow data.

The remainder of the paper is structured as follows. Section 2 provides a discussion of the concepts used for measuring cross-border portfolio investment flows in Balance of Payments accounting. It considers the evolving concept of IPI, against a background of the evolving patterns of IPI.

Because of the importance of OFCs for international financial markets, Section 3 examines their role directly. OFCs are integral to the conceptual difficulties encountered by Balance of Payments accounting in tracking IPI that are examined in Section 2.

Section 4 presents the CPIS data as geographic networks. The dominance of OECD financial markets, particularly the US, UK and Japan is noted. However, the network analysis deployed here also reveals that OFCs are now critical mediation points in international capital markets. OFCs are now integral to the functioning of global capital markets and the hosts for hedge funds, special purpose vehicles (SPVs), and shell and brass plate companies and so on. Their presence is also part of the diversification of organisational forms by MNCs, and international investment institutions generally. OFCs are also acting as hubs for hybrid security issues, where they function effectively as a sort of 'security transfer station'.

Economically significant amounts of IPI flows are funnelled through OFCs and 'recycled' into all forms of capital flow. What may enter as long-term debt, or commodity trade, can just as easily leave as an equity holding or even a foreign exchange hedge.

Section 5 provides some concluding comments and suggested directions for further research.

2   Measuring international investment and finance

Foreign investment and finance have received considerable attention from academics and policy makers over the last two decades, as international capital flows have grown, and as national government attitudes to it have changed. But most of that attention has been directed towards Foreign Direct Investment (FDI), which is now known in the IMF Balance of Payments Manual as International Direct Investment (IDI). In part, this is due to the fact that this renewed interest has focused on the association of IDI with the 'real sector' (that IDI is thought on the one hand to contribute to expanding the capital stock and improving managerial performance, and on the other to contribute to loss of national economic control of those resources), and because it has been found that IDI is the most stable of international capital flows (Lipsey 1999).[6]

This conceptual predisposition towards direct investment flows is reflected in the fact that in Balance of Payments Accounting IPI has been defined largely as a residual category, dependent on what is constituted as direct investment (and increasingly also 'Other Investment'). A review of the concept of IPI must, paradoxically then perhaps, begin with IDI.

Initially, in the immediate post-war period the definition of direct investment left portfolio investment being associated with *short-term* flows involved in arbitrage of cross-national interest rate differentials and accommodating temporary imbalances. This distinction developed because direct investment was defined as cross-border investments that exercised direct ownership *and* managerial control (and, as initially defined, did not involve transactions on the stock exchange). The criterion was devised to analyse the early post-World War II phenomena of internationalisation by multinationals using wholly owned subsidiaries (Jones 1994). The theoretical importance of the measure was to link IDI to changes in the ownership and control of the 'real' economy, particularly (foreign) control over output and employment. The criterion of 'control' over the subsidiary formed the behavioural assumption for distinguishing IDI from other capital flows. Direct investors in particular were said to exercise *long-term control* (and thus to earn profits over the long term). Portfolio investment was therefore defined as capital flows that had an absence of control, motivated simply by temporary differential returns (Rafferty 2003).

As multinationals grew in number and size, and extended their operations in more diverse forms, the definition of IDI evolved in an attempt to absorb the empirical impact of those changes.[7] It has however meant that IDI has been a quite unstable category within Balance of Payments accounting, with obvious implications for measuring IPI. These ongoing changes in the definition of IDI have thereby impacted on the definition of IPI. The current IMF Balance of Payments Manual defines IPI as follows: 'Portfolio investment covers transactions in equity securities and debt securities; the latter sub-sectored into bonds and notes, money market instruments and financial derivatives' (41). The distinction between forms of capital flow based on the time horizon of the investor remains, but is now embedded in a descriptive taxonomy, rather than stated explicitly. The IMF itself has recognised the problem with the notion of distinctions based on the time horizon of the investor:

> It is widely recognised that innovations in financial markets have diminished the usefulness of such a distinction for many purposes (IMF 2004: 82, 91).

As the maturity qualification has been gradually sidelined, the definition of portfolio investment has also been relaxed. At present, IPI is defined primarily on the basis of a descriptive list of security and transactor types (mainly by terms and conditions of the contract).

Faced with these growing statistical discrepancies in recording transactions in global financial assets and liabilities, the IMF has now tried to further clarify capital flows by collecting data on a bilateral geographical basis – that is, showing country of residence of the issuer and holder of securities. The IMF CPIS, which began in 1997 and was further developed in 2001 and 2002, aims to use this geographical segmentation of cross-border capital flows to 'check' against the Balance of Payments measures of portfolio investment positions. The data is taken in survey form separate from the Balance of Payments systems, but relies on the same concepts and methods as the IMF Balance of Payments Manual.

With this introduction to the categories of international investment and the cautionary note about their conceptual integrity, we move towards our network analysis of the CPIS data. Before doing so, the paper provides some background on the origin and development of OFCs, because as the subsequent analysis shows, they are now integral to any analysis of international capital flows.

3   The rise of OFCs and their changing role in global accumulation

While the emergence of OFCs is a 20th century phenomenon, their recent rapid growth has prompted one report to describe the flood of funds passing through them as 'the gold rush of the last decade' (Campbell and Bhatia 2005). Estimates of the scale of capital flows through OFCs, however, vary significantly. At the higher end, up to US$10 trillion in financial claims could be located in OFCs.[8] An IMF calculation based on Bank for International Settlements (BIS) data, which excludes the significant role of OFCs in Off-Balance-Sheet transactions (contingent liabilities), provides a more conservative estimate: something in the order of US$4.6 trillion in 1999 (cited in IMF 2000: 8).[9] Dixon, also using BIS area data, has provided a lower estimate, of around US$800 billion, or 9% of all BIS claims in 2001 (Dixon 2001: 105).

Whatever the actual figure, the recent growth of OFCs and their importance in international capital markets poses interesting questions for conventional explanations about their evolution. Deregulation of financial systems should be creating a pressure towards regulatory harmonisation, and would presumably undermine the competitive rationale for OFCs (Johns 1994). Why is it then that these centres have proliferated and grown during a phase where they should be declining? This paradox goes to the heart of the history and definition of (offshore) financial centres, and the form and nature of international capital flows that pass through them. The next section takes up this issue.

3.1 A short history of OFCs

OFCs existed prior to World War I, but then mainly as locations for 'flags of convenience' shipping (that is, Panama and Liberia). In an early test of 'economic residence', well before the recent period, shipping profits could be domiciled in another country so that dividends were paid to 'non-residents' whilst attracting no withholding tax (Sikka 2003).

The history of OFCs as we understand them now, however, begins in the interwar period. In the UK and US, taxation had risen as part of the postwar expansion of the nation state. Initially, overseas income of British resident companies was tax exempt. However, the British courts ruled that resident companies now had to pay tax on foreign income (Sikka 2003; also Picciotto 1999). In the 1920s and 1930s, tax havens developed to provide residence for these companies; initially in Canada (through trusts), then Switzerland and the Bahamas and later, other British territories (Channel Islands, Anguilla, the Virgin Islands, and Panama). Until World War II, however, these tax havens existed at the margins of global finance, almost exclusively for extremely rich individuals with foreign source income (Dwyer 2000).[10]

After World War II, these tax havens started to become used by multinational corporations to avoid national taxation regimes (through transfer pricing), and also to avoid liability for the insolvency of subsidiaries. The global expansion of US transnational corporations was particularly important here. Their international investment was often in the form of intercorporate loans and retained earnings, and only subject to taxation when repatriated (Sikka 2003). This expansion encouraged the formation of a series of shell or 'brass plate' companies in OFCs for minimising tax obligations.

The development of the Eurodollar markets in the late 1950s was an important step in the modern evolution of OFCs. What started as an innovation to store Soviet-held US dollars outside the US, developed into a way for US-based multinationals to hold US dollars offshore, outside the control of the Federal Reserve (Naylor 1987). When interest rates increased during the Vietnam War, US multinationals were able to draw on a cheaper supply of US dollars, while lower prudential regulatory requirements made these markets attractive for depositors. The City of London[11] and Switzerland became a focus for the Eurodollar market, but many smaller entrepôts also developed Eurodollar markets. The Cayman Islands, for example, joined the Eurodollar markets in the 1970s (Roberts 1995). In 1968, the Asian Eurodollar market developed in Singapore. As the US Federal Reserve attempted to rein in domestic inflation and stem capital outflow it imposed capital controls, reserve requirements and capped interest rates (Cassard 1994; also Sikka 2003). OFCs provided a way to circumvent attempts by monetary authorities to control the money supply and manage exchange rates.

This early history has stamped the popular image of OFCs as peripheral financial centres, used to avoid tax obligations and regulatory restrictions as well as in the seamier instances, provide money laundering for criminal activities. However, the period of financial deregulation challenges this image in a number of ways. As national tax and regulatory regimes across the OECD have become more predisposed to the prerogatives of financial capital (for example, floating exchange rates and relaxation of capital controls and so on), the older competitive advantages of OFCs as tax havens have been eroding. One consequence of this has been the development of semantic debate about 'harmful' and 'fair' tax regimes between OECD countries and OFCs; a debate that itself signals the increasing difficulties in distinguishing OFCs from other international financial centres (Dwyer 2000).

As their earlier regulatory advantages have been waning, OFCs have increasingly become participants in more mainstream financial services in addition to their notorious functions. One major change here has been the development of OFCs as active primary and secondary markets for the trade of securities. In 1992 OFCs' net issuance of new securities was –0.1% of total global issues. By 1996 this had increased to 13% of global issues. Much of the growth had occurred in the Cayman Islands, Netherlands Antilles and Luxembourg (Dufey and Bartram 1997). Other OFCs have also become crucial to the global insurance industry. Bermuda, for example, has an extensive international insurance sector with US$130 billion in insurance activities and estimates suggesting this may account for at least 30% of the world's captive insurance market (Dixon 2001: 109).

Another change to OFCs involves a decline in their official on-balance sheet assets activities (down to 50% of total cross-border flows from a high of 56%) and the growth of off-balance sheet transactions (Dufey and Bartram 1997). This reflects the fact that OFCs have become major participants in derivative transactions and other services such as securitisation and investment consultancy. One of the more conspicuous developments here has been the formation and registration of a number of hedge funds in OFCs. Most major hedge funds in the US and other OECD economies now have an offshore vehicle generally registered in the British Virgin Islands, Bahamas, Bermuda, the Cayman Islands, Dublin or Luxembourg. One estimate suggested that of the estimated US$68 billion invested in hedge funds in 1998, US$31.7 billion was invested through offshore entities (Brown *et al.* 1999).

At issue here is what this change of role means to the operations of OFCs and international financial markets. For the emergence of hedge funds and their presence in off-balance sheet activities suggests important qualitative changes in the global role of OFCs. While tax competition and money laundering no doubt remain features of OFCs, their continued growth emphasises their regulatory flexibility in the innovative and fluid world of global finance. In particular, OFCs have become critical to 'recycling' currencies and securities. The role of OFCs in issuance, trading and distribution of derivatives, specialist equity, specialist bonds and the development of new financial instruments like asset-backed bonds and novel insurance arrangements makes them a central part of today's international capital market infrastructure.

OFCs have become places where securities can be gathered on a global scale and quickly transferred to other global centres. They are also places where assets forms can be changed, so that OFCs now function almost as transfer stations of international capital. This no doubt makes them a focal point for the transmission of regional and global financial crises. However, it makes little sense to continue seeing them simply as outposts of hot money. Instead, OFCs are now an integral part of the competitive circulation of capital. This point has been increasingly recognised even by regulatory agencies. In the words of one Bank of England economist:

> The pattern of financial flows through them (OFCs) may occasionally give a clearer reading of the developments than data on flows through other international financial centres, such as London and New York, where activity relating to the domestic economy is greater. Interpreting the available data entails looking at the types of financial transactions that lie behind the aggregate statistics not captured by banks' balance

sheet data, and might involve intermediation *via* entities located in (or at least domiciled in) OFCs (Dixon 2001: 105).

3.2 The definition of OFCs and Balance of Payments accounting

What distinguishes a domestic financial centre from an offshore centre is very much a contested issue. Traditionally, a distinction has been based on whether clients of financial institutions cross formal national borders to conduct transactions within the financial centre (Tschoegl 2000). In other words, OFCs are understood to provide an exceptionally large part of their financial services activity to non-residents (IMF 2000). At a broader level, OFCs are understood as a spatially concentrated agglomeration of financial institutions, where financial intermediation takes place (Coakley 1992).

The BIS definition of OFCs benchmarks those centres where assets and liabilities are out of proportion to domestic transactions at greater than 50%. And while much of the academic literature focuses on the functional financial services provided by OFCs (for a review see Tschoegl 2000), they still tend to continue to tie the discussion of tax and regulatory structures to a definition of national residence,[12] placing emphasis on where money was domiciled to avoid tax and regulatory obligations. This implies that 'real' financial centres undertake value-added financial transactions for domestic residents, whereas OFCs are about regulatory arbitrage.

However, the emergence of OFCs such as Hong Kong, Singapore (and even some of the Caribbean centres), which issue equity, debt, and derivatives, act as securitisation and repackaging centres, and are active primary and secondary trading markets in their own right, is increasingly making this stereotype obsolete. On the other side, some of the more traditional and 'legitimate' international financial centres like the UK are taking on more of the 'brass plate' and SPE-style functions that have in the past been associated with the tax haven stereotype.

SPEs are often formed for the purpose of securitising loans for on-sale, and this can create difficulties for Balance of Payments accounting. While securitisation is strictly an off-balance sheet transaction (itself an issue for Balance of Payments accounting – see Kester 1995) it nevertheless shows up as a series of transactions. Figure 1, from Dixon (2001: 114), shows the effect of securitisation on Balance of Payments accounting. Bank X provides a loan to an Indonesian company, *via* a funded credit enhancement to a Cayman SPE (recorded on the SPE balance sheet). If other banks then purchase bonds from the SPE as part of the securitisation process, these purchases will also be recorded as claims on the SPE, recorded in the Cayman Islands. Where this really starts to distort Balance of Payments accounting is in terms of which institution bears responsibility for the risk. Prior to securitisation the responsibility rested with Bank X. Post-securitisation, this risk transfers to those banks purchasing the asset-backed security. It is recorded as an exposure to the Cayman Islands and not a loan to an Indonesian company. Significantly many of these data difficulties involving 'brass plate' companies concern transfers within the same banking group. Dixon, comparing BIS locational and consolidated bank claims, estimates that in the Bahamas around 85% of all cross-border intermediation is intra-bank group activity (Dixon 2001: 112).

One problem for any distinction between legitimate international financial centres and OFCs, is that the definition of economic residence remains intractable. Establishing the residence of the transactor underpins the entire system of Balance of Payments accounting by defining when a cross-border flow takes place (that is, between a resident and non-resident) and from this, in what forms and in which direction.

The CPIS data on OFCs presented below is perhaps the most evolved attempt at a definition of economic nationality. Nonetheless, even with these advances in bilateral data, ambiguity arises because modern MNCs often have multiple centres of interest.

If establishing the country attribution of a security issuer is difficult, finding the country attribution of a security holder can be even more problematic. Custodians, insurance companies, funds managers, trusts, pension funds and mutual funds as collective investment schemes, are often not aware of the nationality of the security holder they are investing on behalf of. The nature of pooled investments is that savings can come from a variety of country residences, and this creates problems for attributing indi-

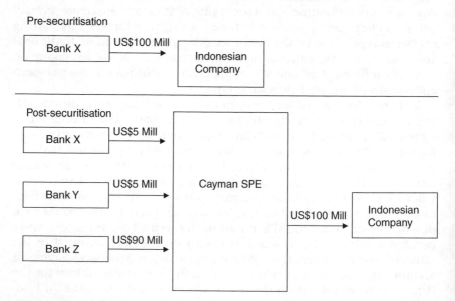

Figure 4.1   Securitisation and Cross-Border Lending
Source: (Dixon 2001: 114)

vidual investments to individual security holders. In practice this means assuming that all holders in the fund have the same country attribution, something we know not to be true (Coates 2003). When these cross-national pools are relatively small, this is perhaps only an awkward but acceptable assumption. But when they become larger, the potential impact on Balance of Payments measures makes them too significant to ignore.

In an era of high capital mobility then, nationality may be unstable, but it must still be contrived for Balance of Payments purposes. The danger is, particularly with data sources like the CPIS, that companies and individuals can have their investment counted multiple times because they have multiple centres of interest. In addition, where a company or individual qualifies for residence, might have little to do with the transaction taking place.

4 Geographic network analysis of portfolio capital flows

It was noted earlier that one of the reasons behind the production of the CPIS by the IMF was the series of currency and financial crises in 'emerging' countries during the 1990s. Nonetheless, CPIS data remains limited. Apart from the confidentiality problem, the most significant limitations with the data is that all derivative and contingent liabilities are excluded from reporting. This has serious repercussions for the CPIS data because derivative transactions are often attached to, or part of, a series of on-balance sheet transactions. To exclude them is to only capture the partial picture (for a review of the limitations of CPIS data in regard to derivatives see Coates, Rafferty and Nicoletti 2005). Only tentative evidence can therefore be offered concerning the wider significance of OFCs in international capital markets. Nonetheless, this evidence provides a clear indication of their importance to on-balance sheet global capital flows.

IMF CPIS data organising bilateral flows of portfolio investment into a matrix form allows a better presentation of the IPI interrelationships between countries. The bilateral flows are only measured on the assets side of each balance sheet and then counter-posed against each other to give the matrix format. In this sense that being measured is only gross total assets which each country is recording against other nations in its Balance of Payments – and this has a number of limitations.[13] Using a hub analysis, through network software, we show the countries that dominate global capital flows.

Figure 4.2 presents IPI in global networks. The distance on the vertical scale indicates their order of importance, while the width of the lines indicates the size of IPI flow. The importance of US capital markets to the functioning of international capital markets is clearly evident here. The US is the major international investor, and also a recipient of significant amounts of inward portfolio investment. This no doubt reflects the tendency for most international portfolio investors, outside the US, to invest in US capital markets when undertaking international diversification.[14]

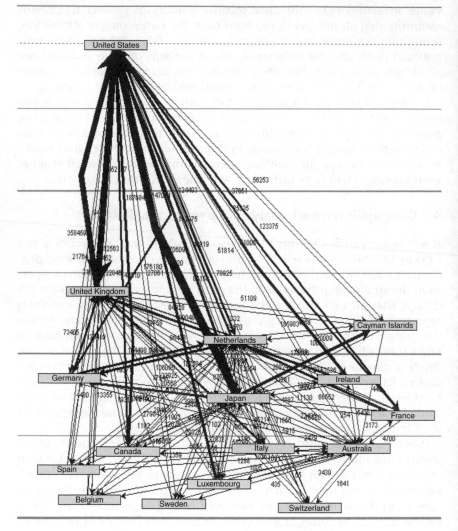

Figure 4.2   Hub Analysis of IPI for Top 15 Countries by Total Asset, 2002 US$ millions
Source: CPIS.

The UK is the next largest hub, and in particular, is a big recipient of US investment as well as a very significant investor in the US. Japan is the third biggest hub of cross-border portfolio investment flows. The next tier of countries includes Germany, the Netherlands, Cayman Islands and France. After that, the third tier capital markets include Italy, Canada, Switzerland, Ireland, and Luxembourg. Finally, Spain, Australia, Belgium and Sweden can be considered as fourth tier hubs. The importance of OFCs becomes immediately apparent with the Cayman Islands, Netherlands, Switzerland, Luxembourg and Belgium all acknowledged as OFCs, with Ireland a more recent instance.

Figure 4.3 aggregates these country patterns into key regions and includes all smaller countries previously too insignificant in scale to show up in Figure 4.2. The US, UK and Japan, because of their significance to international capital flows, are included in their own right. The rest of the OECD economies are present as 'Other OECD', while all the smaller developing and transition economies are classified as 'emerging'. Because of the problems with confidentiality in the CPIS data, we have included a category of confidential transactions; so that the main centres undertaking such transactions can be identified. The hub analysis shows each region

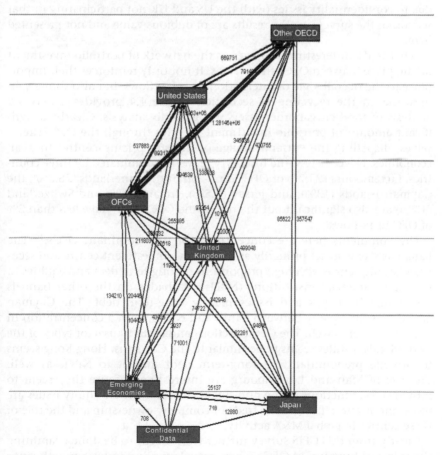

Figure 4.3 Hub Analysis of OFCs' Role in International Capital Flows
Source: IMF CPIS data.

and country's inward and outward (asset transactions) as a proportion of total global flows.

Figure 4.3 shows that Other OECD, excluding the US, UK and Japan, is the largest grouping of capital flows, representing 31% of all cross-border portfolio capital. The US has 24% of all portfolio asset flows, but most critically OFCs as a group[15] come in third with 20% of all flows. Collectively, they are more significant than even the UK (with 14%). Figure 4.3 also exposes the concentration of global capital flows between the OECD and OFCs, with emerging economies comprising only 5% of all capital flows. Finally, the problem of confidentiality in CPIS data is highlighted, at 2% of portfolio investment, by including this as hub in its own right. The amount of confidential transactions involving the UK in particular is notable.

In terms of flows out of OFCs into major countries, again the data suffers due to confidentiality issues (with the US and UK not participating in that section of the survey), so the results are of dubious value and not presented here.

What is also interesting, however, is the network of portfolio investment taking place between OFCs themselves. It not only reinforces their importance to the overall logic of international capital flows, but also shows sub-networks in the recycling of securities. Figure 4.4 provides a network analysis of total cross-border assets using a hub analysis. Clearly, a significant amount of portfolio investment recycles through the OFCs themselves, dispelling the entrepôt image of transfer pricing centres to 'real' economies. Nevertheless, the intra-OFC flows are dominated by three countries: Luxembourg (29.7% of OFCs intra-activity); Netherlands (28.3%); the Cayman Islands (13%); and Jersey (8.5%), Ireland (5%) and Switzerland (4.2%) are also significant but the rest of the OFCs each have less than 2% of OFC intra-flows.

The comments here are concentrated on the dominant OFCs.[16] The Bahamas seems to act primarily as a collective investment centre and securities issuing centre with high proportions of long-term debt and equities to non-bank financial institutions (NBFIs). Barbados on the other hand is dominated by banks and issues mainly long-term debt. The Cayman Islands is split equally between banks and NBFIs, with a concentration in long-term debt as well. The OFC functions and main transactor types of the Netherlands Antilles seems to be similar to the Caymans. Hong Kong seems to provide predominantly a long-term debt market to NBFIs as well. The Isle of Man and Luxembourg are interesting because they seem to provide OFC functions to the non-financial sector, where equity issues are more important, reflecting the trade of company ownership and the role of these centres in global M&A activity.

Clearly from this CPIS survey further work needs to be done examining the role and function of OFCs. Their prevalence and indeed growth since the deregulation of OECD financial markets means they play a critical

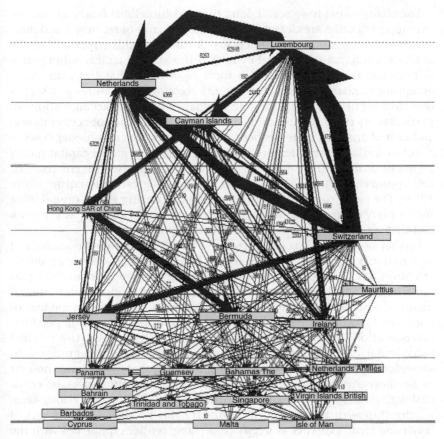

Figure 4.4   Intra-OFC Total Assets, 2002 US$ millions

role in the turnover of securities on international capital markets. One way to think about them is as a sort of short-term 'parking station' for capital during regional asset price adjustments, as well as transfer stations in a string of interwoven securities transactions. This is of course largely conjectural. The nature of OFCs as confidential financial centres makes the data collected on them limited and also brings us back to the original conceptual problems with IPI data.

5   Conclusion

The paper has attempted to make two basic points, one methodological/statistical, and the other analytical.

The changes that have been taking place within global financial markets over recent decades are clearly affecting the integrity of recording and measurement of cross-border transactions. A theme of this paper is that the analysis of international capital by both orthodox and radical political economics has tended to 'lock in' a form of analysis that has come from accepting standard Balance of Payments accounting measures as a sort of objective set of data about the role of finance in global accumulation. In particular, by treating the nation state as a coherent unit of accumulation and unit of analysis, there has been a tendency to see cross-border flows as a sort of 'leakage', or at least to frame an analysis of global capital movements in terms of their national impacts. In a slightly different context, this approach has been referred to as 'methodological nationalism' (Gore 1996). The paper suggests that the project of analysing global capital must increasingly confront that methodological approach, and ask, as Warnock and Cleaver (2002) do, whether the data are up to the task.

Furthermore, there has been a relative neglect of IPI in the analysis of international capital. It is surely somewhat ironic that so little academic attention has been focused on understanding the determinants and patterns of IPI, and their role in the functioning of modern international financial markets (with the possible exception of studies on home bias of portfolio investment and debates about appropriate levels of portfolio diversification). Perhaps the relative neglect of IPI reflects the residual behavioural underpinnings of international capital flow definitions. In these definitions IPI was associated with international investment thought to be motivated mainly by risk diversification or differences in cross-national returns, but with no intention of establishing any long-term relationship with the market. In short, IPI was thought to live a sort of Jekyll and Hyde existence as sleepy respectable rentier capital, but with the capacity to become dangerous hot money where turbulent circumstances existed. While even orthodox economists have questioned Friedman's reassuring notion of stabilising speculation (1953: 157–204), it has not been very fashionable to study hot money.[17]

The data used here provides the first opportunity to present portfolio investment flows as geographical networks, an opportunity not available to researchers depending on Balance of Payments accounting. This paper used network analysis as a way of presenting that geographical data, and provided an analysis of several important features of that data. To our knowledge, this paper is the first to present IPI data in a way that permits geographic analysis of bilateral patterns.

The analysis permits several interesting conclusions to be made. Firstly, it helps to consolidate the previous impressions of the dominance of the main OECD economies in IPI transactions, especially the US, UK and Japan. They dominate not only as source countries of IPI, but also as destinations. There then exist several tiers of IPI nodes, most of which are both destination and source countries. The CPIS data also shows the importance of OFCs in IPI transactions. Indeed, several OFCs are more important to IPI than large industrial economies. The network analysis revealed how they play a role in relation to major capital markets such as the US, UK and Japan. Here their role seems to be in intermediating cross-border IPI, changing its form, and perhaps nationality. There are also strong links between many of these OFCs, where they seem to provide a role as transfer points in the cycling and recycling of global capital flows.

While we offer some analysis of the evidence, there are significant problems with the data. These problems go back to a series of long running conceptual difficulties with defining and measuring international capital flows in Balance of Payments accounting. The conceptual confusion associated with contemporary capital flows are unlikely to be resolved in the near future, and despite the improvement in CPIS data significant limitations remain. Considerable caution needs to be exercised in interpreting these results. The paper makes the case that it is necessary to make clear just how conceptually driven the data actually is. Our analysis must be considered at best a preliminary one, and further analysis is indeed being undertaken. Given the difficulties we have identified in modern capital flow measurement, we suggest that this sort of network analysis has many advantages over other methods for presenting such data. It has certainly highlighted several areas where more analysis would be fruitful.

Notes

1. The authors wish to thank Robert Nicoletti for excellent research assistance.
2. Bryan concluded for instance that '...the spatial movement created by the historical process (of globalised capital accumulation) has superseded the spatial dimension of the analytical categories (based on national Balance of Payments accounting)' (1995: 121).
3. Walker concluded that '(p)erhaps, then, we have come to a time when capital is outgrowing the corporation, as presently constituted' (1989: 63).
4. These hedge fund issues have prompted a recent statement by the Financial Economists Roundtable (FER) expressing concern about the role of hedge funds in global capital markets (FER 2005). For a useful introduction to the hedge funds literature, see Eichengreen and Mathieson (1999), and Temple (2001).
5. As well as the development of the CPIS data, the formation of the Financial Stability Forum of the BIS, and the initiation of a semi-annual Global Financial Stability Report by the IMF are also products of this period.
6. In many ways this finding is an artefact of the definitions of IDI itself, which are based on the motives of the investor. IDI is defined as investment seeking (long term) control. Among other things, the definition contrives to make retained earnings a cross-border capital flow. However, Dooley, Claessens and Warner (1995) provide evidence that challenges the notion that IDI flows are any more stable (long term) than IPI flows.
7. It is significant that economic historians applying this late-20th century distinction between FDI and IPI, produced significantly different results to those that were produced using mid-20th century distinctions and which had indicated that

IPI was the then dominant form of international capital flow (c.f. Svedberg 1978; Platt 1980).

8. This estimate assumes a stable stock of assets is held within the jurisdiction of OFCs.
9. Reporting of OFC transactions to the BIS tends to be limited to major financial centres. Of the smaller OFCs like Bermuda, Liberia and Panama, most do not report to the BIS.
10. A form of onshore tax haven existed instead for the middle class in the form of life insurance schemes and pension funds.
11. Economic historians have pointed out that England was a financial centre of the world long before it was the workshop of the world. It is also interesting that the modern history of the city of London and the Eurodollar markets is one closely associated with 'offshoring', even though it is not defined as an OFC due to the size of Britain's industrial economy. What this suggests is that the formation of OFCs is more about the internationalisation of capital and accumulation itself.
12. Variations on this approach define financial centres as where the majority of financial institutions are foreign banks, or centres where the time zones are linked to a major capital market (Jones 1994),
13. There is a discrepancy between global assets and liabilities, with the latter far more significant than the former. Considering that corporate and national accounting systems are balance sheets, that is, they balance, this signals significant issues in data error.
14. This strategy is prominent among institutional investors in particular.
15. Countries included as OFCs are: Bahrain, Barbados, Belize, Bermuda, British Indian Ocean Territory, Cayman Islands, People's Republic of China, Gibraltar, Guatemala, Guernsey, Hong Kong SAR of China, Ireland, Isle of Man, Jersey, Liechtenstein, Luxembourg, Morocco, Netherlands, Netherlands Antilles, Panama, Singapore, St. Helena, St. Kitts and Nevis, St. Lucia, St. Pierre and Miquelon, St. Vincent and the Grenadines, Switzerland, Trinidad and Tobago, Virgin Islands, British Virgin Islands, US.
16. Though two larger OFCs, Singapore and Netherlands, are absent. These results are still preliminary, and therefore not available.
17. Nor has it been particularly easy. A problem confronting researchers scrutinising portfolio flows has been that the data has not been very detailed or robust. Until the 1990s, national statisticians, like their academic counterparts, had been content to leave the significant anomalies in portfolio data alone.

5
Who Do Derivatives Markets Serve? Rhetoric Versus Reality

Sasha Breger

> *The test of our progress is not whether we add more to the abundance of those who have much, it is whether we provide enough for those who have little.*
>
> Franklin D. Roosevelt

The last four decades have been a time of tremendous change and volatility in the world economy. Producers and consumers are facing an increasingly challenging economic environment. One of these new challenges is the rise of new types of economic risk. The financial sector has risen to the occasion, spawning new markets for risk management. 'Indeed, the advances since the mid-1970s in the ability to identify and isolate the key financial risks commonly found in modern economies, together with the development of financial institutions and markets that can efficiently commoditise, trade and price such risk, are the crowning achievement in the evolution of modern market economics' (Steinherr 1998: xviii). Although financial instruments that manage risk have been exchanged for centuries, the last 30 years have seen the development of markets that facilitate the standardisation, pricing, and trading of risk management instruments. The growth of these markets has complemented and overdetermined the erosion of governmental support for risk management.

The agricultural sector is a seedbed for these complementary processes. Government management of risks associated with producing and selling agricultural commodities, such as price-supports and subsidies, are buckling under fiscal pressures, international trade pressures, and advocacy of market-based risk management methods. In the agricultural industry the incredible growth of derivatives markets and the hedging opportunities they offer are frequently conceived as substitutes for such governmental risk management strategies. Derivatives are financial contracts designed to create price exposure to an underlying commodity, asset, rate, index or event. They are used by participants in the economy to hedge, speculate, and arbitrage. In the context of the farmer, derivatives provide a kind of insurance against volatile commodity prices. Scholars like Alfred Steinherr juxtapose more market-based risk management strategies employed by farmers in the US to the European Common Agricultural Policy in which 'society' is made to bear the costs of risk management (Steinherr 1998: 128). For those wary of government intervention in the economy, the former is conceived to be far superior to the latter.

Such arguments suggest that privatisation of risk management is a boon for the economy insofar as risks can be diversified, diffused, and better matched to those best able to bear them, with costs being borne by the individual producer. Indeed, the farmer is an oft-cited example of the type of person who stands to benefit from innovation in the risk management sector. The farmer, it is argued, can use derivative instruments like futures to hedge against market risk thereby protecting her livelihood from the risks inherent in a global economy. And not only are these instruments priced efficiently and tailored more specifically to the needs of the farmer through what is called 'financial deepening', they are also equally available to all types of farmers. Barriers to entry are thought to be non-existent, not least due to the amount of leverage one can obtain by putting forth only a minimal premium in advance.

It is this contention about the ability of farmers to use derivative markets that this essay seeks to explore and call into question. Statements from some scholars refer to farmers as a homogenous group, implying that all farmers will reap the benefits of derivatives market development: 'Farmers can, on a moment's notice, receive a quotation for and sell to their local elevator a crop that has not even been planted or has not yet been harvested' (Peck 1985: 73–4). Others specifically address the small farmer who, through cooperative farming arrangements, can utilise derivatives markets: 'This way small farmers can have access to the same risk management tools as the larger producers' (Steinherr 1998: 128).

Yet, this rhetoric stands in stark contrast to empirical evidence available on farming, farmers and futures markets in the US. Seventy-five per cent of farmers in the US are classified by the US Department of Agriculture as 'small' (USDA 2001). And, while they produce only about 20% of agricultural output in the US, the importance of small farms to the vitality and prosperity of rural communities, and to environmental sustainability, makes the issue of market accessibility critical. The following analysis points out that farmers do not all have the same access and capability to use derivatives markets, thereby compounding the difficulties already faced by small farmers.

This exploration begins with a discussion of the rhetoric surrounding farmers and derivatives markets. The third section gives an abbreviated portrait of farming in America. The fourth section relates the empirical evidence available on small corn and wheat farmers and futures market accessibility in the US along three lines: 1. the size of standard contracts;

2. the quality of 'mini-futures' markets; and, 3. the prohibitive nature of the 'capabilities gap'. The fifth section speaks of the consequences of these findings for small farmers in the US and for agricultural policy in both developed and developing countries.

The rhetoric

The rhetoric surrounding derivatives markets draws a picture of an economic world in which they are the 'crowning achievement', enabling any and all willing participants to hedge effectively against risks that threaten their livelihoods, while also eliminating the need for governmental risk management programmes. This discourse exists within a larger narrative that more generally celebrates the proliferation of free markets and 'financial deepening'. This section provides a few of the more colorful exclamations on free markets, 'financial deepening', and derivatives markets.

The Oratorical Glory of the Free Market.[1] Echoing many observers throughout the past few centuries, one of the more vivid proclamations of economist Milton Friedman paints in broad strokes the ideological basis of the arguments for privatisation and market expansion and deepening: 'The greatest advances of civilisation, whether in architecture or painting, in science and literature, in industry or agriculture, have never come from centralised government' (1982: 3). Proponents of *laissez-faire* are among those who suggest, in the context of derivatives markets, that privatisation of risk management delivers individuals and firms from what Smith (1776) called those 'impertinent obstructions' that are the work of governments. Risks are better matched to those best able to bear them, are priced more efficiently, and are thus better managed by markets than by governments.

Salvation by Financial Deepening.[2] Within the narrative on the virtues of markets and the evils of government there arises a more sophisticated discourse about why markets are good. In the context of finance the argument takes the form of an explication of 'financial deepening'. 'Financial deepening' refers to the combined processes of: financial innovation; the continued creation, growth and integration of financial markets; the increasing quality of markets in terms of liquidity; and, the increasing efficiency of markets in transmitting accurate price information and reducing the costs of doing business. 'Financial deepening' implies that individuals and firms are better able to navigate the world economy at a lower price and take advantage of new opportunities.

Within discussions of derivative products, 'financial deepening', if we are to believe the narrative, means that derivative products are becoming as readily available and as easy to use as bathroom cleanser and sandwich bread: 'If you can measure it, you can make a derivative for it! Whereas derivative trading used to be an arcane and complex world accessed only by big companies with a lot of money to lose, the costs will soon be low enough to allow individuals to participate...' (Gascoigne 2003). Derivatives trading, says the discourse, is on its way to becoming a household activity.

Discursive Homogeneity: 'Farmers' and Derivatives.[3] The rhetoric surrounding privatisation and 'financial deepening' comes into focus in the person of the 'farmer'. The inherently volatile nature of agricultural production combined with agricultural market integration makes farming a risky endeavor. The futures market is proclaimed the answer to the farmer's prayers. Futures trading, it is argued, provides an opportunity for farmers to hedge against price risks that jeopardise their livelihood. The rapid deepening of futures markets offers farmers previously unavailable risk management opportunities and services. The statements of Peck (1985) and Steinherr (1998) at the outset illustrate two dimensions along which this rhetoric is problematic. As the passage below will also illustrate, farmers are: 1. conceived of as a homogeneous group; and, 2. thought to be uniformly capable of benefiting from futures trading.

A 1995 article in the *Financial Times* captures the rhetoric along both of these dimensions:

> Farmers are a paradoxical bunch. Renowned for being conservative and averse to change, they work in the riskiest business of all ... Contracts have been adapted to farmers' needs, just as volatile grain prices and currency movements have made insurance more necessary; they have become more available in exchanges around the world; and they have become increasingly popular with governments keen to reduce expensive and cumbersome price support programmes... (Harding).

So, the *generic* 'farmer' can use futures to his advantage. Failure to differentiate between different types of farmers implies that *all* farmers can access, utilise and benefit from futures trading. Holding this assumption proves dangerous to the small farmer who, in reality, cannot navigate these markets adeptly (or even at all); this is the import of the analysis in section four. Also notable is the way in which the author implies that the deepening of futures markets is being used as a rationale by governments for reductions in public spending on price supports; this is addressed in section five, as are other consequences of uneven access to risk management tools for American farmers and agricultural policy.

The rhetoric on free markets, 'financial deepening', and farmers and derivatives perilously denies the need for governmental action in the arena of small farm risk management.

Snapshot: farming in America

The United States Department of Agriculture (USDA) regularly collects data to take stock of farms and farmers. Overwhelmingly, the picture is a gloomy one for small farmers. What follows is a snapshot of farming in America based on USDA data over the past few years from the National Agricultural Statistical Service (NASS), and aggregated along those dimensions deemed relevant to this analysis.

Farm Size. The average farm in the US is 441 acres. Yet, the mean is deceiving – skewed due to a small number of large farms. Based on 2002 data, 8% of farms are comprised of nine acres or less; almost 27% of farms have between ten and 49 total acres; about 87% of US farms are comprised of 499 acres or less. The *median* farm in 2002 had between 70 and 99 acres. Based on farm size by acre and average annual yields, it will be shown that many US farmers do not grow sufficient amounts of their product to participate in futures markets.

Uneven Distributions: Land, Sales, Government Payments. Farmland in the US is incredibly concentrated, as are sales and government payments. According to 2004 data from the NASS, the highest sales bracket, US$500,000 or more annually, represents just 3.6% of farms; yet these farms own and operate about 22% of farmland. The lowest sales bracket, less than US$10,000 annually, represents almost 56% of farms working on just less than 13% of farmland.

In 2002, 87% of US farms recorded sales of less than US$100,000. Astoundingly, this 87% made up only 12% of national agricultural sales and government payments. The 3% of farms recording sales of US$500,000 or more in 2002 represented 62% of national agricultural sales and government payments. The Environmental Working Group estimates that between 1996 and 1998, the top 10% of farms by income received some 60% of US federal farm subsidies (Rhagavan 2000: 1). The Heritage Foundation estimates that the wealthiest 10% of farms in the US received upwards of 65% of federal farm subsidies in 2002 (Reidl 2004). Another observer notes, '[F]arm subsidies are corporate welfare *par excellence*...by last year nearly three-quarters of the money went to the richest 10% of American farmers' (Cassel 2002).

Small Farm Finances. Small farmers in the US are also, on average, debtors. Considering only income from farming (most small farmers must engage in non-farm work in order to make ends meet), over 71% of US farmers recorded negative net cash income in 2002. Looking at USDA Agricultural Census data (2002b), one observes a not unexpected phenomenon: the larger the farm, the greater the net income. However, what cannot be explained by reference to the sheer size of large farms or to economies of scale, is that, on average, farms in the US$24,999 or less annual sales bracket (71% of farms in 2002) were producing at a net loss. It is unfortunate, yet unsurprising given US socio-economic policy more generally, that those farms that are least financially solvent receive the least government assistance. Furthermore, as will be suggested below, it is likely that some of this disparity in income might also be attributed to differential risk management capabilities between different types of farmers.

While this description is certainly incomplete on any account, it does paint a rather vivid picture. Small farmers comprise the vast majority of agricultural producers in the US. They operate in an agricultural environment dominated by a few large producers. Small farmers receive the least, and sometimes no, government subsidies. And, a huge percentage of small farms are operating at a loss. While a complete discussion of the reasons for these trends is not within the scope of this paper, it is my contention that small farmers also have a disadvantage in terms of risk management capability which, at the very least, aggravates the difficult circumstances they already face.

Empirical analysis: Small US corn and wheat farmers and futures contracts

While much good work is being done on the international and systemic consequences of derivatives trading,[4] there is little being said within the quickly-growing literature on derivatives about who is trading them. Who has access to these markets? Who understands how they work sufficiently well so as not to create more risk and confusion than is eliminated by their use? Adam Tickell (2000) is among the few scholars who has pointed out the problematic unintelligibility of derivatives contracts; in the context of foreign exchange derivatives, this has resulted in an incredible concentration of dealers, with 15 financial firms controlling over 75% of dealership in the market.

These observations, while helpful, do not specifically address the accessibility of derivatives markets to participants in the economy. In the remainder of this section, the accessibility for small US corn and wheat farmers to futures markets will be called into question. The choice of corn and wheat reflects, albeit, a somewhat arbitrary choice; yet, corn and wheat are among the more widely-grown crops in the US and futures markets for them have been firmly established for decades (the Chicago Board of Trade started trading in corn and wheat futures in 1848). If equality in accessibility exists in any market, it would likely be found here, in long-established markets with large investor bases.

Corn and wheat futures are traded in Chicago with the Chicago Board of Trade (CBOT). Wheat only is traded in Kansas City with the Kansas City Board of Trade (KCBOT), and in Minneapolis with the Minneapolis Grain Exchange (MGE). For all of these exchanges, a standard wheat or corn future specifies 5,000 bushels of the product. And while such standardisation has made the development of a market possible in the first place, it appears that 5,000 bushels is prohibitively large for many small farmers. Do small farmers grow enough to participate?

It must be noted that while farmers don't necessarily have to have this much wheat or corn to back up the contract, not having the product in

the case that delivery is ultimately required increases farmers' risks exponentially. Not having the product to back up the contract transforms a
hedging maneuver designed to mitigate risk into a speculative transaction
that increases risk. Furthermore, many farmers, large and small, use
forward or cash contracting to lock in a future buyer and price for their
crops. Forward contracting, however, has some disadvantages relative to
hedging with futures, suggesting that small farmers might want access
to both. Hedging allows greater flexibility in delivery and flexibility to
change one's market position in response to changing conditions; it also
allows for a potentially longer pricing period than might be obtained *via*
cash contracting. Market integration and price volatility have arguably
increased the costs of inflexibility in the global economy.

Before discussing accessibility more specifically, it helps to look at
whether farmers, and what *kinds* of farmers, actually use futures markets
to manage risk. A 1996 survey, the most comprehensive recent survey of
farmer utilisation of risk management strategies, suggests that use of
hedging through futures (and also options) markets is directly proportional
to the farmer's net income. While all farm operators used cash on hand to
deal with emergencies more than any other strategy, operators in the
largest income category, US$250,000 or more in gross income, were most
likely to use hedging, forward contracting, and virtually all other risk management strategies (USDA 2005: 1). Based on the 2002 Agricultural Census
data, this income figure corresponds to roughly the wealthiest 160,000
farmers, all of whom farm over 1,000 acres. Farmers with less than
US$50,000 in gross income were significantly less likely to use any kind of
hedging strategy. Less than 20% of lower-income farmers utilised futures to
hedge against risk, whereas close to 45% of high-income farmers did so
(USDA 2005: 2). What factors might be precluding the use of futures
markets by small farmers? The rhetoric suggests that all will benefit, and
that farmers are 'paradoxical' for not utilising them. Is this really the case,
or is there something else going on?

The Standard Contract. Tables 5.1 and 5.2 below give rough estimates
of how much wheat and corn farmers actually grow based on acreage
farmed and average yields.

The following observations can be made: 1. Over 51% of wheat farmers in
the US do not grow enough of their product to sell one standard future contract in Chicago, Kansas City or Minneapolis; and, 2. Slightly under 40% of
corn farmers do not grow enough of their product to sell one standard
future contract in Chicago. One factor in making futures markets accessible
to small farmers is simply the size of the standard contract. The 5,000 bushel
standard prohibits a majority of wheat farmers and a large minority of corn
farmers from gaining access to these risk management tools.

The Mini-Futures Contract. While discussing the Commodity Futures
Modernisation Act, the Vice Chairman of the House Subcommittee on

Table 5.1   Wheat farms, bushels produced, 2002[5]

Farm size (by acres harvested)	Number of farms	Percent of total	Average yield[6]	Bushels produced
1 to 14.9	19,232	11.3	40.2	40–599
15 to 24.9	15,781	9.3	40.2	603–1,001
25 to 49.9	25,174	14.8	40.2	1,005–2,006
50 to 99.9	27,384	16.2	40.2	2,010–4,016
100 to 249.9	34,401	20.3	40.2	4,020–10,046
250 to 499.9	21,018	12.4	40.2	10,050–20,095
500 to 999.9	15,636	9.2	40.2	20,100–40,196
1,000 or more	10,902	6.4	40.2	40,200–

Table 5.2   Corn farms, bushels produced, 2002[7]

Farm size (by acres harvested)	Number of farms	Percent of total	Average yield[8]	Bushels produced
1 to 14.9	69,000	15.3	138.2	138–2,059
15 to 24.9	44,589	9.9	138.2	2,073–3,441
25 to 49.9	73,263	16.2	138.2	3,455–6,896
50 to 99.9	79,734	17.6	138.2	6,910–13,806
100 to 249.9	95,497	21.1	138.2	13,820–34,536
250 to 499.9	51,781	11.5	138.2	34,550–69,086
500 to 999.9	28,276	6.3	138.2	69,100–138,186
1,000 or more	9,171	2.0	138.2	138,200–

General Farm Commodities and Risk Management, Representative Nick Smith is recorded as asking, 'With some of my small farmers...*would it be possible to have a smaller trade than 5000 bushels* (USGPO 2003: 60, emphasis mine)?' What Representative Smith did not know is that there *is* a smaller contract. Previously traded on the Mid American Commodity Exchange (MidAm), which has since been absorbed into CBOT, there exist mini-futures contracts for wheat and corn that specify 1,000 bushels. What a boon for the small farmer!

However, a closer examination of the mini-futures markets reveals significant deficiencies. While futures markets for standard contracts have been well-developed, mini-futures markets are not as liquid or as deep as their standard counterparts. The wealth of literature on equity markets in the developing world provides some insight into how underdeveloped markets are to be evaluated. There are two common indicators of market liquidity and depth, deemed by many to be keys to a vibrant capital market: trading volumes and open interest (see Singh and Weiss 1998; Levine and Zervos 1998; Merchant 2000). The former speaks to the liquidity of the market in question. It tells us how relatively difficult or easy it is to sell off the security or derivative for cash. Investors tend to steer clear of those markets in which liquidity is low. Open interest speaks to the nature of participating investors, and therefore to the relative depth or shallowness of the market. It reflects the number of contracts outstanding, and suggests to observers how many investors are holding on to the instrument, and who is merely buying and selling quickly for speculative purposes. A market with low open interest reflects a more volatile and shallow market.

These two indicators are employed below to see whether mini-futures markets provide a viable option for those small farmers who don't grow enough to participate in the standard futures market. Mini-futures are not traded in Kansas City or Minneapolis; Table 5.3 below gives monthly trading volumes for standard and mini- wheat and corn futures traded on the Chicago exchange.

Even from a brief glance one can see that the standard futures market is far superior to the mini-futures market in terms of liquidity. In August 2004, for example, the standard wheat futures market was 303 times, or 30,300%, more liquid than the mini-wheat futures market. In August there were only 112 daily trades made in mini-wheat on average, compared to almost 34,000 daily trades in standard wheat on average. A similar pattern is noticeable across all months for both wheat and corn. Thus, it is not surprising that Representative Smith had no idea that mini-futures existed.

Not only are absolute liquidity levels in the mini-futures market so low that one's risk might actually increase through hedging, relative liquidity levels between the mini and standard futures markets suggest a distinct advantage for the large farmer. In the case of wheat, the 51% of farmers that cannot trade in standard futures might be able to resort to the mini-futures market. However, this puts them at a disadvantage to larger farmers who are aided by a more liquid standard market. It is very likely that the illiquidity of the mini-market would deter many small farmers from participating at all, giving larger farmers an advantage in the availability of diverse risk management techniques.

Open interest data for standard and mini-wheat and corn futures is recorded in Table 5.4 above. While open interest is indicative of the types of investors active in a market, the open interest figures for the mini-futures in both corn and wheat are so small as to make this sort of analysis rather unhelpful – for who would speculate in such an illiquid market? What is useful is to compare open interest data over consecutive years in order to determine whether interest in mini-futures is growing relative to that of standard futures markets. This sort of open interest comparison is

Table 5.3 Monthly volume for commodity futures in Chicago, 2004[9]

	Jan	Feb	Mar	Apr	May	Jun	July	Aug	Sep	Oct	Nov	Dec
Standard Wheat (5000 bu)	656,879	771,699	783,139	286,167	606,051	786,524	501,733	747,393	520,293	478,674	913,699	402,286
Mini-wheat (1000 bu)	3,167	2,874	3,570	3,475	2,111	3,479	2,063	2,466	2,085	1,704	2,987	1,063
Standard/Mini (Wheat)	207	269	219	83	287	226	243	303	250	281	306	378
Standard Corn (5000bu)	2.026 million	2.367 million	2.191 million	2.871 million	1.855 million	2.539 million	1.741 million	1.883 million	1.447 million	1.476 million	2.473 million	1.170 million
Mini-corn (1000 bu)	7,280	10,294	12,702	11,722	4,589	5,285	4,778	6,372	5,978	5,102	8,082	4,587
Standard/Mini (Corn)	278	230	173	245	404	480	364	295	242	289	306	255

Table 5.4   Open interest on commodity futures, 2002–4[10]

	Average month-end open interest 2002–2003	Average month-end open interest 2003–2004	Percent change
Standard Wheat	100,709	137,573	36.6%
Mini-wheat	695	1,257	80.9%
Standard Corn	421,730	574,759	36.3%
Mini-corn	2,989	4,154	39.0%

often utilised in emerging markets analyses as an indicator of growth of investor participation.

From 2002 to 2004 investor interest in standard wheat futures grew by roughly 37%, while in mini-wheat interest grew by almost 81%. For the same time period, investor interest in standard corn futures rose about 36%, and investor interest in mini-corn futures rose 39%. Comparing these relative growth rates it looks like growth in investor interest in mini-wheat is outpacing that of standard wheat, while the growth of investor interest for mini-corn is roughly on par with that of standard corn. While this might seem to bolster the relative quality of mini-futures compared to standard futures, the growth rates must not be confused with the absolute amounts of open interest in mini-futures relative to standard futures. If growth in investor interest in mini-wheat futures were to stay constant at say 80%, and investor interest in standard wheat futures were to experience no growth at all, it would take about *nine years* for investor interest in mini-wheat to surpass that of standard wheat! And, this assumes the unlikely scenario that the rate of growth in standard wheat falls to zero. The quality of mini-futures markets in wheat and corn appear inferior to markets for standard wheat and corn futures.

Cooperatives. Some scholars claim that small farmers can gain access to derivatives markets through participation in cooperative farming arrangements. Small farmers can pool their crops, aggregating enough to trade in standard futures. Based on 2002 USDA Census data, some 16,000 farms participated in 'cooperatives, estates or trusts, institutional, and so on'. This means that fewer than 1% of US farms participated in any of these activities, with cooperative arrangements accounting for even less. Fewer than six in every 1,000 farms of 500 acres or less were members of a cooperative, estate, trust, institutional, and so on. It appears as if cooperative arrangements are not a generally viable means of accessing futures markets for small US farmers at this time.

This does not, of course, preclude the development of cooperatives in the future that might enable farmers to collectively gain access to derivatives markets. Yet, if current government initiatives to engender cooperative creation are any indication of future possibilities, the outlook is not good. The USDA Value Added Producer Grant Program, established by the 2002 Farm Bill, was designed, in part, to fund efforts to build cooperatives. Since the passage of the bill over 60% of the programme's funding has been cut by Congress (Hassebrook 2005). Such public support, however, is vital. The National Council of Farmer Cooperatives (NCFC) notes a number of requirements for successful cooperative start-ups. These include: business and cooperative specialists, legal counsel, financial counsel, technical advice, and equity capital (NCFC 1996). While all of these requirements are costly, the USDA states that, 'One of the greatest challenges facing cooperatives is raising equity capital (USDA 1997: 32).' The USDA goes on to tell the prospective cooperative creator that equity requirements are generally funded by the co-op's members, either out-of-pocket or through retained earnings. Without public assistance, it seems unlikely that small farmers, already burdened financially, would be able to embrace cooperative arrangements for futures market access.

A Capabilities Gap? Aside from the size of standard contracts and under-developed mini-futures markets, small farmers also face other access difficulties. The term 'capability' will be used here to describe those skills, capacities, tools, knowledge and aptitudes necessary to accomplish some sort of task or fulfill some kind of function that is valued by the individual in question. The notion of capabilities has been well-developed by development economist Amartya Sen (see Sen 1988, 1992, 1999). In considering the small farmer and futures markets the following question arises: what capabilities are required in order that a small farmer could, if she so chooses, successfully navigate and participate in futures markets?

While there are many capabilities that might be important in managing risks in this fashion, *informational* capabilities come to the fore. What is a future? How are contracts structured? How are future prices arrived at? How does one hedge? How does one go about buying and selling futures? How does one keep track of his trades? What do these trades mean for the farm, for the family? These questions and many others are raised when a farmer is deciding whether to employ futures trading to manage farm risk. Do small farmers know the answers? And, if they do not, are there ways to find out? While this discussion of capabilities is certainly speculative in nature, it is vital that such questions be asked if policy makers seek to make futures trading accessible to all farmers.

What indicators are there that small farmers are lacking those informational capabilities necessary to navigate futures markets? The USDA suggests the following trends in regard to use of hedging by farmers: 'results indicate that prior use of forward contracts, possession of a bachelor's degree or above, membership in a marketing club, and gross sales had the greatest positive impact on the probability of using futures and options' (USDA 1999: 6). With the connection between income/sales and use of futures having already been established,[11] it remains to investigate informational capabilities in the context of prior experience and education. With very little information available on marketing club participation rates, this aspect of capabilities will not be addressed here.

Prior experience using futures creates an informational base on which to continue participation in futures markets. Futures are currently utilised by less than 20% of small farmers.[12] Since past experience is an indicator of future participation one would expect to see repeat futures customers and very low rates of first-time small farmer participation. Large farmers, on the other hand, with futures market participation over 45%, have more experience. Large farmers seem to have superior informational capabilities than small farmers insofar as past experience is concerned.

The USDA reports that those most likely to use futures to manage risks have a bachelor's degree or above. How educated are small corn and wheat farmers relative to large corn and wheat farmers? Less than 20% of all wheat farm operators surveyed by the USDA have completed college (USDA 2002a: 13). But, because the data on wheat farmers is not aggregated by farm size, this is an inconclusive piece of information. Corn farmers, however, are aggregated in a 2001 USDA report according to production costs; three categories, low, medium, and high, are used (USDA 2001: 8). Small farmers generally have the highest production costs (USDA 2001: 1). Thus while the data does not correlate directly, one can extrapolate based on this production cost grouping. About 71% of high-cost producers had a high school education or less, compared to 55 and 56% of medium- and low-cost producers, respectively. For those corn farm operators that completed some college, only 17% were high-cost producers, compared to 30 and 27% for medium- and low-cost producers, respectively. Finally, only 12% of high-cost producers completed college, compared to 16 and 17% for medium- and low-cost producers, respectively. Education levels appear to decrease in direct proportion to farm size. That 71% of small corn farm operators have a high school education or less speaks not only to limitations they face in navigating futures markets, but also to a not insignificant disadvantage in relation to larger farmers.

But, there are other ways of learning about futures and hedging that do not require a college education. The Internet has a wealth of information about financial lingo, tutorials on futures and hedging, and specific hedging strategies that offer an alternative to the small farmer. However, that 'operators of small farms often cited radio and television broadcasts as the most useful source of marketing information' is telling of the degree to which Internet education has permeated small farm life (USDA 1999: 5). Less than half of farms of 500 acres or less have Internet access (USDA 2002b). Closer to 60% of farms with 500 acres or more have Internet access, illustrating some disparity in access to risk management education between smaller and larger farmers.

While there are certainly other educational options (for example, marketing clubs or university agricultural extension services), one other central option remains for the small farmer. She can hire someone to gather, interpret and apply the information for her. Brokerage services become a potential avenue by which small farmers can fill in the gap between themselves and larger farmers. But, hiring a broker, or financial consultant, is costly, and this expense might be difficult for heavily-indebted farmers to bear. It is not surprising, then, that only 'operators of larger farms and those with at least some college education tended to cite marketing professionals as most useful' (USDA 1999: 5).

Implications for small farmers, agricultural policy and developing countries

It has been noted that: 'With less government intervention in farming and greater trade liberalisation, farmers appear to be increasingly relying on forward contracting and other risk management tools to reduce their farm-level risks' (USDA 1999: 5). Yet, the analysis of small wheat and corn farmers and their relationship to futures markets illustrates that this increasing reliance has been unevenly distributed across the farming community. Large farmers not only receive a disproportionate share of what little public assistance is left, but also have better access to and greater capability to use market-based risk management approaches.

The present discussion of farming in America is relevant to broader discussions about farm subsidies in the developed countries that disadvantage farmers in developing countries. The US and EU have been targets of these concerns, and the Doha Round of trade talks that began in 2002 specifically addressed this issue. In this context, small US farmers share some common ground with developing country farmers insofar as both face a competitive disadvantage due to farm subsidies.

This analysis suggests that farm subsidies are not the only source of competitive disadvantage for small farmers in the US. Uneven access to risk management techniques for small farmers in the US is creating a 'double disadvantage': unsubsidised production costs, as well as poorer access to and capabilities to utilise market-based risk management techniques. Even without subsidies large US farmers might retain a significant competitive advantage over small US farmers and developing country farmers in the form of superior risk management capabilities.

In the US, and also perhaps in the developing world, there are concrete steps that can be taken to ensure equality of access to market-based methods of risk management:

1. Attention must be paid to the size of standard contracts. In the US a 5,000 bushel standard is not small enough for small farmers.

2. If alternative markets (that is, with smaller contract specifications) are created in order to address this first problem, the quality of such markets, in terms of liquidity and depth, must be noted and addressed.
3. Increased public assistance to make new agricultural cooperative start-ups viable might be an additional means by which to address market access difficulties.
4. Educational initiatives to inform small farmers of their risk management options, and assist in strategising and utilisation, are vital components of a market access agenda.

Although agricultural risk privatisation is quickly becoming a global norm, this analysis suggests new ways in which developed and developing country governments might use public funds to assist farmers. As we have seen, 'farmers' are not a homogeneous group. Public funding might be employed to address access difficulties to market-based risk management techniques for segments of the farming population. Paradoxically, even privatised derivatives markets require public support to operate effectively.

Notes

1. Classic statements of the superiority of market over government management can be found in: Smith (1776), Ricardo (1821), Friedman (1982), Hayek (1980) and Obstfeld (1998).
2. Shaw (1973), McKinnon (1973), and Viksnins (1980) make powerful cases for 'financial deepening'.
3. I have yet to find a substantive discussion of farmers and derivatives that distinguishes between different kinds of farmers in terms of farm sise aside from that of Steinherr (1998). The Mississippi State Agricultural Extension has a partial study on risk management techniques used by 'limited resource' farmers (Vergara 2001). Peck (1985), and the Chicago Board of Trade website (www.cbot.com) are good illustrations of the way in which the term 'farmer' is used rather uncritically in discussions of derivatives usage in the agricultural sector.
4. See, for example, Dodd (2002) and Dodd (2005).
5. Based on data from USDA (2002b) Agricultural Census.
6. Based on data from the USDA Economic Research Service's, 'US Crops and Products Supply and Utilisation, 2002'. The average yields are assumed to be uniform across farms of different size.
7. Based on data from USDA (2002b) Agricultural Census.
8. See Note 6 above.
9. Data from the Chicago Board of Trade.
10. Data from the Commodity Futures Trading Commission Annual Report 2004.
11. See p. 97
12. See p. 97.

Part II
The Popularisation of Finance

Part II of this volume brings to our attention the ways in which the deepening and broadening of financial activities after 'deregulation' continues to have a social impact in the everyday lives of millions across the global political economy. It deals with the social consequences of the popularisation of finance through, for instance, wider ownership of securities, the increased promotion of consumer credit, annuities, and pensions. This expansion in markets for financial consumer products should be seen in the context of neoliberal deregulation and a broad programme of welfare retrenchment, particularly within Western Europe. The shift from collectivist welfare to an anti-collectivist ideology is apparent in the discourse of the Financial Services Authority (UK), which promotes financial inclusion as a partial remedy to social exclusion:

> We [FSA] share a vision of better informed, educated and more confident citizens, able to take greater responsibility for their financial affairs and play a more active role in the market place for financial services.[1]

Placing the FSA's discourse of financial education and literacy under scrutiny, Froud, Leaver, Williams and Zhang in Chapter 6 argue that falling information costs have promoted a process of product proliferation which increasingly outruns consumer knowledge. In this context, the problem of financial literacy, in the absence of a driving scandal, has been framed in the language of prudence, regulation and social exclusion. The authors argue that the problematisation of financial literacy in terms of social exclusion obscures a process of 'adjusting consumers to meet neoliberal norms rather than adjusting financial products to meet prevailing attitudes, behaviour and needs'.

One central concern in promoting financial literacy is the 'pension problem', analysed by Mary Condon in Chapter 7. This author considers whether and to what extent gender can play a role as an analytical category in understanding the shift to 'defined contribution' (DC) from 'defined benefit' (DB) pension plans. In this respect, the chapter is a welcome addition to feminist political economy of finance, where gender analyses remain rare. Condon documents the political, economic and discursive shift away from the norm of DB to the DC pension plan now taking place across the industrialised world. Various explanations for this shift are explored, including the rise of post-Fordism and the feminisation of labour markets under the new economy, all of which, the author contends, have a gendered content. Indeed, she argues that the very discourse of 'retirement' itself is gendered. Condon's feminist approach shows that choices in terms of pension provision are embedded in specific material and psychological constraints, as well as in the broader set of social and familial relations. Overall, a clear case is made that the shift to the financialised provision of pensions is creating new forms of gender inequality, new forms of discursive discipline and new forms of gendered insecurity. New forms of collective endeavour will, therefore, need to take account of the gendered nature of retirement and its associated investment risk discourses.

Questions of risk in terms of the social consequences resulting from the expansion and popularisation of financial products take a different turn in Chapter 8, where Johnna Montgomerie focuses on the credit card market. The author seeks to account for the current unprecedented levels of profitability within the credit card industry, directing attention to the deregulation of the banking industry in 1986 and the emergence of innovative methods of securitising credit card receivables. These processes reduced the costs of credit card issuers considerably, setting in train unparalled profit growth in this market, and the geographical and social expansion of the credit card in everyday life. The consequences of this innovation in securitisation have led to cooperation between third party issuers and large multinational corporations (MNCs), which encouraged the widespread use of credit cards credit to facilitate the increased consumption of MNC goods. Montgomerie infers that there is an inherent instability in this process, ultimately concluding this strategy may be difficult to sustain, and the alchemic pretensions of the banks may prove groundless.

This expansion in financialisation and credit in the wake of deregulation are addressed further in Chapter 9, where Or Raviv examines the mechanisms through which global finance has expanded into the 'emerging markets' of Central Europe. Raviv argues that in the process of capitalist penetration, the neoliberal mode of regulation and global private finance are closely coordinated. In contrast to the orthodox appreciations of financial liberalisation and deepening as positively associated with flexibility and efficiency, 'Central Europe in the EU Financial Embrace' is primarily concerned with the concentration of disciplinary power in a foreign-owned banking sector and its implications for the local non-financial sector, local state regulators, and households. The author carefully elucidates the specificity of financial predation here, arguing that the peculiarity of European finance has allowed banks to retain 'a much more significant disciplinary role'. Ultimately, he argues that the influx of foreign banks into Central Europe has failed to optimise investment, the efficiency of economic management, and general welfare patterns. Instead, new EU member countries have seen the regulation and configuration of their national financial systems and by implication, their economies as a whole pass into foreign hands.

Finally, Gérard Duménil and Dominique Lévy offer a timely class analysis of how financialisation in France and the United States has generated the emergence of new, but divergent, trends in social relations. Focusing on the last century, they argue that neoliberalism has been successful in enabling the restoration of capital income growth through the control of labour costs, maximisation of the profit rate, high real interest rates, and a lavish distribution of dividends on the back of rising stock markets. By contrasting households' shares of financial income in the United States and France, the authors conclude that in France, the social compromise shifted to the right under neoliberalism. In this respect, the distance between managerial and capitalist classes in terms of income and politics remained considerable, with management actually being 'disciplined' by capital. In contrast, in the United States the managerial class was split, and society shifted significantly further to the right than in France.

Note

1. http://www.cpag.org.uk/info/Povertyarticles/Poverty114/financial.htm

6
The Quiet Panic about Financial Illiteracy

Julie Froud, Adam Leaver, Karel Williams, Wei Zhang

> *Financial literacy is important. The need to improve financial literacy is also urgent.*
>
> John McFarlane, CEO of ANZ Bank and Chairman of the
> Australian Bankers Association 2003

> *This book is the first major study of financial education at the international level. It highlights the economic, demographic and policy changes that make financial education increasingly important, identifies and analyses financial literacy surveys in OECD countries, describes the different types of financial education programmes currently being offered... and suggests some actions that policy makers can take to improve financial education and awareness.*
>
> *Improving Financial Literacy*, OECD 2005

These two quotes epitomise the current panic about financial illiteracy. From the mid-1990s, establishment figures including politicians and bankers in the UK, USA and Australia have discovered the problem of financial literacy, which is now recognised at national level through inquiry and initiatives. By the mid-2000s, the recently discovered problem went global on the assumption that all high-income countries have a literacy problem requiring attention. The OECD book of 2005 is important because it provides an overview, including a consensual statement of the problem and an endorsement of literacy education as the fix. Interestingly, this is a relatively quiet panic, especially if we make the comparison with the problem of corporate governance, which was also discovered in the decade of the 1990s. Financial illiteracy has not been the object of Congressional inquiries; nor has it figured in front page headlines as governance did in the early 2000s.

In this paper we are not primarily concerned with the conceptual definition of financial literacy, which is relatively unproblematic. In their report to National Westminster Bank, Noctor *et al.* (1992) defined *financial literacy* as 'the ability to make informed judgments and to take effective decisions regarding the use and management of money'. Schagen and Lines (1996: 91) broke this capability up into its constituent general elements of knowledge and attitude. They argued that the financially literate would have: an understanding of the key concepts of money management; a working knowledge of financial institutions, systems and services; a range of analytical and synthetic skills, both general and specific; and attitudes which allow effective and responsible management of financial affairs. These general definitions can be inflected to cover the situation and requirement of specific groups of consumers, so that a study of poverty defined financial literacy as 'a knowledge of sources of credit and rights in relation to specific creditors, budgeting skills, and an understanding of basic financial terminology' (Rogaly *et al.* 1999).

This chapter is about the socio-economic problematisation of financial illiteracy, which leaves the problem discovered yet unsolved. The first section develops an updated concept of *panic* as the prism through which we can analyse the whole process of economic problem definition and policy response in present day capitalism, which aims to combine the economic benefits of neoliberalism with social responsibility. The second section is about problematisation and policy response. It begins the analysis of a quiet panic by explaining how fears about the consequences of illiteracy were both a weak driver of diffuse concern and a muffled policy response managed by different coalitions in the US, UK and Australia. The third and final section looks at the intractability of the problem. Economic problematisations often work not by exaggeration but by understatement, which makes a problem appear amenable to treatment by the standard fixes. In this case we respond by reworking evidence from official and unofficial inquiries into illiteracy to explore the problem.

These sections deliver a further instalment of our analysis of new policy areas in present day capitalism. Our main interest here is in the problem/policy cycle through which behavioural and attitudinal deficiencies are discovered and then rediscovered under conditions that create panic, while policy fixes recurrently fail to solve the primary problem about motivation and capability. This analysis of ineffectual good intentions complements our previous work on a related panic, corporate governance (Erturk *et al.* 2004, 2005a).

Economic panics under neoliberalism with responsibility

In thinking through the policy problem of financial literacy we return to the idea of (public, moral) panic, introduced through the work of Jock Young (1971) and Stanley Cohen (1972) on sub-cultural deviance and subsequently widely used in media and cultural studies. In this section, we begin with the history of the concept of panic in the UK, before setting it in the economic context of neoliberalism. This will allow us to present an outline framework for understanding economic panic in present day capitalism.

In a much-quoted passage Cohen defined panics:

> Societies appear to be subject, every now and then, to periods of moral panic. A condition, episode, person, or group of persons emerges to become defined as a threat to societal values and interests; its nature is presented in a stylised and stereotypical fashion by the mass media; the moral barricades are manned by editors, bishops, politicians and other right thinking people, socially accredited experts pronounce their diagnoses and solutions; ways of coping are evolved or (more often) resorted to; the condition then disappears, submerges or deteriorates and becomes more visible. Sometimes the subject of the panic is quite novel and at other times it is something which has been in existence long enough, but suddenly appears in the limelight. Sometimes the panic passes over and is forgotten, except in folklore and collective memory; at other times it has more serious and long-lasting repercussions and might produce such changes as those in legal or social policy or even in the way society conceives itself (1972: 9).

Cohen's ideas about media 'over-reporting' (1972: 31) and amplification of deviance were inserted into a more politicised cultural studies through Stuart Hall *et al.*'s (1978) classic study of 'mugging'. But, after the mid-1980s, changes in the political landscape and in epistemology led to a series of both explicit rejections (for example, Hunt 1997) and critical reactions against the concept of panic (for example, McRobbie and Thornton 1995). McRobbie and Thornton argued that the concept of panic needed updating, even if paedophilia or internet porn could still occasion old fashioned panics. We would add that the updating needs to consider more than changing epistemologies and the new pervasiveness of media in a more fragmented society because present day capitalism assembles many components that are outside the field of the visible for cultural studies. If we make the shift from cultural studies to cultural economy, we could start by observing that there is a long history of economic panics around issues such as productivity which, as part of the prevailing division of intellectual labour, are discussed by historians of economic thought, not sociologists.

One important cultural economy question is, what is new and different about the economic panics of our time. Two points are relevant here if we consider the UK. First, Thatcher after 1979 promised private ownership, competition and the market but, as Moran (2003) demonstrates, the outcome was the Financial Services Authority, utility regulators and a massive reinvention of regulatory controls on business. Second, under Blair's New Labour after 1997, the language of the post-war social settlement was selectively used to justify a hybrid we have termed 'neoliberalism with responsibility', whereby competition and private business management deliver an economic dynamism whose disruptions can be rendered politically palatable by regulation and the enforcement of social responsibility.

The second point is that in this context the economic panics are now as much about process as about outcomes, illustrated by the growing insistence in the 1990s on (the need for better) corporate governance in the advanced countries, beginning with the UK's Cadbury report (1992) and culminating in the OECD's *Principles* (1999). In our view, the more subdued and low-key panic about literacy represents more of the same. The benchmark reference in economic panic in Britain in the 1900s or 1950s was about relative performance and competitiveness *vis à vis* other advanced capitalist economies; in the 1990s and after panics are about the gap between neoliberal ideals of process and the awkward actualities of self-serving directors and ignorant consumers. The concept of panic is useful here because it takes us away from rationalistic ideas of policy acting on objects through an ends/means calculus so that symptoms are cured, palliated or managed by specific interventions that solve primary problems. Panics are much more emotional, operate through discursive logic and aim for closure through the addressing of problems in ways which have often had large secondary effects while leaving the primary problem unsolved.

From this point of view, it is useful to start by thinking about the features common to the 1990s panics about governance and literacy. These are ostensibly about different things: in the one case about self-serving managerial elites in giant companies and, in the other, about the absence of capabilities in mass consumers. But they exist in a common frame that defines the necessary actions of key economic agents and the possible political reactions of social actors.

(1) The panic is economic because it is about the threatening and deviant motives and behaviours of actors constructed as key economic agents. The discrepancy between ideal type characterisation and actual behaviour threatens the fabric of an economy which, in the neoliberal frame, only works to produce economic dynamism when key agents satisfy specific behavioural preconditions: workers participate in the labour market; shareholders take the responsibility of ownership seriously; senior managers act for shareholders; and consumers choose rationally to generate market signals and safeguard their own welfare. These basic presuppositions define the field within which panic then occurs: the different agents should represent a narrowly defined rationality but more often display dysfunctional attitudes and deviant behaviours which challenge the utopian reform project of making the world more like a particular kind of economic theory.

(2) The actualities of attitude and behaviour are such that many basic preconditions are not met for long periods of time without any panic
ensuing. But, behavioural discrepancy becomes public problem
through an episode with specific drivers that then resonate to create
general panic. *Episodic panic* responds to drivers such as dysfunctional
behaviour with dramatic consequences in terms of winners and losers.
This was the case with dishonest management in Enron or WorldCom
and with overpaid self-serving CEOs in many other companies. *General
panic* then typically works by enlisting all in a polity where many of
the traditional divisions between left and right politics have become
blurred and universal agreement masks the various motives of different
players.

(3) Media indignation and political opportunism about (sometimes unrep-
resentative) egregious behaviour or blameless losers is important in
stoking public indignation. But the technical nature of the issues is
generally such that the problem definition and the argument about
lines of response are quickly captured by official reports representing
the mainstream, consensual views of big business and the political
classes, as was the case in the series of British reports on governance
that followed Cadbury (1992). One of the most interesting points is
that the empirical definition of the problem in official reports typically
works not *via* exaggeration but understatement because a problem
about the behaviour of one class of agent (directors or consumers) is
represented as amenable to treatment through standard policy fixes
(proceduralised governance or educational programmes) acceptable to
big business. The fundamental intractability of the problems posed by
the inappropriate behaviour of whole classes of agents cannot be confronted because that would raise unanswerable questions about ineffectual responses and quixotic projects.

(4) In the absence of left/right oppositional politics, reform does not
comprise concessions extracted from unwilling government and/or
big business. Instead, the solution is initiatives, proposed and directed
by coalitions of the political and business classes in and around
government, regulatory agencies and giant firms. The leading role can
be taken by any combination of these players whose weakness and
conflicted motives further complicate the articulation and development of policy. Initiatives combine new policies with repackaged old
ones and focus on low-cost forms at accessible points of intervention.
The preference is often for formalised policies creating paper trails
of compliance, and repeated failure does not prevent the recycling of
standard fixes such as remuneration committees in governance.

(5) The problems are perennially unsolved because the behaviour of the
agents remains dysfunctional and the same misbehaviour is rediscovered in the next episode of panic. Not only is the behaviour of agents

generally difficult to control, but the outcome of persisting behavioural discrepancy is tolerable because, although many of these deficiencies have distributional consequences for individuals and groups, they are not immediately system threatening.

Quiet panic: weak drivers and muffled response

Establishment authorities like bankers and politicians dutifully emphasise the seriousness and urgency of the problem, however most high income countries have done little to investigate or solve the problem. Table 6.1 shows that only 6 of 28 countries surveyed by the OECD have conducted a public survey of financial literacy; and in most of those 28 countries the policy response to illiteracy has taken the (low effort) form of web sites and brochures. Interestingly, the OECD study also clearly shows that three high-income countries, the UK, USA and Australia, have been considerably more active. This section tackles two questions. First, why did the problematisation of financial literacy produce such a low-key panic in the high-income countries and, second, how and why have the more active countries found it difficult to frame effective policy to change attitude, capability and behaviour.

This uneven and subdued response can be immediately explained by focusing on the weakness of episodic drivers and the consequent failure to capture public attention. The key consideration here is the absence of any intelligible major scandal that has clearly produced winners and losers. In this case, the issue is not about whether victims exist but how their misfortune is labelled and explained. Thus, millions have lost out through various forms of endowment mortgages and personal pensions in the UK; indeed, most of the British who took out a mortgage to buy their homes in the late 1980s are victims. The dominant product then was the endowment mortgage on which the estimated collective shortfall is £40 billion, with around 80% of endowment policies unlikely to generate enough funds to pay off the mortgage (House of Commons Treasury Select Committee 2004: 5). But these losers are invariably represented as victims of 'mis-selling' by financial institutions (not of illiteracy). In this case, the appropriate response is compensation for victims, backed by education of the salesman and regulation of the industry, not education of consumers. As we have argued elsewhere, in the case of the Equitable Life crisis about guaranteed annuities, it is in any case quite unreasonable to expect the consumer to have the technical information and expertise to identify risks, especially when key policy decisions were not disclosed to the Board or policy holders (Erturk *et al.* 2005b: 20–1).

In the absence of a driving scandal, the problem of financial literacy has been explained through less compelling, forward-looking arguments about the benefits of literacy. Furthermore, the force of these arguments was limited by the way in which they were framed in different languages about prudence, regulation and social exclusion, which appeal to diverse constituencies.

We can begin with prudence about retirement needs which is the first reason the OECD gives for increasing interest in financial literacy:

> An increasing number of workers will have to rely on defined benefit contributions and their personal savings to finance their retirement as governments begin scaling back the benefits of state supported social security programmes and as the number of employers offering defined benefit plans decreases (OECD 2005: 11).

This argument engages with current debates and involves constructing a scenario for the future where literacy becomes more essential, supported by factoids suggesting current systems are unsustainable. Thus, the Australian banker John McFarlane (2003) emphasised that the proportion of the Australian population above retirement age would increase from 1 in 5 in 2002 to 1 in 2 by 2050. Similarly, the UK Pensions Commission reports (2004, 2005) have stressed the need to make decisions about retirement age and public expenditure on pensions over the periods to 2020 and 2050 to deal both with demographic change and current meagre state pensions. But this is a long run that is difficult for most individuals to engage with, limiting the direct effect on individual behaviour or political calculation.

Similar points can be made about the market efficiency argument which sketches another future world where less regulation would be required if literate consumers met responsible suppliers. In the UK, a 2004 FSA report includes a virtuous circle account of how a national strategy for literacy contributes to the development of efficient markets:

> ...more people review their financial situation regularly; people are more discriminating when shopping for financial services; fewer people buy unsuitable financial services and products; the financial services industry designs products that more closely meet people's needs; products are promoted and sold in a fashion that is more suited to people's needs; the FSA is able to take a less interventionist approach to the regulation of the financial services industry (FSA 2004: 11).

The OECD and national agencies repeat the efficient market arguments that 'well-informed consumers are better placed to recognise the need to save and invest appropriately' (OECD 2004), which could lead to lighter touch regulation. In reverse, 'a less financially capable population acts to reduce the quality of the financial services market; enabling poorer quality providers to continue in business using the same practices' (Raven 2005). But such arguments again have limited appeal because the pay-off is distant, diffuse and general, except for a narrow constituency of regulators and large financial services conglomerates, like Prudential and NatWest in the UK, ANZ in Australia and Citigroup in the USA, which have all used their involvement in financial literacy initiatives to position themselves as responsible producers.

The third argument about social exclusion further complicates matters because it does not quite fit with the other two. Exclusion draws attention to a sub-problem about how the poor, the unemployed, the old and the badly educated are disproportionately likely to be both financially illiterate and unbanked in a country like Britain where up to 9% of households have no bank account of any kind and many more are under-served in terms of access to credit and other financial services (Kempson *et al.* 2000). This not only implies a criticism of high street banks, but it invokes social democratic language and values that fit uneasily with the language of efficient markets. Thus, Kempson talks of the 'risks of long-term social exclusion' (*BBC News* 22 March 1999) while Rogaly *et al.* (1999) writes of 'economic citizenship which is undermined by non-participation'.

In sum, the various advocates of financial literacy have diverse motives and use different languages to argue for literacy. This heterogeneity is undoubtedly an intellectual weakness because the problem is represented differently within at least three different problematics about prudence, markets and social exclusion. And in the long run this complicates evaluation of policy effectiveness because a decline in social exclusion does not, for example, necessarily mean any increase in market efficiency. But heterogeneity could immediately become a political strength if the constituencies came together to agree an initial programme. However, there is a further complication about implementation. Under neoliberalism with responsibility, policy on issues like financial literacy is typically a matter of initiatives sponsored by combinations of representatives from government and regulatory agencies. The USA, UK and Australia have experimented with different kinds of combinations, which give the leading role to different actors, without so far finding a recipe for effective policy that would have any measurable effect on the literacy of any large group.

The USA has given the leading role to federal government *via* the Federal Reserve and simplified the policy problem by concentrating on school children. Early recognition of the problem of 'overspending' and debt in the 1980s (Schor 1999), broadened into a later concern about consumers' capacity to 'manage their money'. The resulting initiatives focused on school children and the most successful of the non-profit organisations promoting financial literacy is the *Jump$tart* Coalition for Personal Financial literacy, first convened in 1995. This was followed in 1998 by the federal government's launch of a national campaign, FL2010, intended to increase the average high school student's awareness of personal finance and investment (www.fl2010.org). In 2003, the Fair and Accurate Credit

Transaction Act (FACT) became law, establishing the Financial Literacy and Education Commission with the purpose of improving the financial literacy and education of persons in the USA (www.mymoney.gov).

Most of this was irrelevant to the current generation of adult decision makers and the US effort to influence the next generation encountered problems with subsidiarity, because federal government initiatives only become effective through discretionary state action and results in many cases depend on private sector contributions in a system where there is often no clear locus of responsibility. The federal government's own initiatives mainly took the form of information through the establishment of a website to circulate educational materials, a 'toll-free telephone number' to provide advice, and the publication of teaching guides. More effective action depended on state level follow through, which was variable. Against this patchwork background, it is perhaps not surprising that annual official surveys show that the financial literacy of US school children has actually declined since the late 1990s: the 1997 sample of high school students correctly answered 57% of questions but the 2004 sample got no more than 52% right (OECD 2005: 101).

British policy set itself more ambitious objectives because it aimed to influence adults as well as school children and the leading role was given to the FSA which, as Kempson *et al.* (2005: 7) point out, has the promotion of public understanding of the financial system as one of its statutory responsibilities. The then British Education Secretary, David Blunkett was clear that 'financial literacy should be improved among both pupils and adults...' (*BBC News* 19 January 2000) and in 2000 the Adult Financial Literacy Advisory Group (*AdFLAG*) was established to make recommendations on ways to improve the financial literacy of the adult population with a specific emphasis on the disadvantaged. This was the first attempt to look at access to financial services and the findings were presented to the Secretary of State for Education and Employment (AdFLAG 2000). The leadership role in developing and implementing a national strategy for financial capability was then handed to the FSA, whose key committees include members of the financial services community.

The project of 'Building Financial Capability in the UK', launched in November 2003, is currently dealing with seven lifecycle priorities including schools, young adults, workplace, family, retirement, borrowing and advice. The webpage of the project (http://www.fsa.gov.uk/financial_capability/) contains detailed information about how the organisation works and discloses modest spending of £35–40 million per year but does not discuss effectiveness. Although centralising initiatives on the British pattern may improve coherence, it is not in itself the key to well-funded effective action. Significantly, state action has also been supplemented by the activities of financial services firms. NatWest Bank's Financial Literacy Centre started research in the early 1990s and Prudential carried out a

Financial Literacy Project which produced on-line resources in 2003, targeted at both learners and tutors (www.moneymatterstome.co.uk). After the completion of this project, Prudential continued to provide sponsorship for the OECD's project on financial education.

If British problematisation of financial literacy could be constructed as a joint effort by government and business, the Australians took this approach further by handing over the leading role in policy to a financial services conglomerate. A first comprehensive adult financial education programme in 2004 was based on the findings of ANZ's national survey of literacy in 2003, which had identified a strong association between socio-economic status and financial literacy. As in the UK, the Australians have defined a broad problem and tried to formulate a national strategy on improving financial literacy to encompass development of skills both through life stages and across particular circumstances. *MoneyMinded*, the financial education programme sponsored by ANZ, consists of six topics separated into 17 workshops, each of which includes speaking notes, case studies, activity sheets and definitions of key terms. Although the Australian initiative recognises the differences between individuals' circumstances and the support they require, policy makers are clearly setting more ambitious targets without mobilising large resources or inventing new policy tools.

Underestimating the intractability of the problem

Traditional kinds of moral panic generally worked through exaggeration, which captured the mass public imagination and often involved media sensationalism. The new kinds of economic panic about process are interesting because they often work through understatement, which justifies and channels informed public attention in official reports and think tank publications circulated among the political and business classes. Under a kind of law of proportionality, the problem definition requires empirical support and grounding but the empirics cannot be so bleak that they raise fundamental questions about the appropriateness of the policy response. This is what we see in the panic about literacy, which rests on readings of literacy surveys that demonstrate a problem but do not admit that the problem is beyond treatment by the standard fixes. We will now demonstrate this by first considering the OECD's anodyne overview of the problem before putting forward an alternative reading in the form of a series of propositions.

Chapter 3 of the 2005 OECD book provides an authoritative overview of the current state of knowledge about illiteracy, and the nature of the empirical problem is summed up in four propositions based on financial literacy surveys:

> 'One result common to all the surveys is the low level of financial understanding amongst respondents'

'The surveys that included questions about respondents' social characteristics find that financial understanding is correlated with education
and income levels'
'Respondents often feel they know more about financial matters than is
actually the case'
'Consumers feel financial information is difficult to find and understand'
(OECD 2005: 42–4).

Each proposition is accompanied by illustrative empirics, with the complexity of the detailed evidence consigned to an appendix. The chapter
then makes the connection between the packaged problem and the
standard policy fixes in a section titled 'Lessons for financial education programmes', where each of the four propositions turns out to have a corre-
sponding policy lesson. Thus, the specific problems of low income and
education groups can be met by 'targeting financial education programmes
to those groups of consumers who are most in need of it'; and on
overconfidence, 'policy makers need to think about the best way to reach
these consumers and convince them that they need financial education'
(OECD 2005: 45).

Through such devices, the official accounts encourage the reader to
believe in the possibility of a virtuous circle whereby policy addresses the
problem after suitable lessons have been drawn. But it is perfectly possible
to construct another reading of the empirical evidence. In the five propositions below, we bring together evidence about illiteracy from different
sources in the UK, USA and Australia; these countries can fairly be grouped
together because they are all at the neoliberal end of the spectrum, with
high levels of home ownership and traditions of stock market investment
linked to distinctive private systems of provision for retirement pensions.
In these countries we would expect to find the most sophisticated financial
consumers and the highest degree of literacy; instead what we find are
similar patterns of aversion, ignorance and incompetence.

*(i) A fundamental absence of interest or aversion to thinking about financial
affairs amongst a majority of the population*

Most education programmes rest on the assumption that citizens or consumers are generally willing to learn if issues are brought to their attention.
But the empirical evidence shows that this is not so for a significant part of
the population. A 1996 Mintel survey into retirement planning in the UK
found that only 30% of respondents were 'very interested' in finance as
against 10% who never thought about finance and 60% who thought
about finance only when 'absolutely necessary' (see also Whitehouse 2000).
On this evidence, the population as a whole has an attitude problem about
finance, which has so far only been really taken into account by the behav-

ioural finance researchers at Wharton Business School (Mitchell and Utkus 2004) who have tried to think through the consequences of popular attitudes for pension design and structure. The Wharton researchers have certainly confirmed the aversion of a majority of citizens to long-term financial planning. Thus McFarlane (2003) found that more than half of 1,141 randomly selected US respondents: had no strong retirement goals (and moreover lack the discipline to pursue such goals); consider financial matters a 'source of stress, anxiety and confusion'; or are uninterested in the future. Furthermore, the evidence shows that those citizens who are willing in principle may also lack three other key prerequisites: conceptual understanding, behavioural consistency in acting on that understanding and basic calculative competence.

(ii) A blurred and indistinct conceptual understanding of the basic financial concepts and relations

This point emerges most clearly from the US survey by Harris for the National Council on Economic Education (NCEE) (1999), which interviewed just over 1,000 adults and simultaneously administered a questionnaire to around 1,000 senior high school students. The survey was designed to evaluate knowledge of 'basic economic principles' and included relevant evidence of misunderstandings about what inflation means and how it impacts on borrowers and lenders to create winners and losers. This is important because hedging against changes in the value of money is one of the most fundamental objectives of long-term savings plans. One might suppose that most adults would intuitively understand changes in the value of money after living through a period of rising prices in and after the 1970s; but fewer than two in five adults (37%) and students (30%) recognised that the statement 'money holds its value well' in a period of inflation is incorrect (NCEE 1999). There is as much or more confusion about who wins and loses from such price changes. Only one in three adults recognises that people who borrowed money are most likely to be helped by inflation; a similar proportion (32%) believe that creditors or banks that loan money will benefit.

Clearly, part of the problem here is the abstract nature of the concept of inflation. But the level of ignorance and confusion remains distressingly high if questions about general relations are framed in common-sense terms echoing the 'health warnings' included in many investment-related documents. The most fundamental of those warnings is, of course, that the value of investments can go up or down, but in the ANZ survey of 2003, 19% of Australian respondents believed 'good investments are always increasing in value' (OECD 2005, Annexe A, p. 115), only 63% 'accepted short-term fluctuations in market value' with managed investments and only 12% were prepared to accept that the market values of property could fall (ANZ 2003: 52). Furthermore, even if consumers are able to recognise fundamental general relations, the evidence shows they do not necessarily act on this knowledge in making specific decisions.

(iii) Some consumers with good knowledge of fundamental general relations may yet not apply that knowledge in specific decisions

The problem of inconsistency between general knowledge and specific decisions on savings and investment emerged clearly from the ANZ survey of more than 3,000 individuals in 2003, which followed up some interesting general questions about risk/reward relations with a specific question about how much respondents would invest in a high return investment. Here, 85% of Australian respondents knew that high returns generally mean high risk. But, faced with an investment that advertised 'well above market rates at no risk', only 46% would consider it too good to be true and not invest; while an equally large group or some 44% would 'invest lightly to see how it goes before investing more heavily' (ANZ 2003: 6). This pattern of response helps to explain the millions lost in investment scams and bubbles and raises fundamental questions about how many consumers can reach that informed Socratic state where they can dispute the professional optimism of an advertisement or financial services salesman. The OECD (2005: 70), for example, believes that an educated consumer should be able to stand up to sales pressure because: 'more financially confident consumers would be better able to challenge financial intermediaries selling them credit contracts, and take better charge of their debts in general'. Even if consumers can maintain an appropriate scepticism about whether what looks good really is, sensible decision making often requires appropriate calculative competence that many lack.

(iv) Most consumers are incapable of making very simple calculations about rates of return and such like

The general level of calculative competence was explored in the UK 2004 survey by MORI for the Institute of Financial Services (IFS) by asking respondents two questions: first, they were asked to choose the right answer from several alternatives about the sum of interest earned on £2,000 over two years at 4%; second, they were asked to define APR (annual percentage rate) which is universally used in British financial services advertisements and brochures to provide benchmark comparisons of the cost of credit. Two-thirds of UK respondents failed the most elementary test of calculative competence because they did not choose the correct answer of 'around £160' in interest earned; moreover, 79% of all UK respondents could not explain APR. The ANZ survey of 2003 demonstrated similar levels of calculative incompetence in Australia and at the same time highlighted 'the disconnect between perception and understanding' because the percentage of Australians who believed they understood and could calculate was much higher than the percentage who could demonstrate calculative competence. The results here were all the more striking because the general level of mathematical capability amongst Australians was quite reasonable so that, for example, 87% of respondents could correctly perform percentage calculations (ANZ 2003: 19). But, on compound interest, while 67% of respondents reported that they understood the term, only 28% were able to demonstrate this when given a practical example at a more advanced level. The higher socio-economic groups, with more education and income, always get more of these questions right but that is a small consolation when, as we argue below, they also tend to have a delusional confidence in their own abilities.

(v) Those in the higher socio-economic groups have a misplaced confidence in their own understanding of financial matters

On any test of calculative competence, the higher socio-economic groups get more questions right, but that is not much consolation because the MORI (2004) survey of more than 1,000 UK respondents highlights a distinct problem about the misplaced confidence of the higher socio-economic groups in their own understanding of financial issues and products. Nearly half of middle class respondents in the AB groups got the interest answer right compared with just over a quarter of skilled workers in the C2s. But, as Table 6.2 shows, the middle class ABs are much less likely to return an honest 'don't know': on the interest rate question, only 11% of ABs admitted they did not know the answer, compared with 28% of C2s. If we define functional literacy broadly as knowing the answer and knowing when one does not know the answer (with the ultimate aim being to avoid making bad decisions), the results are worrying: adding up the correct answers and the don't knows, the ABs and C2s are the worst performers with 44% failing to produce the correct answer, while the DEs are the socio-economic group least likely to make the wrong decision. More broadly, the AB social groups often have a (delusional) belief in their own ability to judge financial products and choices. Here, 60% of MORI's AB respondents think, 'they understand the financial products available' as distinct from just 35% of C2 respondents. The combination of limited calculative competence and misplaced confidence is seriously alarming if consumers are now increasingly required to make individual purchases of complex products.

Conclusion

Britain's leading brand of polyurethane varnish is famously sold with the slogan 'does what it says on the tin'. This chapter demonstrates that neoliberal policy has a rather different efficacy, at least when it results from economic panics about process and where problems are addressed in ways that speak to social concern. The current dominant problemat-isation of consumer illiteracy sets us on a trajectory of adjusting con-sumers to meet neoliberal norms rather than adjusting financial services products to meet prevailing attitudes, behaviour and needs. The long-term consequences are unclear but this problematisation is more likely to safeguard current sources of profit in financial services and in the long-term may well make it easier to hold the individual consumer responsible for mispurchase of financial products or failure to make adequate financial provision for old age.

Table 6.1   Number of countries offering selected financial education initiatives

	Public initiative Number of countries	Private initiative Number of countries
Literacy survey	5	1
Internet websites	22	11
Brochures	16	10
Publications	15	9
Course and seminars	8	9
Media campaigns	7	2
Other services	13	2

Source: Based on the responses of 28 countries to the OECD Financial Education Survey, reported in Smith (2005).

Table 6.2   Responses by socio-economic group to the question '*If you were to put £2000 on deposit at 4% for two years, what interest would you expect to receive at the end of the two years? Would it be around ....*'

	AB	C1	C2	DE
Unweighted base (number of respondents)	410	463	418	629
A: £80	35%	31%	32%	22%
B: £40	9%	12%	12%	14%
C: £160	46%	39%	28%	21%
D: Don't Know	11%	19%	28%	43%

Note: Fieldwork dates – 30 September to 6 October 2004
Source: Market & Opinion Research International (MORI), table 62.

7
The Feminisation of Pensions? Gender, Political Economy and Defined Contribution Pensions

Mary Condon[1]

Introduction

The conditions under which employers in many industrialised countries are prepared to offer occupational pension benefits to their employees are currently undergoing significant normative revision. In particular, there is a well-documented shift from the norm of a 'defined benefit (DB)' pension plan, to one of a 'defined contribution (DC)' plan.[2] In the former, the employer remains liable for funding a calculable 'pension promise' for its employees and pension contributions are invested on a collective basis, while in the latter, the employer undertakes only to make specific contributions into the employee's plan and, in some forms of DC plans, individual employees may make their own contribution investment decisions (Bajtelsmit and Jianakoplos 2000; Blackburn 2002; Langley 2004; Munnell and Sundén 2004; Myners 2001). The political, economic and discursive implications of this shift will be taken up in greater detail below, but an obvious development to note immediately is that space is thereby created for individual employees to interact much more directly with financial products and securities markets in making pension investment decisions. Specifically, DC pensions ultimately make financial outcomes in retirement heavily dependent on the market performance of the investments made. The research question that animates this chapter is whether, and to what extent, gender can play a role as an analytical category for understanding the development, and implementation, of DC pensions. The chapter proceeds by situating the attempt to develop a gendered analytics of DC pensions in the context of a feminist approach to political economy. It asks to what extent gender is implicated in the systemic shift to the DC form of pension provision in the US, the UK and Canada. The discourses of choice and risk that are central to an understanding of the implications of DC pensions are then interrogated from a gender perspective. Of specific interest here are the mechanisms by which the gendered financialisation of daily life is enacted and reproduced through research findings in the field of behavioural economics as adopted in the 'personal financial wellness' literature.

Gendered approaches to political economy

The project of developing a 'gendered political economy' which purports to analyse economies as 'gendered structures' has had a somewhat uneven trajectory to date (Cook and Roberts 2000: 3–4). The analysis is possibly most advanced in relation to the economic sectors of (i) labour markets (ii) the household, unpaid labour and caregiving (Humphries 2000; Lewis and Giullari 2005; Nelson and Williams 2000) and (iii) the study of economic globalisation (Aslanbeigui and Summerfield 2000; Beneria 2003; Bergeron 2001). With respect to the analysis of gender and labour markets, researchers have documented the 'feminisation' of labour markets, by which is meant the growth in non-standard, contingent and short-term employment (Cook 2000; Vosko 2000; Walby 2000). An hypothesis with respect to occupational pensions then is whether, if labour markets are being feminised so that they look more like women's traditional patterns of employment rather than men's, is the same phenomenon also affecting modes of pension delivery? A major recent contribution of feminist political economists has been to insist on the need to disaggregate the analytical category of 'gender' into more class-sensitive and race-sensitive elements (Bakker and Gill 2003: 7; Cossman and Fudge 2002; Walby 2000). It is argued that, in part as a result of the accomplishments of the feminist movement itself, there is emerging a new 'gender order' such that women are stratified according to the extent to which they interact with the full-time labour market and have access to professional occupations. Many women are in a position to thrive socially and economically within this new gender order, but a non-trivial number cannot. As Walby puts it, 'there are very significant divisions between full-time and part-time working, and developing divisions around age' (2000: 169). The economic stratification among women is exacerbated when considered in the context of globalised labour markets (Beneria 2003). This point about a new gender order is particularly salient with respect to occupational pensions (Condon 2002). As Ginn and Arber put it, 'The immediate cause of women's pension disadvantage in later life lies in their lower earnings and more complex employment patterns, both of which reflect their family roles' (Ginn and Arber 1999: 75).

Meanwhile, relatively little attention has been paid to the gender aspects of the processes whereby economies have been 'financialised' such that they accord primacy to the 'dictates of finance capital' and specifically, the attainment of 'shareholder value' by corporations (Cutler and Waine 2001; Langley 2004: 541). A notable exception to this silence is the work of de Goede who argues that the 'commercialization of risk in finance' should be seen as a 'profitable cultural process that rests upon gendered constructions of danger and security' (de Goede 2004: 197). She highlights the domain of finance capital and risk management therein as 'a heroic masculine enterprise' (ibid: 207). This reminds us that it is important to pay attention to the ways in which gender is a constitutive element of the discursive construction of markets and economies as well as their systematic material effects.

The political economy of DC pensions

It is not hard to document the shift away from DB occupational plans to DC plans in a variety of industrialised countries.[3] So far it has been most pronounced in the US, such that, according to the US Department of Labor, 'more than four-fifths of all workers covered by employer-sponsored pension plans are participants in DC plans' with 401(k) plans now holding 'approximately 34% of all assets held by qualified pension plans' (Bajtelsmit and Jianakoplos 2000; de la Torre and Moon 2004: 58). This is especially the case for smaller, non-unionised employers (Shuey and O'Rand 2004: 464). But it appears that the UK is not far behind. Thus Ring reports that research undertaken by the Association of Consulting Actuaries suggests that 'over 60% of defined-benefit schemes have been closed or replaced by defined-contribution schemes' (2003: 67). According to Watson Wyatt, 'four out of five FTSE 100 companies now provide a DC pension scheme for at least some of their employees' (2004). The Myners report also predicts that 'defined contribution is likely to be the dominant model for future pension provision' in the UK (2001: 98). The DC sector is growing at a slower rate in Canada than it is in the US or the UK, with the occupational sector still dominated by a number of extremely large DB plans. In Canada 'the vast majority of DC plans are with small or medium-sized employers, representing less than Cdn\$10 million in assets each', but a continued exodus of employers from DB to DC plans is predicted to occur there also (Benefits Canada 2003: 36).

What information is available as to the participation by women in DC pension arrangements? With respect to the US, Shuey and O'Rand note that 'An increase has occurred over time in the participation rates for women at all earnings levels owing in part to an overall increase in DC pension sponsorship in industries where women tend to be concentrated and where DB sponsorship has traditionally been low' (2004: 463). In other words, women tend not to have jobs with access to DB pensions, so we find them contributing to DC plans as the only viable occupational alternative. It therefore becomes important to have a clear understanding of the gender implications of this shift. With respect to variation by size of compensation, Bajtelsmit and Jianakoplos report that 'Employed women with defined contribution plans are more than twice as likely to earn less than \$25,000 per year than employed men with defined contribution plans, but almost 5 times less likely to earn more than \$100,000 per year' (2000: 1). In the UK the 2004 report of the Pensions Commission concluded categorically that 'The DB-DC shift will ... tend to worsen the situation for female private sector workers' (2004: 266). A number of reasons are provided for this, including the facts that their employment and earnings rates are routinely lower and their employment has tended to be concentrated in sectors which were less likely to provide DB plans, DC schemes are less generous than DB ones, the survivor provisions of DC pensions are almost non-existent, the impact of career breaks on pension accrual is now greater in DC schemes than in DB schemes, and women buying their own annuities out of maturing DC pensions obtain lower annuity rates because of higher female longevity. Overall, the research findings of the Pension Commission with respect to women and occupational pensions in Britain confirm the need to be sensitive to 'gender order' issues. Thus it notes that 'women in full-time employment have now become **more** likely to be a member of an occupational pension scheme than men' and that 'the greater concentration of women in the public sector has meant that women are less affected by the rapid erosion of DB provision in the private sector'. But its rather equivocal overall conclusion is that '[T]he relative disadvantage that women have suffered from concentration in private sector services is thus declining, but because of a decline in men's pension provision rather than an improvement in women's' (2004: 276).

A variety of explanations are proffered in the academic literature for the shift to DC pensions. One version focuses on the restructuring of labour markets and the consequences of this for occupational welfare. Thus the shift to DC pensions is taken to be a predictable outgrowth of the rise of post-Fordism and the flexible, contingent and 'feminised' labour markets of the 'new economy' (Castells 1998, 2000; Vosko 2000). If DB plans were about a reward for long-term loyalty to a single employer, the alleged increased portability of DC plans reflect the reality that workers will work for more than one employer, often on contractual or part-time bases, and that those employers are subject to intensified price competition in a globalised economy. An explanation rooted in variations in risk exposure would point out that the shift to DC pensions entails a transfer of the risk of obtaining an adequate pension from employers to employees, by reducing the cost of the contributions required to keep a DB plan funded and by removing the legal and financial liability on employers to guarantee a specific pension amount to employees. Meanwhile employees incur the increased risk of provisioning themselves for retirement by relying on the market performance of their investments. Specifically, Cutler and Waine argue that, especially in the US, this transfer of risk occurred because of the dominance of 'shareholder value' preoccupations over those of occupational welfare for employees over the last few decades (2001). Indeed, the Myners report lists a number of specific costs to employers resulting from the regulatory structure of DB plans in Britain, such as the requirement to guarantee pension improvement and more rigorous accounting regulations concerning disclosure of the funding levels within pensions (2001: 98; Veysey 2002). This transparency is clearly directed at shareholders' ability to assess the financial health of their investments.

It should be pointed out that a 'shareholder value' explanation for reducing occupational welfare by closing DB pension plans contains its own contradictions. This is because one of the ironies is that the entities being privileged by a corporate policy organised around shareholder primacy are often *other pension funds*, or similar pools of capital like mutual funds (Harmes 1998). DB funds themselves participate in the push to shareholder primacy in the name of maximising financial returns on behalf of their beneficiaries. This fracturing of individual identities into those of workers and investor-beneficiaries ultimately legitimises the transfer of pension risk to employees and sustains financialised economies (Minns 2001). From a corporate policy point of view, one might speculate that an important result of abandoning the DB mode of pension provision is not just to potentially reduce pension liabilities for employers, but also to reduce the possibilities of collective action by pension funds investing large pools of capital, by disaggregating that capital into much smaller DC decision making units. Much of that DC capital is invested in mutual funds, which of course re-pool the money, but under different institutional, legal and financialised conditions (Harmes 1998). It should be noted that the increased disaggregation of pension capital comes at a time when, arguably, at least at the level of discourse, the movement towards 'responsible investing' by pension funds has begun to gain broader acceptance (Blackburn 2002; Clark 2000).

At the level of ideology, some commentators advance the thesis that the widespread adoption of DC forms of pension provision represents the primacy of the moral economy of neoliberalism, which privileges individual autonomy and a 'discursive responsibilization of the self' over collective provisioning by the state or the employer (Langley 2004: 552; Knights 1997). Cutler and Waine's (2001) analysis of the legislative enactment of a neoliberal platform in the 1980s suggests to them that it was neoliberal policy shifts at the state level rather than corporate policy that was the driver of change in Britain. While the new forms of subjectivity thereby created are 'sold' in terms of values of choice, prudence and economic rationality, many note that their effect is to heighten insecurity and the 'atomization of social relations' among individuals (Bakker and Gill 2003: 13; O'Malley 1998; Rose 1999). We have noted that, as the task of managing the pre-defined risk of financial insecurity in old age is passed on to individuals, they are required to develop strategies to govern themselves accordingly (Ring 2003). These discursive shifts in individual self-governance themselves spawn new material interests, with cadres of pension providers, pension consulting firms, independent financial planners, human resources specialists and even academic journals[4] stepping up to offer pension and investment-related services to plan sponsors and individual employees (Rose 1999).

The gendered political economy of DC pensions

All of these explanations for the rise of DC pensions have gendered content. At the broadest level, the discourse of 'retirement' is itself gendered, since what is being referenced is retirement from the productive labour force, not the ongoing work of social reproduction for which women take significant responsibility. Thus a number of feminist commentators have argued that pensions for women should be much more robustly based on citizenship rights rather than connections to the labour market (Condon 2002). More particularly, the discourse of retirement is gendered in terms of the relationship that is posed between the time spent in productive work and in nonwork, that is, the 'life cycle' model of pension provision. The traditional norm is that employees should prepare for retirement by contributing to a pension plan over the course of a lengthy period of work, in order to prepare for a shorter period of non-work that follows. It has been pointed out that increased life expectancies have rendered these two periods more commensurate than they were when occupational pensions first developed. But fewer have noted that this version of the retirement 'life cycle' is inherently gendered. Women's relationship with labour markets tend to be much more fractured than those of men during the so-called 'peak earning' years because of social reproduction responsibilities, they are more likely to reenter the full-time labour market later in life, and may be much more interested in working beyond traditional retirement ages, given their greater longevity (Street and Ginn 2001: 32). The aggregate policy implications of removing mandatory retirement ages and expecting workers to work for longer need to be considered with care, and cannot be addressed in detail here. The point simply is that women's trajectories of work and non-work are generally more complicated than those of men and this complexity is not reflected in gendered retirement provision norms. As I argue below, despite the apparent feminisation of pensions represented by the growth of DC structures, they are unlikely to improve this gendered normativity, especially as the mantra of stock market investing is that investors need to be 'in for the long haul'.

More specifically, if the *raison d'etre* for the shift from DB to DC pensions is the transfer of financial risk from employers to employees in the interests of according primacy to shareholder value norms, it is worth investigating whether and how the risk transfer varies by gender. Here, it is important to be cognisant of the 'gender order' point made earlier, that women as a group are not similarly situated with respect to labour market pay or ancillary pension benefits, but rather are stratified by race and class. Yet, it is interesting to note Warren's assessment, in the context of her 2003 analysis of women and pensions in Britain:

> That even the most economically-privileged pole amongst women workers were still facing pension disadvantage compared with most men

confirms the necessity of retaining gender in the analysis of economic inequality ...the fact that the pension savings that the privileged pole had built up in their own right were worth only 42% of their male peers reaffirms the vast differences in the independent financial positions of women and men in top jobs (2003: 623).

But for women facing occupational segregation into low-paying jobs that do not offer benefits at all or offer less desirable ones, the risks of instability and heightened future financial insecurity associated with the shift to DC pensions are intensified (Ginn and Arber 2001; Shuey and O'Rand 2004: 465). We have noted that employers tend to contribute less to DC than to DB forms of pension (Langley 2004: 551) and that individuals are required to thereby navigate ups and downs in the market performance of investments to a much greater degree.

With respect to the explanation rooted in neoliberal ideology, a number of feminist scholars have pointed out that neoliberalism generally is coded masculine (Bakker 1996; Brodie 1997; Cossman and Fudge 2002). Policy preferences for the technocratic rationality of markets and limited state regulatory 'intervention' in those markets, the heightened responsibilisation of individuals to manage their own well-being, as well as attacks on the redistributive efforts of states by way of welfare provision have all been critiqued from a gender point of view, both because of their disproportionately negative effects on women generally and because of the impoverished version of social relations and social citizenship they instantiate (Condon and Philipps, forthcoming). In particular, reducing the public pension exposure of states has been an important plank of a widespread privatisation agenda promulgated by the World Bank, the OECD, and the so-called Washington consensus, though this agenda has played out differently in different states (Blackburn 2002; Condon 2002; Ginn, Street and Arber 2001; Rittich 1998). With respect to specific shifts within the private sector from DB to DC pensions, it becomes important to investigate the gender content of the 'governance of the self' that is thereby called into being (Rose 1999). The next section of the chapter turns to this issue.

Choice, risk and gender

A key feature of the major forms of DC pension plan is that they offer employees the opportunity to direct the investment of the contributions made into their plan. They thus accomplish a major discursive shift in pension provision, which is to transform employees directly into investors in financial markets[5] and to tie their personal financial fate ever closer to the well-being of those markets, in a context in which the risk-spreading feature of collective pension funds is absent (Condon 2002; Gold 2003; Langley

2004). In neoliberal terms, this opportunity to exercise investment choice provides welcome autonomy to individual investors, enabling them to have greater control over their financial destiny. At a general level, the economic discourse of rational choice that is taken to underlie the enterprise of stock market investing has been subjected to a feminist critique. Feminists have argued that the model of 'separative sel(ves)' who optimise selfish choices uninfluenced by their multiple identities or the social construction of their desires, without regard for the existence of 'empathy, altruism or a sense of social solidarity', is inherently gendered. It takes account of neither the material or social constraints under which people make choices nor the embededness of their lives (Condon 2000; England 2005; Waylen 2000: 17–19). At a different level of critique, the neoclassical economic definition of rationality has also been problematised by behavioural economic analysts, who have undertaken a variety of social-psychological tests designed to demonstrate that individuals are subject to systematic biases in their decision making that deviate from a neoclassical rational choice approach (Langevoort 2002; Nofsinger 2005; Sunstein 2000).

Specifically with respect to DC pensions, a highly significant location of choice-making is the initial decision to enroll as a contributor. The removal of mandated enrollment requirements as a systemic feature of occupational pensions is consistent with neoliberal privileging of individual autonomy. But it also operates at the discursive level to uncouple employment from a robust sense of entitlement to ancillary benefits like a specific pension. The rise of voluntarism has spawned a great deal of attention in the behavioural economics literature about the motivations behind choices to enroll or not enroll in a pension plan. Here the assertion is that individuals are not particularly 'rational' about retirement planning, by their own admission and by 'objective' evidence (Mitchell and Utkus 2004: 5ff). Mitchell and Utkus characterise this as a gap between desire and action (a 'lack of willpower'), which may be related to the fact that the consequences of failure to join a pension plan will be distant, as opposed to short-term (ibid: 6–10, 61ff).[6] A feminist approach might be more likely to examine how such choices are embedded in specific material and psychological constraints as well as in a broader set of social and familial relations. As Joan Williams argues in relation to the 'choices' women make about navigating full-time work or family caregiving responsibilities, '[A]llowing women the 'choice' to perform as ideal workers without the privileges that support male ideal workers is not equality (2000, intro)'. Feminists might also be less inclined to privilege autonomy for its own sake at the expense of robust regulatory requirements requiring both employer and employee pre-commitments to pension funding.

Shifting the focus from the choice to save in a DC plan at all to the decision about what to invest in requires a broader exploration of the norms of risk governance embedded in pension arrangements (Beck 1992; Ericson

and Haggerty 1997; O'Malley 1998), and in particular, the extent to which
this is gendered terrain (Hannah-Moffat 1999). As de Goede points out,
'financial risk management is cast as a domain of technical expertise'
(2004: 207). Professionalised DB pension funds are expected to be conver-
sant with modern norms of investment risk management in making
asset allocation decisions, including portfolio theory (which valorises
diversification in order to reduce firm-specific risk), risk-return ratios, asset-
liability management (ALM), and value at risk investing (VaR), as well as
distinctions between active ('beat the index') and passive investing (Clark
2000; de Goede 2004; Langley 2004; Luckhaus 2005; Mitchell and Utkus
2004: 13–15). As de Goede cautions, 'financial risk management does not
just *react to* but *creates* particular definitions of insecurity... while pretend-
ing to eradicate uncertainty from business ventures, finance identifies and
invents more and more possible uncertainties to be hedged'[7] (2004: 213).
The tendency to instability caused by a number of the investment strategies engaged in by DB funds have been noted by academic commentators
(Clark 2000; Harmes 1998; Langley 2004).

If risk management by DB funds can have perverse effects of heightening
instability, is it likely that individual DC employees, now increasingly
required to navigate the technocratic enterprise of investment risk management, will escape this? Empirically, there is significant variation, across
jurisdictions and across types of DC plans, in terms of the latitude provided
to individuals with respect to investment choices. Less choice has typically
been provided in the UK and Canada in the occupational pension sector
than with respect to US 401(k) plans, but stakeholder pensions in the UK
are changing this (Byrne 2004). It will be recalled that a significant feature of
the Enron debacle for its employees was the latitude provided to both
employers and employees under 401(k) plans to make contributions in the
form of own company stock (Blackburn 2002, on Enron; Mitchell and Utkus
2004: 15).[8] Employees' acceptance of this invitation, in disregard of the
principles of diversification, significantly worsened their financial situations.
The typical scenario is for individuals to be offered the choice of investing
contributions across a menu of investment funds, variously characterised as
balanced, growth, value or international equity funds, depending on the
level of 'risk tolerance' desired. Financial products pegged to various indices
have also developed to allow investors the benefits of diversification
without the need to engage in more active investment strategies.

The rise of the so-called 'ownership society', rooted significantly in the
advent of DC pensions, has spawned an extensive literature investigating
the behavioural or psychological biases exhibited by individuals investing
in financial markets, such as insufficient asset diversification, or the perils of
'asset allocation confusion,'[9] momentum-chasing,[10] and over-confidence'[11]
(Deaves 2005: 6; Mitchell and Utkus 2004: 15). Some researchers posit that
employees are unduly influenced by peer pressure or social norms[12] (Bailey,

Nofsinger and O'Neill 2003). As Bailey, Nofsinger and O'Neill summarise, '[O]n average, employees do not really know how to pick a portfolio that represents their desire for the future' (2003: 150). One finding within this literature that is considered particularly problematic is that 'many employees show limited... interest in their pension arrangements' (Byrne 2004; Peggs 2000). Thus, in the DC context, where employees are given choices about where to invest their retirement contributions, the evidence suggests they do not exercise those choices, but tend to stick with the initial default options provided (Mitchell and Utkus 2004: 11, 17–18; Stabile 2002). This empirical evidence has not yet destabilised the discursive power of neoliberal individual autonomy. Indeed, recent pension literature directed at plan sponsors raises the issue of whether sponsors should take any action in relation to those members who engage in frequent trading, without their personally being responsible for the trading fees payable. It is suggested that sponsors might consider charging transaction costs, but in any event, they should require their record keepers to monitor transaction volumes and bring 'unusual trading behaviours' to their attention (Benefits Canada March 2004: 8–10). The exercise of individual choice, therefore, may bring with it enhanced surveillance.

Not surprisingly, a particular preoccupation of the behavioural economics framework is whether individuals exhibit appropriate levels of 'risk tolerance' in order to adequately fund their retirement goals. Here a consensus appears to be emerging that individuals are 'too risk averse' in making asset allocation decisions, and become increasingly so as they age (Blake 2003; Dodge 2005; Greenwich Associates 2005; Myners 2001). Several strands of analysis investigate whether risk tolerance varies by social location, with gender, race, earning levels and marital status being subject to detailed attention (Bajtelsmit, Bernasek and Jianakoplos 2000; Roszkowski, Delaney and Cordell 2004; Shuey and O'Rand 2004; So-hyun Joo 2002; Yao and Hanna 2005; Zanglein 2001). Hallahan, Faff and McKenzie summarise recent findings in the context of its implications for the funds management industry. They argue:

> Our research, in providing support for the widely held view that women have lower risk tolerance than men and that... age has an inverse....relationship with risk tolerance, has important implications for the funds management industry: as the baby boomer cohort ages and moves into retirement we could expect to see demand shift away from the relatively more risky growth asset classes towards the less risky income asset classes, reflecting the decline in risk tolerance associated with increasing age. Moreover, this effect would be compounded by the greater life expectancy of women: as the population ages, the gender composition will shift in favour of women, who on average have a lower risk tolerance. Thus, the changing age and gender demographics of the popula-

tion will provide a dual force for change in the composition of the overall demand for investment products (2004: 75).

Analysts of risk perceptions generally would not be surprised by these findings in the context of investment decision making. Thus Slovic argues that:

[R]ace and gender differences in perceptions and attitudes point toward the role of power, status, alienation, trust, perceived government responsiveness and other sociopolitical factors in determining perception and acceptance of risk. To the extent that these sociopolitical factors shape public perception of risks, we can see why traditional attempts to make people see the world as white males do, by showing them statistics and risk assessments, are often unsuccessful (1999: 693).

The apparent passivity and lack of investment knowledge of women investors is, as we have noted, interpreted within this framework as a problem to be overcome, because of its alleged consequences for women's retirement well-being. The solution that is proffered in the personal finance literature is to better equip women to make these technocratic decisions, either by education and guidance about how to take more risk, or by the purchase of services in the 'advice market' (Charupat and Deaves 2004; de la Torre and Moon 2004).

The latter solution provides yet other opportunities for disciplining DC contributors in accordance with gendered knowledge about risk tolerance. As De Goede argues '[T]he identity of the masculine financial risk manager – the late modern master of the future and imperial adventurer – is now underpinned by scientific authority and mathematical models, which appear as profoundly apolitical' (2004: 213). It appears likely that the risk profiles generated by investment advisors and financial planners as a guide to the provision of advice to employee-investors take the findings discussed above into account. For example, the personal finance literature offers suggestions to financial advisors 'faced with spouses conflicting in their risk tolerance' (Roszkowski *et al.* 2004: 139). In an interesting example of legal norms being employed to buttress the risk-related disciplining of individuals, Yao and Hanna state bluntly that:

Although clients should ultimately decide whether they would like to take a certain level of financial risk, as a fiduciary of the client, a financial planner has the duty to act in the client's best interest – to evaluate the client's situation and make appropriate recommendations. It is the job of financial planners to educate clients (especially unmarried females) who choose inappropriate investments with low financial risk about their need to take more risk; and to educate male clients who have inappropriate investments with high risk about the importance of preserving wealth (2005: 75).

These exhortations to female DC employees to take more risk in their own financial self-interest obscure the possibility that women's systematic reluctance to engage with investment risk-taking discourse is in fact an exercise of agency rather than a lack of it; a sign of a desire to resist the 'financial responsibilization of self' and the reproduction of the social world in the image of the heroic risk-taker, in favour of alternative discourses of citizenship-based provision for pensions or other forms of collective responsibility for well-being in old age. The plausibility of this interpretation of behavioural economic findings need to be subjected to further qualitative investigation of course, but this chapter suggests the need to take gendered risk aversion seriously on its own terms, and to probe further the possibilities for discursive heterogeneity in response to ever more invasive pressure for financial self-discipline.

Conclusion

This chapter has sought to argue that the turn to financialised provision in pensions is creating new forms of gender inequality, new forms of discursive discipline, and new forms of gendered insecurity (Bakker and Gill 2003: 10). The power of financial institutions resides in part in the ability to *define* the risk of financial problems in retirement and to offer their own, market-based, solutions to these. Individual employees, especially lower-income women, are being governed more intensely by this financialisation. In contrast, employers are being regulated less pervasively, that being, on some accounts, the goal of the shift from the outset. Yet one reading of the findings of the behavioural economics literature may be that there are signs of a desire to resist the atomisation, individualisation and feminisation of occupational pensions occasioned by the shift to DC. If this is so, the task for the future is to find ways to harness gendered risk aversion to define and pursue alternative projects in relation to retirement preparedness. The first aspect of this is to continue to destabilise the hegemony of risk-based pension provision (Graham 2005), and to rethink the pros and cons of a compulsion to save for retirement. Furthermore, to counteract the disaggregating trends occasioned by the demise of DB pensions, individuals will need to enact new forms of solidarity, both at the level of general democratic participation in social and economic policy choices around pensions, and at the level of new forms of collective endeavour to invest pension contributions. Such collective enterprises will need from the outset to take knowledge of the gendered nature of retirement and its surrounding investment risk discourses into account.

Notes

1. The author wishes to thank Libby Assassi for her support of this project. Thanks for support are also due to the Social Sciences and Humanities Research Council of Canada and the Centre of Criminology, University of Toronto, as well as to Kim Brooks, Stephanie Benlshai and Toni Williams for their comments on an earlier draft.
2. I am using the term 'defined contribution plan' as an umbrella concept to capture a number of different types of pension arrangement, whose details vary but whose overall distinctive feature, that they do not guarantee any specific pension outcome to the worker, is the same. They include; occupational money purchase schemes, group personal pensions, stakeholder pensions (UK); defined contribution plans and group registered retirement savings plan (RRSP) (Canada), 401(k) plans (US). One important plane on which a number of these arrangements differ is the extent of investment choice they provide to the employee. This chapter will specify where this is a distinctive feature of some but not all of these arrangements.
3. Countries that have recently moved in this direction include Taiwan, Thailand and India. See *Benefits Canada* DC Forum, September 2005: 4.
4. See the *Journal of Personal Finance*, inaugurated in 2002.
5. The analytical separation of employees from a defined benefit pension plan, of which they are considered 'beneficiaries', is of course, a major accomplishment of pension law. See Blackburn 1999.
6. The literature makes a number of policy-related suggestions to mitigate this, such as what Mitchell and Utkus call 'commitment devices or even pre-commitment devices' (2004: 12).
7. Italics in original.
8. There may be cultural variation here between the UK and the US. See Byrne (2004: 17) arguing that employees in the UK are less interested in investing in their employer's stock.
9. A tendency to be swayed by the format in which the menu of investment options is presented rather than an 'objectively rational' allocation decision (though what this latter would be is itself controversial).
10. Engaging in the cardinal error of making investment decisions based on recent past success of individual stocks or mutual funds.
11. Overestimating one's knowledge, abilities or the precision of the information available, thus trading 'too frequently' (Deaves 2005: 11).
12. Thus, Duflo and Saez use peer effects to explain why 436 librarians in 11 buildings on the same university campus exhibited large differences in participation rates in the same 401(k) plan among librarians working in different buildings.

8
The Alchemy of Banks: The Consumer Credit Industry After Deregulation

Johnna Montgomerie

In 2004, after-tax profits in the American credit card industry were US$24.44 billion, that is a 50% increase from 2003 with reported profits of US$14.24 billion dollars (Simpson 2005). We should consider that in the same year (2004) all commercial banks averaged 1.98% return on all assets, while the credit card market, on the other hand, made a 3.55% return on before-tax earnings (Federal Reserve 2005). This astronomical profit rate has not always been the case. Credit cards first emerged at the beginning of the American post-war boom, and for the following 30 years they were considered high-risk and low-profit endeavours. Thus, this chapter asks: what can historically account for the current unprecedented profitability of the credit card industry? It is argued that the turning point in the credit card industry came after the deregulation of the banking industry in 1986 and the newly created ability to securitise credit card receivables, which, in turn, became the cornerstone of profitability. The process of securitisation means that banks and non-banks with large pools of outstanding credit card loans (receivables) can package them together under one master trust and then issue shares in that trust (securities). This form of asset management by credit card issuers is used primarily to re-capitalise existing loan pools, meaning that the original amount of money extended through credit cards is recycled by securitisation because it is taken off-balance sheet, which technically frees up these funds to be re-lent. By doing this credit card issuers have been able to dramatically reduce their costs because they no longer have to pay interest on new funds to be lent-on for credit cards; instead they use the same pool of funds again and again.

By focusing on the creation of securitisation in the context of the US financial market deregulation in 1986, we can locate the historical starting point for the unprecedented growth of profitability in the credit card market. This new financial instrument became the catalyst for the broader geographical and social expansion of the credit card in everyday life. As a result of its new profitability new actors, especially large Multinational Corporations (MNCs), were attracted into the credit card industry, and new marketing strategies were created, which aimed at altering consumer habits towards revolving balances. The entrance of an increasing number of non-banks into the credit card market has now made the creation and maintenance of large credit card portfolios the objective of many market actors, compelling them to constantly seek out new borrowers to replenish their receivables pools. By understanding the changing structure of the US credit card market historically, we can elucidate how this ostensibly detached financial process is inextricably linked to the everyday practice of credit card use. This chapter limits its focus on the shifting supply structure of credit and how this has brought about change in the organisation of markets and the imperatives of market actors. In this way we can better explore how financial power works in the creation and marketing of credit cards.

This chapter begins by examining the creation of the universal third-party card in the post-war American boom and how the social organisation of finance and production under Fordism largely dictated the form and function of the limited credit card industry. As a result of these conditions, the modern mass credit card was created but it was a very limited product known for its high operating costs, limited market, and low returns. Yet, the robust nature of the consumer market initiated a period of consultation on the possibility of deregulation in consumer credit and credit cards, to facilitate more access to credit. In the end, the deregulation of the banking industry was a political project rather than an act of social engineering. The next section examines how 'after deregulation' the credit card industry experienced far-reaching structural change emanating from the new ability to securitise credit card receivables. Specifically, I consider how the growing number of new actors in the credit card market, drawn in by its new-found profitability, changed the orientation of credit card marketing towards frequent use to increase the likelihood of revolving monthly balances. These new marketing initiatives are considered, here, as the embodiment of the changing structure of credit card finance. The chapter concludes by considering the tension between the resilience of these financial instruments in creating profit and flexibility in the credit card market and the inherent instability of its unabated expansion.

Creation of the universal credit card

The first universal third-party credit card was the Diners Club Card. It was created in 1948 when Frank McNamara, Ralph Snyder, and Alfred Bloomingdale pooled their personal credit together and offered the financial service of becoming the middlemen between traveling businessmen and restaurant merchants: extending credit to one, providing customers for the other, and charging both for their services. In 1951, using its long-standing market expertise in travellers cheques, American Express also launched its own credit card. The creation of these new credit card companies, with no goods to sell or customer loyalty to promote, meant their management had purely financial interests. These financial interests transformed the modern credit card into a financial product to be sold, meaning it has become an end in itself, rather than simply a means to an end.

The significance of the credit card's emergence in post-war Fordist America cannot be underestimated. Similar to the creation of Fordism itself, which developed as an American innovation based on its unique geopolitical and socio-economic circumstances, the credit card industry grew as a result of the economic, social, and technological characteristics of the US post-war economy. As a result of World War II the US had an enormous industrial base that allowed for its continued post-war economic expansion. The socio-political movements in favour of Keynesian demand management and full employment policies, which came as a direct consequence of fears of returning to the depression state before the war, meant filling this industrial capacity was a priority. For the first time in its history, the US had a majority of people earning income in excess of what it took to pay for their basic needs (Klein 1999). A major Keynesian response to the Great Depression was to stimulate credit growth. The Roosevelt government introduced and maintained what it called 'fair lending practices' by offering banks government-backed and guaranteed low-interest loans so that all the citizens had an equal opportunity to obtain credit from a bank (MacDonald and Gastman 2000: 221). Also, new banking regulations helped expand the amount of consumer credit available. In the US, the 1933 Glass-Steagall Act segmented the financial services industry, creating a separation between commercial and investment banking activities. This induced many commercial banks to look for new ways to expand lending to households to generate profits.

The concomitant creation of mass consumption patterns under Fordism was also necessary for the cultural acceptance of credit cards. The rapid socio-economic transformation that occurred in the post-war era where suburban neighbourhoods supplanted the urban neighbourhoods of major metropolitan centres, resulted in new consumption patterns: 'private automobiles replaced public transportation, private lawns replaced public parks, and national retail chains in local malls replaced mom-and-pop shops in downtown business districts' (Klein 1999: 10). It is no coincidence that credit cards were invented in the same decade as the first McDonald's, first fully enclosed shopping mall, first mass-produced suburban housing in Levittown, New York, founding of Best Western and Holiday Inn motel chains, the beginning of mass production television sets and of national television broadcasting, and opening of Disneyland (Ritzer 1995). The new mass consumerism of American Fordism was equally as important in spurring an historical change in societal attitudes towards borrowing. Previously, wage-earners considered it right to save first, in order to buy later. The opposite became true in post-war America, where this model was reversed: people bought first and saved in the form of monthly repayments (Gelpi and Julien-Labruyáere 2000: 108). John Kenneth Galbraith (1967) observed that the structure of borrowing and debt had been established in the Fordist era of post-war expansion. According to him, within a generation debt had become not only the norm but the expected right of virtually the entire middle class and a good section of the working class.

The inseparability of the emergence of credit cards and American Fordism can also be seen in the credit card firm structure. The internal organisation, marketing campaigns, and revenue strategies are complementary to larger tendencies within American Fordism. For instance, all four credit card companies (Diners Club, American Express, Bank Americard and MasterCharge) were configured as large-scale clearing houses. In the case of the first two bank cards, Bank Americard and Chase Charge-it Card, their respective banks put up the necessary credit, distributed the credit card to bank customers, and maintained, integrated, and promoted these exchanges, which proved decisive in establishing market dominance. The prime profit making strategy of these four major credit card companies remained the same for almost 20 years: pursuing economies-of-scale. The main reason was that as the card sponsors, the mass production of credit cards reduced the cost-per-unit for distributing and servicing customer accounts and increased the income from merchant commissions as more customers obtained cards. This meant that the marketing campaigns for the expansion of the credit card market concentrated on two things: the merchants and the consumers.

These early marketing strategies focused on establishing market share, since merchants would not sign up unless there was a sufficiently large number of card carriers in their area, and consumers would not sign up unless there was a sufficient number of merchants who accepted the card. Therefore, both the merchants and consumers required credit card companies to solicit new customers on a mass scale. Merchants needed to be convinced that they would receive more business as a result of this new technology, justifying the 7% discount rate on purchases. On the other hand, customer expansion was limited to strictly defined creditworthy individuals, meaning that banks were essentially all chasing the same customers. Standard business logic at the time dictated that the key to profitability was the proportion of mature customer accounts held by the bank (an account with a solid record of timely payments) but this limited the scope of expansion for credit card firms. In response, Amex introduced the Gold Card aimed at coaxing mature bank customers over with price protection guarantees, insurance on purchases made on Amex cards, travel insurance, and no credit limit (but Amex was a charge card, so balances could not be revolved).

Both Diners Club and Amex had their inherent weakness in the credit card market – the inability to offer revolving balances – meaning the whole balance had to be paid at the end of the month. Since both were not banks it was almost impossible for them to allow revolving balances and still be profitable because they had to service their own debts to the banks. It was not until 1958, when New York's Chase Manhattan Bank and California's Bank of America launched their respective credit cards, that the banks targeted the credit card market, and the revolving debt option was offered. The nature of the relationship between the parent bank and the credit card operation proved important to the revolving third-party credit cards' success (Wolters 2000). In terms of revenues the non-bank credit card issuers were limited to two revenue streams: a monthly fee from cardholders and a 7% discount rate from the merchants. Bank credit cards added new revenue streams through revolving credit option by charging very high interest rates on unpaid balances.

In 1966, Bank of America decided to license its Bank Americard to other issuer banks across the US in order to augment its diminishing market share in California. This action effectively created a national network for credit card transactions. Other banks interested in becoming issuers of credit cards joined together to establish a rival national network called Interbank Card Association, which created the MasterCharge card. These two national credit card systems enabled the cardholder to use a credit card for purchasing goods in areas served by other banks. Such an arrangement made it possible to transfer sales drafts from the bank of the merchant who accepted payment with the credit card to the bank of the cardholder for collection. The interchange, in effect, transformed local cards into national cards. In the late 1960s, both Bank of America and Interbank promoted their new national networks with a series of carefully calculated mass mailings of unsolicited credit cards. Its success in signing up millions of new customers meant merchants responded by wanting to sign up to gain access to new customers. This was short-lived since legal limitations made these mass mail-outs a loss-making marketing strategy, but the principles of firm expansion remained unchanged.

The legal and institutional norms of Fordism ultimately limited credit card competition to poaching mature accounts. Interest rate ceilings, segmentation in the financial service industry, limitations to total amounts allowed to lend customers in specific income categories, and legal restrictions on implementing an annual fee, all stifled profitable credit card expansion up until the late 1970s (Gelpi and Julien-Labruyáere 2000). Also, there was little change in the historical social practices of limiting use of credit cards to special purchases, especially for consumer durables (Olney 1991). The success of Fordism in providing the necessary conditions for acceptance of consumer credit has also tempered the expansion of the consumer credit industry. The same government acts that gave incentives to banks and credit unions to lend also imposed interest rate ceilings and mandatory deposit requirements, putting limits on profitable expansion of credit cards. Also, government programs such as social security, worker's compensation, unemployment benefits, and disability benefits may have contributed to a growing sense of overall economic security, giving the individuals confidence to borrow, but also limiting their need to borrow.

The institutional mechanisms that embodied the Fordist project, namely high-paid employment based on wages tied to productivity, contributed to growing household incomes, which increased the number of mature accounts for credit card companies to solicit because the overall creditworthiness of individuals increased. It was in this context that the US began its initial public consultation on the deregulation of the consumer credit industry in 1972, with the creation of the US Commission on Consumer Finance. The conclusions of this commission meant that, from 1974 to 1980 seven different US laws were amended to pave the way for deregulating consumer credit markets, with provisions for clarity and equal opportunity replacing ceilings and regulation that controlled over-borrowing and over-lending.[1] Also, a US Supreme Court ruling in 1978, weakened the broadest measures of state usury laws but kept intact protections for consumers from excessively high interest rates and fees. The rulings allowed national banks to charge the highest interest rate permitted in the bank's home state – as opposed to the rate in the state where the customer resides. As a result of these changes, many banks and non-banks sought out credit cards portfolios for profitable expansion (Draut and Silva 2003).

The alchemy of credit cards: securitisation and profitability

The most significant development from this initial wave of deregulation was the new ability of banks, and non-banks, to offer asset-backed securities (ABS). The impact of ABS on the credit card industry has been unprecedented growth and tighter competition between banks and non-banks to expand their credit card portfolios. Initially, the relationship between bank and non-bank actors was a partnership between credit card issuers and large MNCs to create intensive marketing strategies to alter credit card consumption patterns toward revolving balances. This boosted the profitability of the credit card portfolio of banks and non-banks alike. The increased competition between the various market actors to bolster credit card portfolios contributed to the successful marketing plan of Affinity credit cards, which relied on popular civil society organisations or images of celebrities on the cards as means of attracting new customers. Using these card programs as a template for the global expansion of the American credit card, banks and non-banks alike used these highly developed marketing campaigns to enter new countries with the view of reproducing the same profitable overspending habits that existed in America. It is only 'after deregulation' that the American credit card industry becomes the cultural icon we know today. It is argued here that this came about as a consequence of the increased access to renewable finance from securitisation. Thus, the previously high cost, tightly regulated and low profit credit card created in the late 1940s, becomes a sophisticated financial instrument capable of mass social change.

The creation of an ABS is known as securitisation and the name of the financial vehicle that deals with credit card loans is known as CARDs (certificates for amortising revolving debts). First created by Solomon Brothers Bank in 1986, the growth and increasing complexity of CARDs has provided an alchemy for banks by transforming often risky loans into attractive packages for big investors (Cocheo 1993). Securitisation involves the bundling and sale of credit card receivables into a pool of loans that are placed in a special subsidiary or trust. These trusts are backed by a certificate and investors can buy the certificates or shares in the trust and receive interest and principal payments as the loans are repaid.

The process of securitisation improves bank profitability because, unlike syndicate loans, ABS create liquid, fixed-rate, investment-grade obligations with spreads of 10 to 100 basis points over US Treasury obligations of comparable maturity. The income earned on the loan pools pays the interest on the securities. The bank earns a profit because it receives a higher interest rate on the loans than it pays on the securities. This arrangement is maintained in exchange for the issuer's obligation to service the loans. But as a result, the issuer removes the loans from its books. Then it can use the proceeds to make new credit card loans, meaning securitisation also creates a new method of raising funds. Securitisation used primarily by credit card issuers to generate revenue is not necessarily a 'risk management' strategy because securitisation is mainly used to re-capitalise funds. Increasingly, banks are not relying on deposits for capitalisation for loans; instead they are using new ABS issues to re-capitalise their existing deposit base. This means that ABS provides a competitive advantage to third-party issuers attempting to increase market share because when the loan capabilities of the bank exceed funding growth, securitisation allows the institution to expand loan volume faster than deposit growth (DeSear 2004).

Also, having securities offered as low-risk, fixed-rate investment, has allowed third party issuers to lower the cost of funds in relation to the interest they charge cardholders, thereby increasing profits (Simpson 2005). According to one banker, 'securitization has totally changed the credit industry in terms of how fast the market can grow as well as sparking competition that led to lower interest rates and annual fees' (Hull and Annand 1987: 138). Alongside ABS third-party issuers use other financial instruments to diversify the risk of these loan pools through vehicles like interest rate 'swaps', meaning interest payments contracts can be exchanged, bet, or hedged, on different markets. From the standpoint of the investment marketplace the relatively short maturity of the instruments secured by credit card receivables makes them particularly attractive (Punch 1998).

New marketing strategies

The new ability to recycle pools of funds, thereby reducing the overall costs of funds, through securitisation increased the supply of credit available to issuers. The first observable consequence of securitisation on the credit card industry was cooperation between third-party issuers and large multinational corporations. Freed from restrictions of capitalisation requirements and the lower cost of funds, third-party issuers sought out new, bolder, avenues for expansion. The main focus of marketing initiatives between issuers and MNCs was to alter consumption patterns among credit card users to facilitate revolving balances, the most profitable stream of revenue for issuers. The complementary effect would be advertising, promotion, and more consumption of MNC goods. This union created the first 'product benefits card' which gave holders points for every dollar purchased using credit cards. These reward schemes were intended to encourage more widespread use of credit cards to increase merchant discount volumes as well as interest from revolved balances. The most famous product benefit card is the *Air Miles* card, which gave air travel points based on the billed amount each period. Also, credit card companies teamed up with industrial producers in order to create co-branded product benefit cards. For example, in 1992, General Motors, General Electric, and Ford entered the credit card market with co-branded cards. These MNCs' incentive was to stimulate the sale of their product during a recessionary period.

Today, new reward schemes are targeted at existing 'revolvers', as they are known, a remarkable change from the 'mature account' approach of the 1960s. For example, the TravelPlus airline card offered by the American Bank One is aimed at holiday makers because vacationing was revealed to be the most likely place individuals will over-spend on their credit cards (Lucas 1994). Also, there has been a large migration from classic store cards to co-branded retail credit cards. This means the customers' new retailer/bank co-branded credit cards earns them loyalty points at the parent store, with more points earned for money spent in-store than money spent elsewhere. In this case both major retailers and issuers have teamed up to distribute new types of store cards explicitly to access the millions of existing store card holders, knowing that historically these groups rarely default on their card debts, and sell them other related bank financial products (Aldridge 2004).

Another important marketing initiative, created 'after deregulation', was developed based on the success of the reward card schemes and was called the Affinity Card. There are two types of affinity cards: lifestyle cards, which are marketed to people with a particular interest, often a charitable cause, and which provide the charity with some form of remuneration for the use of the cards; and personality cards, which have sought to cash in on the public's fascination with certain individuals, such as Elvis Presley or Madonna (Schlegelmilch 1995). Most affinity card issuers did not focus on 'poaching' existing customers away, instead they anticipated that most new customers would already have multiple credit cards but would sign up for an affinity card for their novelty. This marketing campaign was successful because personalised cards provided an incentive for consumers to accept a new card as opposed to merely switching from a previous card (Worthington 1997). It also allowed the banks and issuers to target groups with known financial attributes resulting in reduced credit risk and often increased credit card spending volume. The success of the Affinity card programme formed the basis of the expansion of US credit card banks across the globe. MBNA, the largest credit card bank, used Affinity card programmes to create a client base in the United Kingdom, Europe and East Asia.

The introduction of non-banks to the credit card business came as a result of exemptions to the 1987 Competitive Equality Company Act, which excluded credit card banks, and a few other special purpose banks, from the new definition of a 'bank.'[2] Originally, only AmEx and Sears Reobuck were major non-bank players in the credit card market, but the advent of ABS made it a viable investment for any large corporation with enough capital to become a third-party issuer (Lerner 1990).[3] Now firms like AT&T, General Electric Capital Corporation, First USA, ADVANTA Corporation, and Ford Motor Company became part of the top twenty-five largest credit card issuers (Meyercord 1994).

The large scale participation of non-banks in the credit card market signifies the wholesale shift in the form and function of the credit card industry 'after deregulation'. Admittedly, the first two credit card companies were non-banks, but the dominance of Bank Americard (now Visa) and MasterCharge (now MasterCard) from the 1950s to 1980s was exclusively based on banks' support in acting as third-party issuers. The strong trend towards increasing non-bank participation in credit card markets has come as a result of securitisation and the building of large credit card portfolios through successful marketing strategies. In an effort to create more lucrative portfolios, and as a consequence of the increased competition in the credit card market, issuers have sought to expand their market by extending ever more credit card offers to individuals, specifically to those that revolve their debts (Lucas 1994).

The current buying and selling of credit card portfolios between non-banks and banks confirms the demand for these lucrative profits. A credit card portfolio comprises the sum of the issuer's non-delinquent accounts and can be bought and sold on the open market. Until the end of the 1990s, the sale of credit card portfolios was usually part of merger negotiations but today they are bought and sold like stocks. The buying and selling of credit card portfolios has allowed many non-banks to enter the credit card market as well as allowed banks to consolidate their own credit card operations pre- or post-merger (Simotas and Weisel 1991).

Conclusion

This chapter sought to account for the historical rise in the profitability of the American credit card industry since its deregulation in the mid-1980s. The ability to offer asset-backed securities, a process known as securitisation, is the linchpin in the credit card industries turn around from a high-cost low-profit venture in the immediate post-war era to the mainstay of financial services' profitability today. This is because securitisation allowed third-party issuers to free up funds, not merely through low interest rates, but essentially moving the existing pool of funds off-balance sheet, and re-issuing the same amount of capital again to new credit card customers. The ability to recycle the same funds continuously not only drastically reduced the cost of credit card operations but also gave issuers incentives to find new customers or extend the limits of its existing customers. Bolstering the customer base to create a successful portfolio became integrated into the credit card issuers' profit strategies. Currently, the buying and selling of credit card portfolios happen on an almost weekly basis as new actors enter and others exit.

These developments are a stark contrast to the meager origins of the universal third-party card in post-war America where the Keynesian organisation of finance and production largely dictated the form and function of the limited credit card industry. It was as a result of these conditions that the modern mass credit card was created but it was also a very limited product, known for its high operating costs, limited market, and low returns. The robust nature of the Keynesian consumer market initiated a period of consultation on the possibility of deregulation in consumer credit and credit cards, to facilitate more access to credit. After this deregulation the credit card industry has experienced far-reaching structural change emanating from the new ability to securitise credit card receivables. Drawn in by the astronomical profitability of the credit card market, the growing number of new actors changed the orientation of their credit card marketing towards frequent use in order to increase the likelihood of individuals revolving their monthly balances. Securitisation has proven to be the alchemy of the banks turning high-cost credit card operation into the most profitable financial industry in the global political economy.

That being said, the securitisation of credit card bills also has inherent problems. For accounting purposes, and so that securities can gain an AAA rating, the securities are considered to be a sale by banks. This has proven to be merely an off-balance sheet financing that enables banks to avoid posting capital for the loans and to finance credit cards at lower rates of interest, by virtue of the AAA rating offered through third-party financial guarantees. Critics have argued that securitisation is 'the glue that has prevented credit card profitability from deteriorating sooner... and a decline in securitization that is bound to follow will create rising credit card delinquencies, which will adversely affect capital adequacy and costs of funds for the banks' (Celarier 1996: 10). But, whether securitised cards belong to the bank or investors is a matter of semantics because the securitisation of credit card loans is only a temporary transfer of risk. This is because when card receivables are securitised, the bank still manages the individual account: it can increase the credit limit, change the interest rate and so on.

The pool of securities, known as a master trust, is a complicated structure that is constantly being replenished by new loans, so that its outstanding level remains stable. Likewise, to keep paying investors, charge-offs must be compensated for with new loans (ibid). There is an inherent instability in using securitisation to both raise more capital as well as maintain the credibility of existing loans, on top of servicing customer accounts. This may prove to be a difficult balancing act for credit card portfolio owners over the long term especially in a market downturn. Thus, the alchemy of the banks may prove to be unachievable: turning millions of small high-risk loans into the most profitable financial product, like converting iron into gold, could remain a failed endeavour.

Notes

1. These acts include: the Fair Credit Billing Act 1974, the Equal Credit Opportunity Act 1974, Regulation B, Consumer Leasing Acts 1976, Fair Debt Collection Practices Act 1977, the Electronic Transfer Act 1978 and Regulation E, Bankruptcy Act 1978 and 1984.
2. Prior to the 1987 Act, the Bank Holding Company Act of 1956 prohibited non-bank companies from owning banks. In the early 1980s several non-financial firms found that they could conduct credit card business by acquiring so-called non-bank banks. Since non-bank banks limit their operations to either deposit taking or lending, they did not legally meet the Bank Holding Company Act's definition of a 'bank' as an institution that engages in both activities, and thus were not subject to the Act's restrictions on bank ownership.
3. Major corporations who entered the market are Household International, General Electric, J.C. Penney, The Associates (owned by Ford Motor Corp) but other retailers, manufacturer, securities firms, insurance companies have also become issuers.

9
Central Europe in the EU Financial Embrace

Or Raviv

Over the past decade, global finance has expanded into 'emerging markets' in search of higher returns. Recurring financial crises have done little to dispel the lure of riches beyond the horizon and awaiting exploitation.[1] In this chapter, I explore the mechanisms through which this exploitation operates, with Central Europe as the prime area of concern. The three case studies, Poland, Hungary, and the Czech Republic, account for more than three-quarters of new member states' total banking assets (ECB 2000). Here, neoliberal economic policy, or as I will argue, the neoliberal mode of regulation and global private finance, have established themselves in a closely coordinated manner. Neoliberal policies, first introduced by the IMF in the early 1990s, were subsequently 'locked in' by EU accession and the requisite preparations. EU membership was offered on the non-negotiable condition of adopting the entire existing catalogue of EU rules and achievements (the *acquis communautaire*), as well as commitment to full membership of the ERM II and the Eurozone – a commitment not required of existing EU members. Their recent 'formal' accession in May 2004 has effectively sealed off any retreat.[2]

Foreign inflows have completely overhauled the ownership structures of the existing financial systems. If in the early 1990s, an overwhelming majority of financial intermediaries and financial assets were still publicly owned, by 2003 private foreign ownership accounted for 70 to 95% of financial intermediaries and banks' assets (over 90% in the Czech Republic; over 80% in Hungary; over 70% in Poland).[3] Such a drastic shift is unprecedented, in scope or in speed. However, similar trends of increasing foreign ownership of emerging market financial sectors are evident now across the globe.

The arguments offered to legitimate the transformation of economic policy along neoliberal lines and the influx of foreign finance under its aegis, tend to be broadly identical irrespective of the area where this occurs. Easier access to global financial markets for individuals and corporations will lead to a more efficient allocation of capital, a reduced cost of capital and improved investment opportunities for businesses and individuals, which, in turn, promote growth and prosperity. This process will also enhance the depth and liquidity of financial markets, thus, reducing systemic risk and promoting stability (ECB 2000). Neoclassical economics, whether relying on endogenous or exogenous growth models, suggests that foreign investment and (closely correlated) technological innovation will combine to generate a 'virtuous growth cycle'.[4] Even if this was the case, given the importance of financial systems for the process of capital accumulation, economic growth, and social cohesion, the level of foreign ownership should raise concerns about the transfer of regulatory power and economic discipline into foreign and private hands.

To analyse the implications of the entry into Central Europe of foreign finance, I rely on the arguments of French Regulation School. In contrast to neoliberal scholars and policy makers, authors in this tradition identify debt-driven asset price inflation as the primary mechanism of capital accumulation in the contemporary global economy (Aglietta 1998). Over the past decade, asset prices have ballooned, unabated by declining GDP growth rates in virtually all OECD countries, suggesting an intrinsic relation to the hegemony of neoliberalism. Indeed the explosion of cheap credit and the assertion of shareholder value are key features of the neoliberal mode of regulation. Consequently, equity markets have come to wield considerable disciplinary power over the state, the economy, and society (Aglietta and Breton 2001: 433). Similarly, authors have noted that the ratio of wage-related income to equity-related income has shifted significantly in favour of the latter over the same time period, suggesting that equity markets also play an important role in the social mediation of the new accumulation pattern through the so called 'wealth effect' (Brenner 2002).

The sustainability of what has been coined, a finance-led growth regime, therefore hinges not so much on the soundness of the economic principles underlying it, but on the 'permanent optimism' of investors. Their expectations of future profits, rather than the calculations of neoliberal economists, are what make finance-led growth tick. However, the capacity of credit expansion and equity-based income distribution as mechanisms of regulation is waning. On the one hand, ever increasing levels of indebtedness require constantly increasing rates of return on equity; on the other, as asset ownership becomes increasingly concentrated, the expected trickledown effect dries up, resulting in extreme inequality in the distribution of income (Duménil and Lévy 2004a: 106–9). This is why global finance is compelled to continually diversify, including by means of penetrating developing economies, where corporate and household indebtedness levels are comparatively low, and asset prices are subject to inflation.[5]

A closer examination of the reality in Central Europe will allow us to critically assess whether foreign finance has delivered on its promises to augment investment, increase competition and enhance risk management and stability; and how has the concentration of disciplinary power in the hands of foreign investors and regulators affected local state regulators, the local non-financial sector and households. I first briefly introduce the features of the finance-led growth model before addressing the specifics of the European integration process in the area of finance. I conclude with the effects of foreign financial regulation on Central European societies.

From industrial-led to finance-led growth

Post-war European integration took shape in the context of a growth regime organised around the mass production of consumer durables, following a pattern originally developed in the US in the 1930s New Deal. The industrial-led growth model (or in the terminology of the French Regulationists, regime of accumulation) was based on the nexus of mass production and mass consumption, made coherent by capital-labour wage compromise – 'Fordism' (Aglietta 1979). This compromise assured the relative stability of income distribution and sufficient aggregate demand by indexing wage increases to productivity growth.

However, 'the term "regulation" gives a name to the stabilisation of a fundamentally contradictory and conflictual process without removing its underlying contradictions' (Görg and Brand 2000: 374). The contradictions reproduced through the mode of regulation will therefore at some point unhinge the compromises around which the accumulation regime is built. As to Fordism, two forces signalled the unravelling of this accumulation regime. First, the stagflation of the 1970s, which demonstrated that in the original area of its development, North America and Western Europe, it could no longer accommodate the competing interests of capital and labour; and secondly, the geographical push into new zones beyond the North Atlantic political economy. This search for new zones of exploitation of labour entailed the transplantation of the Fordist mode of production albeit without the class compromise and was dubbed 'peripheral Fordism' (Lipietz 1982, 1987). Wages in these host economies were not indexed to productivity gains but rather served to maintain profitability, capital accumulation and price stability (cheap imports) in the core economies.

In the 1980s, from the crisis of the Fordist accumulation regime, new modes of regulation emerged, although it took until the mid-1990s before these had been sufficiently consolidated to understand them as a new regime of accumulation. In the nomenclature of the French Regulationists, this then became the 'finance-led growth regime'. As a new and relatively coherent set of regulatory principles, finance-led growth entails '...changes in macro-economic performance, productivity trends, income distribution, capital accumulation and the business cycle' (Aglietta and Breton 2001: 435). Specifically, the new accumulation regime '...combines norms of shareholder value, labour market flexibility, price stability, and a booming stock market fuelled by credit to sustain the rapid growth of consumption, as well as the permanent optimism of expectations in firms' (Boyer 2000: 116). Under a finance-led growth regime, debt-based asset price inflation replaces productivity growth as the driving force in capital accumulation. This is demonstrated by the meteoric growth of equity and securities markets that occurred amidst a slowdown in productivity and growth rates across OECD countries (Aglietta 2000).

Equity and securities markets are key institutions mediating the competing social interests and the underlying contradictions inherent to capital accumulation in a finance-led growth regime. As the accumulation regime is now mediated by a 'wealth effect' on assets rather than wage growth, spending power becomes associated with the growth of an asset-owning democracy; ideally, any loss in wage-related income is compensated by asset-related income.[6] Consequently, the balance between wage-based income and capital gains has dramatically shifted in favour of the latter. However, just as the wage compromise did not eliminate the class contradictions that underlay Fordism, but rather contained them temporarily, the capacity of the 'wealth effect' to socially mediate the accumulation regime is finite. As asset ownership becomes increasingly concentrated and the expected trickle-down effect dries up, the limits of finance-led growth become apparent (Duménil and Lévy 2004a). It has been argued that household credit has been mobilised as an auxiliary social mediation mechanism for finance-led growth; as asset values no longer balance wage erosion, household credit maintains consumption levels and aggregate demand whilst simultaneously exerting a disciplinary effect on society.

Another axis on which finance-led growth seeks to prolong its lease on life is the quest for new markets – in this it follows in the footsteps of Fordism. Just as the slowdown of industrial productivity in the 1970s forced capitalist operators to look outside the developed economies for cheaper labour, global finance has taken the route of geographical expansion to ensure higher returns on equity. Hence the 'predatory' diversification of finance into emerging markets can be equated with the 'peripheral' Fordism of the late 1970s described by Lipietz (1987). But as with the Fordist expansion, the social compromises around which the regime is organised are somehow left behind in the process.[7]

For French Regulation theorists, regimes of accumulation are historically and socially specific constructs insofar as the institutions and cultural habits which reproduce a particular capitalist society can and do vary spatially and temporally. Thus the Fordist mode of regulation, the wage compromise, for example was achieved through varying institutional arrangements in different societies; in some, trade unions played a significant role, in others the state paved the way by enforcing income redistribution through taxation and social expenditures (Lipietz 1987). Even so, the bulk of contemporary Regulation literature has been primarily occupied with the Anglo-Saxon experience of finance-led growth. In the Anglo-Saxon model, traditional intermediation offered by financial institutions has given way to direct financing through equity and debt markets. Banks themselves become part of this process by shifting away from traditional intermediation (extending loans on the basis of deposits) to securitisation and security trading (thus removing both assets and liabilities off their balance sheets) (Seabrooke 2001; Aglietta and Breton 2001; Boyer and Saillard 2002).

Consequently, equity and securities markets move into position as fundamental disciplinary mechanisms in the Anglo-Saxon finance-led growth regime while financial intermediaries are forced to reinvent themselves. It is through these markets that profitability is ensured and capital accumulated, and it is these markets that wield significant disciplinary power over corporations, households and states alike. As markets for corporate control attain dominance, shareholder value and creditworthiness replace actual production levels as primary concerns for non-financial enterprises. Thus, both individual strategies and the overall growth of the non-financial business sector become subject to the discipline of equities and securities markets. The relationship between the financial system and the state has also been transformed, as governments become ever more sensitive to the fluctuating price of their public debt and local regulators put the stability and 'health' of financial systems above all else. Finally, the new regime of accumulation also entails disciplinary effects over households' behaviour, shaping expectations of income, risk (debt), and increased asset wealth in a precarious balance.

However, while the inroads made by direct finance have altered the logic of savings and borrowing practices in all developed economies, the particular institutional arrangements enforcing this mode of regulation differ from one society to another, depending on the particular historical legacies, culture, institutions and the configuration of (external and internal) social forces. It is here that my analysis seeks to broaden the discussion beyond the mainstream arguments of the Regulationists by focusing on the specificities of finance-led growth in continental Europe. While the aggregate financial depth of both regions is relatively similar, there are some striking differences between the North American and Continental European financial systems. Most notably, in Europe corporate finance is still much more heavily based on bank loans than on shares and other securities; in 2001, bank loans to the corporate sector amounted to 42.6% of GDP in the Euro area, and to 18.8% in the US. Conversely, outstanding debt securities of non-financial corporations and stock market capitalisation amounted respectively to 6.5 and 71.7% in the Euro area and to 28.9 and 137.1% in the US (ECB 2005a).

The reasons for this distinction are numerous and require a fuller treatment than possible here. I shall confine myself to discussing two major historical and regulatory differences which played a central role in the divergence. Perhaps the most significant regulation guiding the development of the US financial system towards market-based finance was the 1933 Banking Act (the Glass Steagall Act). The aim of the Glass Steagall bill was to make banking safer and less prone to speculation as a direct reaction to the economic problems which followed the stock market crash of 1929. The provisions of the Act separated the activities of commercial banks and securities firms and prohibited commercial banks from owning brokerages. It also prohibited paying interest on commercial demand deposits and capped the interest rate on savings deposits. In effect, this legislation (along with the poor state of the banking sector during the 1930s), created a kind of 'capital vacuum' in the American financial system.[8]

This void was quickly occupied by institutional investors in the US. One key element in the rise of institutional investors in the US, and the second point of difference from Continental Europe, was the channeling of pension fund contributions into equity investment. From as early as the 1940s, defined contribution (DC) retirement plans began their ascent in the US. These plans do not guarantee a predetermined level of income, and consequently they can be channeled into (riskier) investment in equity markets rather than (safer but lower yield) government bonds (Langley 2004; Condon, this volume). Since the 1980s DC has displaced defined benefit plans as the most ubiquitous form of retirement plan. The significance of pension funds to the rise of non-bank institutional investors in the US cannot be overestimated; it is estimated that in 2005 approximately 40% of American common stock, or US$12.9 trillion originated from pension and retirement funds (Fundamentals, August 2005). Similarly in 2003 institutional investors in the US accounted for approximately 75.9% of the US leveraged loan market (Hickey 2003).

Meanwhile, in continental Europe the tradition of 'universal banking' originating in the 19th century continued unabated. European banks were unrestricted in conducting investment and securities businesses and consequently the European financial sectors did not experience the same 'capital vacuum' characteristic of the US. Furthermore, even to this day most EU Member states maintain predominately state-financed pensions systems (with the exception of Ireland, the Netherlands and the UK). In Continental Europe, pensions have been largely state-run, pay-as-you-go schemes that essentially restrict investments to safe, low-yield domestic bond issues. This has further restricted the scope for the rise of non-bank institutional investors in Europe.

No doubt, over the past decade equity and debt securities have increasingly replaced traditional bank lending in Continental Europe, and while the recourse to market-based finance in Europe is still significantly below that of the US, the gap is rapidly narrowing. But it is also true that by diversifying into this area, European banking groups have been able to 'internalise' the changes in their clients' saving and investment behaviour. In Continental Europe, the increased recourse to equity and securities markets is compatible with the preservation and expansion of the role of financial intermediaries. Notwithstanding increased competition from non-bank intermediaries, the importance of banks has not declined either. European banks have been able to exploit their extensive retail distribution networks in order to reach investors, thus gaining a dominant position that in many EU countries goes beyond 80% of total collective investment (ECB 2000).

Thus, the Continental European finance-led growth regime allows banks to retain a much more significant disciplinary role. This has certainly contributed to the rapidity of their success in taking over the financial sectors of the Central European economies, which can be understood as a historically and socially specific mode of 'predatory finance'. Of course, the underlying contradiction of finance-led growth, which it can mediate and manage to a certain extent, but not overcome, is integral to this expansion. Sustaining continuously rising levels of indebtedness requires sustained increases in returns on equity. Just as the expansion of mass production at some point failed to generate the necessary increase in incomes to sustain mass consumption and production, it must be expected that global finance will no longer find asset owners whose properties can be mortgaged and made subject to income-generating price increases capable of sustaining the finance-led growth regime. Before turning to the question of how this affects Central Europe under the EU umbrella, let us look at European financial integration itself and its policy implications.

European integration as a vehicle of neoliberalism

The 1980s saw the broad introduction of neoliberal principles of privatisation and market regulation across the EU. Originally implemented by conservative governments, these principles were not fundamentally altered when these governments were replaced by nominally left/centre-left cabinets in the course of the 1990s. The EU in no small way was responsible for this continuity. This illustrates how the neoliberal agenda has become entrenched at a level of policy making beyond the reach of the social constituency of national political systems. At this level, effectively removed from public scrutiny, the neoliberal principles of economic policy and social organisation have successfully maintained their hegemonic position. Neoliberalism has become inscribed in the thinking and practice of European institutions, limiting the space for discussion by its encapsulation as a technical matter, and neoliberal orthodoxy as professional competence.

This is confirmed by the rhetoric of key policy makers at the EU level; 'The market-led process should be seen as the predominant driving force towards further integration... Most importantly, it should be determined by the market, once regulatory and other obstacles have been removed. Public authorities have, of course, to play their role, *but it is really up to the market to grasp the opportunities* provided by the regulatory framework and competition policy' (Padoa-Schioppa, March 2004, my emphasis). This has led critiques of the EU neoliberal agenda to conclude, 'the leading political and economic forces in Europe present neoliberalism as a taboo that cannot be violated' (Milios 2005: 209). By equating neoliberal convergence with the goal of enhancing the economic, monetary and political unity among EU Member States the neoliberal strategy is effectively exempted from criticism and placed out of reach for 'any substantial revision or change'. The process of European integration itself thus becomes a mechanism of imposing and observing neoliberal discipline; the deepening and broadening of integration a vehicle of conversion to neoliberalism.

It is this that all new member states and those so aspiring, are directly confronted with. Accepting the EU option means committing one's state to reducing barriers in the internal market and the convergence of monetary and fiscal policies towards maintaining price stability through direct inflation targeting (DIT) (Toporowski 2005: 215–22). The 1992 Treaty of Maastricht, the founding document of the EU, set inflation targets whilst constraining government budget deficit levels. The 1996–97 Growth and Stability Pact has further entrenched these goals. It places in the hands of the EU the power to discipline EMU member states failing to meet targets and impose fines on delinquents. The EU was already contemplating taking such actions against Portugal, but the spectacle of Germany, France, Italy, and the UK (albeit not an EMU member) all failing to meet the EMU requirements, has made disciplinary action self-defeating, and punitive measures have been suspended for the time being. Equally the attempt to 'lock in' neoliberal policy into the integration process by the contested European Constitution, suffered a defeat at the hands of voters in France and the Netherlands in 2005. But even if we accept the claim that this vote provided the first chance for a real public debate about the neoliberal nature of integration since Maastricht, it has not itself suspended the neoliberal principles on which the EU is run (van der Pijl 2006).

As to finance proper, EU regulation has been shaped, in the period 1998–2003, by the Financial Services Action Plan (FSAP). The Plan has represented – in the past few years – the main tool for public action to remove legal, regulatory, supervisory, and tax obstacles to further financial integration. The underlying assumption was that further financial integration was mainly impeded by laws and regulations, and that it therefore had to be pursued by removing legal barriers to operations across borders. The Plan has two main pillars. First, the introduction of the 'Single European Passport' allows financial service providers licensed in any member state to offer services in all others. These providers require no further licence and do not submit to regulation and monitoring other than that of their country of origin. Secondly, under the auspices of the FSAP, regulation on European securities has been harmonised, effectively creating pan-European markets for corporate and public securities.

For accession countries, submitting to these principles amounted to the price of entrance. Not only were they required to adopt the *acquis* (including the Growth and Stability Pact), but unlike existing EU members, they cannot opt out of ERM and Eurozone membership. They are also required to adopt the ERM II for a two-year period, leaving them with the problems of controlling currency exchange in an environment of unregulated capital flows, whilst enjoying none of the benefits of cancelling currency exchange risks by being in the actual Eurozone.

Yet despite the regulatory reforms of the past decade, relatively little consolidation occurred within national financial systems, and even less consolidation took place at a trans-European level.[9] The changed regulatory environment notwithstanding, the liberalisation envisaged by the Financial Passport scheme has not induced substantial changes in terms of market access and transnational ownership in Western Europe.[10] The explanations for this anomaly vary depending on the structure of national financial markets. For Germany, the fragmented structure of the national banking system makes foreign entry unattractive because the acquisition of any one bank will not result in sufficient market share to justify the initial investment. For the UK on the other hand, it has been argued that the current level of bank consolidation at the national level makes any further consolidation unlikely to generate additional substantial efficiency gains. In Italy, domestic politics hindered foreign bank entry. However, the row over the attempted takeover of Italian Banca Nazionale del Lavoro by Spanish BBVA, and of Banca Antonveneta by ABN-Amro of the Netherlands, has led to the recent resignations of Italy's Economy Minister and the Governor of the Italian Central Bank for their roles in organising the defence, perhaps heralding more to come.

Central European financial systems, on the other hand, have experienced a dramatic shift in ownership structures, organisational practices and market consolidation even prior to formal accession. They certainly did not have to wait for their 'Single European Passport' to see a massive influx of foreign financial institutions. Foreign banks began to expand into the post-communist states from the mid-1990s, discovering Central European financial systems that were extremely weak by Western standards, and lacking capital and skills – obvious legacies of communism exacerbated by the recurring crises of the early 1990s. Hence foreign ownership has come to be perceived as beneficial not just on the micro level of the company, which gains access to its new parent's company resources; it also is judged a boon for the entire market by supposedly promoting competitiveness and inducing other players in the market to become more efficient. A deeper, and more efficient financial intermediation system in turn positively influences the private non-financial and household sectors, which gain access to a wider choice of more sophisticated financial instruments at more competitive prices (Reininger *et al.* 2001). Finally, financial services Foreign Direct Investment (FDI) has been argued to contribute to stability at the national economy level. By improving risk management, it enhances the system's capacity to withstand shocks. Hence FDI in the financial sector is claimed to positively affect macroeconomic stability (see for example the Committee on the Global Financial System Working Paper no. 25; Focarelli and Pozzolo 2000; Levine 1996; 1999).

Foreign banks as a result were perceived as essential to achieve reform, ensure accession to the EU, and promote economic growth and convergence. They were deemed crucial to a functioning, comprehensive system of financial intermediation which in turn was essential for growth in the non-financial sector. All this was backed up by a steady flow of studies, reports and recommendations emanating from the various global financial institutions as well as academia, lending the theses credence. Studies of the performance of foreign banks suggest that when entering a developing economy, foreign banks are more efficient and perform better than local banks. This is claimed to have positive effects not only on the bank which was acquired but also on the entire sector, and ultimately on overall macroeconomic stability (Akbar and McBride 2004; Claessens *et al.* 2001; Clarke *et al.* 2001; Moreno and Villar 2004; Naaborg *et al.* 2004). Now, we turn to the reality of financial integration in the CE3, and assess the extent to which foreign finance has delivered on its promises, or alternatively, how has the concentration of disciplinary power in the hands of foreign investors and regulators affected local state regulators, the local non-financial sector and households.

Foreign ownership and regulation of Central European societies

The expansion of neoliberal politics and global finance into Central Europe, then, was expected to herald the advent of a 'cycle of virtuous growth' in the region, entailing a convergence of living standards to EU levels over the medium-to-long run (Dyker 2000). This can now be subject to what may be regarded as a mid-term review. Financial expansion into Central Europe was mainly channeled through financial intermediaries rather than equity markets; intermediaries account for approximately 85% of financial sector assets in CE3 (Backé and Zumer 2005; Racocha 2003). Therefore the primary concern is the concentration of disciplinary power in a foreign-owned banking sector and its implications for the local non-financial sector, local state regulators, and households.

The most fundamental argument in favour of opening Central European financial systems was that this would allow a deepening of the intermediation system. The non-financial private sector stood to benefit from enhanced access to credit, boosting investment and resulting in growth in output and employment. Note first, irrespective of whether this outcome has in fact occurred, the speed of financial development has so far been rather slow, even in the three most advanced transition countries. In Poland banking assets on the eve of EU accession accounted for approximately 65% of GDP (from 62% in 1999); in Hungary 76% (from 68%); and in the Czech Republic 97% (down from 141.7%). This is still considerably lower than the Eurozone average of 260% (Kager 2002; Barisitz 2005). Indeed, according to a Merrill Lynch study conducted in March 2004 the new member states are 'seriously underbanked from mortgage penetration to credit as a percentage of GDP. The financial sector could be a growth area for years to come' (Merrill Lynch 2004).

Furthermore, despite the increase in bank capitalisation and assets over the past decade, credit growth to the non-financial private sector, measured as the level of bank claims on the private sector as share of GDP (Beck *et al.* 1999), has increased to a much lesser extent than total bank assets. In the Czech Republic, the ratio of private sector credit to GDP is slightly over 40% while in Hungary and Poland the ratio is between 30% and 40%. The average share of credit to the private sector as share of total credit in all CE countries still hovers unchanged around 40–45% of GDP, similar to 1993 levels despite the ensuing influx of foreign-owned banks (Naaborg *et al.* 2004).

The advantages of a bank-based financial intermediation system over a market-based one are supposedly in the specificity of bank-client relations which enables banks to gain 'insider' knowledge of their debtors and make risk judgments on the basis of an informal record of trust and reputation. Market-based financial intermediation on the other hand essentially rests on the law of large numbers, which through a logic of homogenisation, renders probability distributions of returns for standardised classes of financial products (Aglietta and Breton 2001). Arguably, therefore, a bank-based financial intermediation system is more suitable for Central European economies; there are a large number of small and medium enterprises (SMEs) which enjoy limited access to equity markets and are thus dependent on bank credit.

However, Berger *et al.* (2001) and Clarke *et al.* (2001) find that foreign bank credit to SMEs as a share of total credit to the non-financial private sector has virtually stagnated over the past decade. Whatever little increase in credit which did accrue to the non-financial private sector was specifically targeted at foreign-owned enterprises and large and established domestic corporations. Evidently, banks have so far 'cherry picked' only the most creditworthy clients. SMEs, on the other hand, although they form the backbone of the economy in terms of employment, are severely underrepresented in foreign-owned bank portfolios. The developmental value of foreign-owned bank portfolios to the local non-financial private sector is thus confined to what we can at best call 'development assistance to the strong' (Tilly 1986). It would seem than that foreign ownership in the banking sectors of these countries has done little to promote productivity or employment-enhancing investment. Already the plausibility of the investment optimisation thesis advocated by neoclassical economics encounter difficulties on the ground.

In contrast to the low and lagging growth in bank credit to the corporate sector, credit extended to households has been the main driver of credit growth in CE3. Household lending as a share of total domestic lending has climbed in the Czech Republic and Hungary from approximately 10% in 1999 to over 30% in 2004 and simultaneously, in Poland, from approximately 30% to almost 50%. The expansion of household credit in Central Europe, much as in other countries, predominately took the form of mortgage lending; which is real estate backed and easily securitised and removed from the balance sheet of the creditor bank. Over the past five years foreign-owned banks have aggressively expanded into mortgage lending and mortgage-based debt consolidation, leading to a dramatic increase in household debt. In Hungary for example, where government subsidies were introduced in 2001, mortgage lending has ballooned in recent years (+130% in 2002, +70% in 2003), albeit from a very modest point of departure. Similar trends have been recorded in Poland and the Czech Republic (Barisitz 2005).

Furthermore, the dominance of foreign-owned banks also discourages personal saving; as these banks are largely independent from the local deposit base, competition over deposit interest rates has failed to materialise. Indeed even in cases where the interest margins contracted, it was due to declining credit interest rates rather than rising deposit interest rates.[11] Consequently, levels of household indebtedness have been growing rapidly in most Central European economies, carrying familiar disciplinary implications. Although still far from the levels of indebtedness we in the West have grown accustomed to (see Montgomerie, this volume), there is little doubt that this trend will intensify – as Merrill Lynch suggests – this is a potential growth area for years to come.

Another troubling feature of credit growth in the new member states is the high (and rising) share of foreign currency-denominated loans. Whereas in Hungary and Poland foreign-denominated loans were virtually non-existent in the early 1990s, by 2004 foreign-denominated credit to non-financials and households have surpassed 40% in Hungary and 30% in Poland and is growing fast (in the Czech Republic foreign-denominated credit on the other hand is relatively limited, and has in fact decreased to approximately 10% in 2004 owing to the low interest rate levels) (Backé and Zumer 2005). Most of the loans referred to are Euro-denominated, and have typically been granted to non-financial corporations, although recently their share in household loans has also soared. In extending foreign-denominated loans, foreign-owned banks have effectively 'externalised' their exchange rate risk to local businesses and households who have been motivated to borrow in foreign currency by the lower costs of borrowing. However, unlike foreign banks, local businesses and households who predominately rely on revenues (or wages) denominated in local currency are much less able to hedge against exchange rate risks, which leaves any asset appreciation precarious (Szaparáry 2005).

Banks have also opted to invest more in liquid securities such as government bonds (de Haas 2002; de Haas and van Lelyveld 2004). In the Eurozone, private credit is about three times as high as public credit, whereas in the transition countries the share of private and public credit is about the same size. The dominance of foreign ownership in the public debt markets of CE also serves to impose foreign bondholder discipline over governments' fiscal policies. Here again foreign-owned banks play a central role in the pricing of public debt both as market makers in the primary markets and as major investors in the secondary markets. The EU Commission may be unable or unwilling to enforce the Growth and Stability Pact targets, but market discipline is swift and unyielding.

Poland has found this out in recent years, as it has not been able to meet EU public deficit requirements and is therefore required to maintain a comparatively high interest rate to stem financial outflows, with all that this entails for domestic economic activity. Even in Hungary and the Czech Republic, where public deficits are kept broadly within ERM requirements and interest rates are comparatively low, central banks are still incapacitated in controlling monetary aggregates. Again, an interest rate hike will only serve to attract yet more speculative finance looking to cash in on interest rates differentials. This is why these economies are in a constant state of 'structural liquidity surplus'; central banks are reduced to the function of absorbing, or 'sterilising' excess liquidity from the market in order to maintain the 'health' of their financial systems and prevent overheating and recurring speculative currency or interest attacks (Schmitz 2004). This is virtually risk-free for investors but imposes considerable costs on central banks, as when the National Bank of Hungary in January 2003 'sterilised' foreign currency to the tune of 4bn Euros before having to slash its interest rates by 1 percentage point twice in two days to fend off foreign currency speculators.

Summing up, the influx of foreign banks into Central Europe has so far not brought the promised optimisation of investment and efficiency of economic management, let alone enhanced general welfare levels. Introducing the finance-led accumulation regime whilst enjoying the advantages of corporate centralisation banks have instead scavenged for opportunities for interest income on asset-backed credit and risk-free lending, whilst passing on risks to the population at large.[12] This confirms the expected effect of the geographical expansion of the finance-led growth model without the related class compromise. That the Central European EU accession countries have also seen the regulation of their national financial systems, and by implication, their economies as a whole, alienated into foreign hands, was perhaps inevitable given the already established European structures. This does little, however, to salve the pain of the EU embrace.

Notes

1. Emerging market equity funds absorbed US$20.3bn of net inflows in 2005, five times more than the previous year and beating the previous record of US$14.4bn of inflows in 2003 (*Financial Times* 2 Jan 2006).
2. The ERM II is in effect an interim mechanism, a 'waiting room' for countries aspiring to join the Eurozone; prior to acceding to the Eurozone countries are required to maintain a 15% plus/minus currency exchange rate bandwidth around the Euro for the minimum duration of two years.
3. For comparison the equivalent rate for the Eurozone was just over 20% in 2003; the ECB defines any majority foreign owned bank as foreign owned (ECB Monthly Bulletin May 2005b: 81).
4. In the exogenous growth model (Solow growth model), capital intensity affects short-term economic growth. In the endogenous model the production of new technology is 'internalised', however, the latter is still predicated on the basis of investment (specifically in R&D, education, and so on).
5. Duménil and Lévy also argue that this is also why US equity abroad displays a higher rate of return than foreign equity invested in the already inflated markets of the US, crucial for the ailing American BOP (2004b).
6. The concept of an asset-owning democracy has been introduced into public popular debate by the Minister of the Exchequer, Gordon Brown and forms a pillar of 'New Labour' philosophy.
7. For a comprehensive discussion of the applicability of the concept of peripheral capitalism to the post-communist states of Central Europe, see Holman, O. 2005.
8. The 1933 Banking Act was finally repealed by President Bill Clinton in 1999 (by the Gramm-Leach-Bliley Act).
9. ABN-Amro's purchase of Italian Banca Antonveneta and UK's Abbey acquisition by Spanish Santander Central Hispano are arguably the exceptions that prove the rule.
10. While integration progressed the furthest in the money market following the introduction of the Euro, and to some extent also in equity and securities capital markets, relatively little integration took place in the area of retail banking.
11. The spread (or margin) between interest paid by banks on clients' deposits held with the bank and the interest charged on credit; a common measure of financial intermediation efficiency.
12. For example the CE subsidiaries of RZB and BA account for 20% and 11% respectively of the total group's assets in 2000, however approximately 40% of the group's annual profit was generated by their CE subsidiaries that year. For Erste Bank, one of the biggest 'regional revolvers', CE equity amounted to 25% of the group's assets, and generated 86% of the group's profits!

10
Finance and Management in the Dynamics of Social Change: Contrasting Two Trajectories – US and France*

Gérard Duménil[+] and Dominique Lévy[++]

Introduction: actors in history

There is, in the left academy, a rather broad agreement concerning the nature of the new phase of capitalism asserted since the early 1980s, commonly referred to as *neoliberalism*. Central to this contemporary economy is the pre-eminence of financial institutions and mechanisms, domestically and internationally: the new discipline imposed on labour and management, macropolicies targeted to price stability, and the opening of frontiers to trade and capital movements, and so on. Although it is a multifaceted phenomenon, it is possible to date neoliberalism from the end of the 1970s, when the Federal Reserve, chaired by Paul Volcker, decided to increase interest rates at any level supposedly required to curb inflation (what we denote as the '1979 *coup*').

We agree with this general framework of analysis, but we also believe it often lacks a clear, explicit, reference to social relations. This chapter is, actually, a bold attempt at assessing both contemporary trends in capitalism and the perspectives now opened for the 21st century, in a framework whose main focus is on classes, and the interplay of class relations and struggles.[1] Thus, the theoretical foundations in the paper are rather strictly Marxist, with the major 'revisionist' proviso that a *managerial class*, to be defined below, is a component of class relations in contemporary capitalism.[2]

The first crucial transformation in the history of capitalism was the separation between ownership and management at the transition between the 19th and 20th centuries. The transformation, around 1900, combined the 'corporate revolution', the 'managerial revolution', and the formation of a new 'modern' financial sector directly backing large corporations. Obviously, this separation was not absolute, but it was so far-reaching that it reshaped social relations. Second, the capitalist class, or *bourgeoisie*, took a new form, that can be labeled *financial*, since its hold on the means of production was maintained through the ownership of securities (stock shares and loans), instead of the traditional individual or family ownership. We denote as 'finance', the upper fraction of this capitalist class and the financial institutions (banks, investment funds, International Monetary Fund) through which the power of this class is enforced. Lastly, management was delegated to a salaried personnel, reaching unprecedented levels of sophistication under new organisational forms. The traditional opposition between a *bourgeois* and a proletarian class was, thus, mediated by new intermediate classes (besides the earlier petty *bourgeois* class which is still active). A managerial class emerged, supplemented by clerical personnel. The new managerial trends reshaped the organisation of both the private and public ('government', as the term is often used) sectors, uniting, to some extent, these various bodies beyond the sectoral divide.

Abstracting from traditional petty proprietaries, class patterns can be summarised as follows: (1) Capitalist owners; (2) Managers (in a broad sense of the term including officials); (3) Clerical workers; and (4) Production workers. In addition to smaller capitalists, managers and clerical workers shaped what has been denoted as 'new middle classes'. The conditions of clerical and production workers tend to converge and, for the sake of simplicity, we will call both of them, considered jointly, as the 'popular classes'. Thus, the following hierarchical configuration can be denoted as the *early 20th century social pattern*:

- Large capitalist owners.
- Managers and smaller capitalists.
- Popular classes of clerical workers and production workers.

The focus of the paper is, broadly, on the last century of capitalism. We distinguish three phases. A first hegemony of finance from the late 19th century to the Great Depression, the 'Keynesian' or 'managerial' compromise from World War II to the late 1970s, and the second financial hegemony in neoliberalism since then. (We restrict ourselves to the examples of the US and French societies.)

Class patterns and powers

This section uses data on income distribution to suggest the emergence of new trends in social relations.

Capital income under neoliberalism

The restoration of high incomes and, in particular, of capital income, was the main purpose of neoliberalism: control of the cost of labour of popular classes and maximising of the profit rate, high interest rates, lavish distribution of dividends, rise of the stock market, and so on.

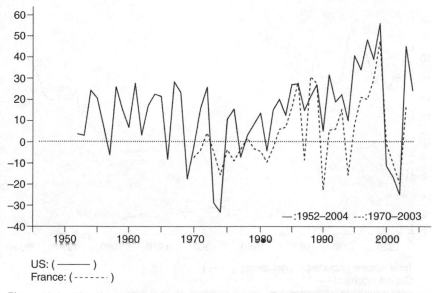

US: (———)
France: (- - - - - -)

Figure 10.1   The Share of Financial Incomes in the Total Income of Households: US and France

In this sense, it was highly successful. It is easy to document this phenomenon. Figure 10.1 shows the share of financial incomes in the total income of households. Capital gains and a correction for the devaluation of assets by inflation are added. Large fluctuations reflect the ups and downs of the stock market. Abstracting from these fluctuations, one observes in the US a significant decline during the 1970s and an upward trend since the 1980s. This rise culminates in 1999, prior to the 'bursting of the bubble'. One can also observe the recovery in 2002. (One can notice that, in 1999, capital gains, mostly virtual, amounted to more than 50% of total household income.) The data for France is only available since 1970, but one can easily observe a similar profile, beginning with very low levels during the 1970s.

Financial incomes are the sum of interest and dividends, plus (virtual or realised) capital gains corrected for inflation. (In France: *Revenus de la propriété mobilière*.) Total income is the sum of compensation of employees, proprietors' income (with adjustments), rental income of persons (with adjustments), and personal income receipts on assets.

As can be easily surmised, high income earners benefit more from financial income than the rest of the population. Therefore, we can infer that they were the main beneficiaries of the restoration of these incomes. But this is also where things become more complex.

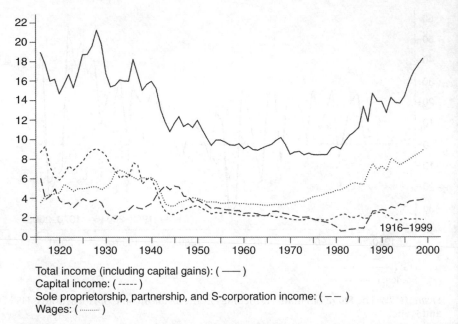

Figure 10.2   Share in the Total Income of all Households of the 1% of Households with Larger Incomes: US, Total Income and its Components
Note: The three components do not add up to the total, since the fourth component, capital gains, is not represented separately.

Capital income and 'wages' at the top of the income pyramid

Indeed, the income of the fraction of the population earning high incomes, dramatically increased with neoliberalism. But, contrary to what could be inferred from the previous section, fiscal data do not identify interest, dividends, and rent as the major elements in the comparative rise of large incomes under neoliberalism.[3] This can be assessed using data from the Internal Revenue Service (IRS).[4] There are two differences with the data used earlier: (1) no correction for the effect of inflation is made (stocks of assets are unknown); and (2) only *realised* capital gains are considered. In addition to the decomposition by income fractiles, one advantage of this data set is that the series are available since World War I.

Figure 10.2 shows the fraction of total income received by the top percentile, 99–100, of households (actually individuals filing a tax return), when they are classified by the level of their income. Incomes are the sum of four components: (1) wages (including the distribution of shares and pension benefits); (2) incomes of sole proprietors, partners, and S-corporations; (3) capital income (interest, dividends and rents); and (4) realised capital gains. The figure also shows the first three components separately. (Only capital gains are not represented, though they are included in the total.)

The consideration of the fiscal income of the top 1% (99–100 fractile) of the income pyramid confirms our view that the situation of classes with upper incomes improved in the 1980s and 1990s. From the 1970s to the early 2000s, the share of total income received by the upper percentile of households, in terms of income, rose from 8% to 18%. This restoration can be viewed as a return to the income concentration levels that prevailed before World War II. Inequality actually diminished sharply throughout the Great Depression and World War II. The top 1% lost 4 percentage points of the total income of the country between its average share during the 1920s (1919–1928) in relation to the average for the 1950s. There was no recovery after the war but, instead, a slow decline until the neoliberal upturn. The intermediate period, that of the Keynesian compromise, can be globally characterised by low incomes at the top of the income pyramid.

The transformation of income composition is telling. Before World War II, interest, dividends, and rent, accounted for about half of the income of the traditional capitalist class. The recovery during the latter decades was due to (1) 'wages', and (2) income from sole proprietors, partnerships, and S-corporations. (An important fraction of 'wages' corresponds to the distribution of shares).[5] These are incomes from tax returns, and it is obviously impossible to determine how much capital income is undeclared. The importance of tax shelters has been growing considerably during those neoliberal years. But the rise of the other categories of incomes remains – unquestionable.

Incomes and classes

There is no straightforward correspondence between income channels and class determination as implied in the patterns of social relations outlined in the first section. Any individual can receive dividends and interest but, for this reason, does not become a capitalist. The case of upper 'wages' is particularly difficult, since the fact of receiving a wage does not mark an individual as a production worker. Marx had already noted in Volume III of *Capital* that, following the separation of ownership and management, active capitalists pay to themselves a wage, and consider themselves as 'workers'. The problem is made even more complex by the fact that the tasks of the active capitalist may be delegated to salaried managers, or 'wages' may reflect mere sinecures.

The case of *sole proprietors, partnerships, and S-corporations* shows that the pattern of social relations is even more intricate than suggested by the separation between wages and profits in a corporation. Since the late 1980s, most of partnership income has corresponded to a financial sector where rich households pool their wealth and engage in financial operations; interest and dividends are, thus, transformed into partnership income. (These

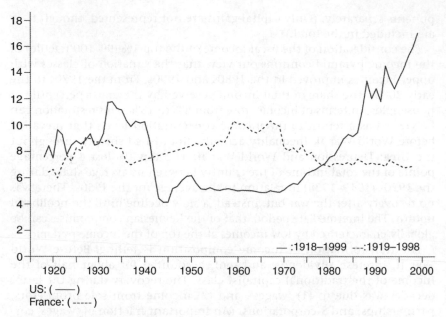

Figure 10.3   Ratio of the Average Wage in the 99–100 Income Fractile to the Average Wage in the 0–90 Fractile: US and France

groups are major users of tax shelters.) Considering the income of the three groups jointly, the income of Finance and Real Estate represents about one-third of the total. The profits of Business Services amount to about a quarter of the total; they correspond to the managerial tasks which are sub-contracted to enterprises where professionals are active, selling their services but are also owners of their enterprise.

At the level of income of the upper percentile, non-wage incomes are large, signaling a status within relations of production, distinct from rank-and-file wage earners. This is even more obvious higher in the hierarchy. (In 1999, incomes other than wages represented half of the income of the top 1%; for the top 0.01%, incomes other than wages amount to 58%.) And fiscal data do not reflect non-realised capital gains, which might account for the bulk of the rising 'virtual' wealth of very rich families. At this level, the capitalist component is quite significant. The remunerations are so high that any individual reaching the top percentile becomes, *de facto,* the holder of large portfolios of securities. Below the 1% upper percentile of the pyramid of incomes, wages (including pensions) are the overwhelming component of income. In the US, in 2001, the income of fractiles below the top 1% were made of wages up to 90%. But this does not mean that this block of 99% of households is homogeneous.

In what follows, we compare three income fractiles: 99–100, that is the upper percentile as above, 90–99, and 0–90. Figure 10.3 shows the ratios of the average wage of the top percentile to the average wage for the 0–90 fractile. For example, 8 on the vertical axis reflects the fact that the average wage in the top percentile was 8 times larger than the average wage in the 0–90 fractile. For the US (–), the figure confirms the sharp reduction of income (here wages) inequality during World War II, from a ratio of 8 or 10 to a plateau of 5 during the 1950s and 1960s. This ratio began to rise during the 1970s but, overall, such 'low' ratios were characteristic of the period of the Keynesian compromise. But the most striking observation is that, from the 1970s onward, the ratio engages into a steep rise, up to 17 in 1999.

A new configuration of class domination in the US?

This singular profile of wages at the top of the income pyramid in the US, and the role it played in the restoration of the income of the better-off fraction of the population, is so sharp that it suggests a new transformation of the institutional framework in which the powers and incomes attached to ownership and control are expressed under neoliberalism in the US.

The main feature of this transformation is that, in the US, capitalist ownership and top management tend to coalesce, defining a hybrid class, in which capitalist owners participate in top management, and top managers, *via* large remunerations, become owners, if they were not before entering the group. Although the structural pattern of capitalist and managerial classes is still at issue, the hierarchical configuration of relations introduced in section 1 must be altered:

- *Large capitalist owners-top managers*, a hybrid complex in which the inter-action between both social relations confers specific features on each component.
- More traditional managers, lower in the hierarchy, and whose involve-ment in ownership is secondary, as in pension funds, and smaller capitalists.
- Popular classes.

(In a very crude empirical manner, we associate the two first components to either one of the two fractiles: 99–100 and 90–99.)

The difficulty in the distinction between the two patterns – *early 20th century pattern* and this *US late 20th century pattern* – is the nature of the relation between top managerial activities and ownership. The first pattern preserves the separation between the capitalist and managerial components: owners may also be registered as managers, but on behalf of ownership, whatever the reality of the tasks. This approach is in line with Marx's analysis of the 'active capitalist'. The second configuration points to a polarisation among the managerial class, between 'top' and 'standard' management, and a hybrid class at the top of the social hierarchy. This polarisation within the managerial class is a replica of that which always existed among capitalists, between the upper fractions of the class and medium or petty owners. (At issue in this polarisation within the capitalist class is the distinction we introduced in our definition of neoliberalism, between the upper fractions of the capitalist class and the rest of the class, although no strict separation can be established.) It is not too surprising that such a polarisation was also asserted within the managerial class, as this class was maturing and gaining social ascendancy. The difficulty in this discussion is the dual logical pattern of 'structural' determinations (capitalists, managers…), on the one hand, and the resulting confinement and concentration of powers and incomes, on the other, among real 'blood and flesh' individuals.

In this new configuration in the US, the grasp of ruling classes, or the 'new ruling class' as it can now be denoted, on the means of production must be interpreted as the combined effect of ownership and top management. It is a new revolution in the institutions of ownership, to be related to that which occurred at the turn of the 19th and 20th centuries. Although the participation of members of capitalist families in management has always been a characteristic of 20th century social configurations, this hybrid character is now becoming a basic feature under neoliberalism. It reshapes incomes channels. The *bourgeoisie*, the 'leisure class'[6] of the early 20th century re-emerged, after several decades of containment, within a set of relations in which its link to top management has been reshaped. Both control and income channels are at issue. The *bourgeoisie* actually 'borrows' from top management its own income channels, wages, inflated to the point of becoming the privileged access to the surplus. Traditional channels, such as interest and dividends, are now shared with broader, though upper, fractions of the population, as in funds. *It is this ruling class whose power and income was asserted in neoliberalism.* The fate of the standard managerial class, as defined above, was distinct: its relationship to the ruling class is one of 'compromise', not 'fusion'. Using the income data of the 90–99 fractile to characterise this group, it appears that its relative wages, in the metrics of Figure 10.3, displays a rather steady upward trend since World War II, slightly steeper during the neoliberal decades, a thoroughly different profile from that observed for the top percentile. We use the phrase *neoliberal compromise* to define the situation of this class under neoliberalism, with its growing share of total income and its pension funds. It is a compromise between the new ruling class and the standard managerial class.

Globally, a new alliance is taking place among upper classes, that we can label as *capitalist* and *managerial*. One way of interpreting this emerging configuration of social relations is to consider jointly the two classes and their internal fragmentation, on the one hand, and the two aspects, fusion and compromise, on the other. This social deal implies a double polarisation: (1) the upper fraction of the capitalist class (capitalists I) and the rest of the class (capitalists II), and (2) the upper fraction of the managerial class (managers I) and the rest (managers II). Of course, in both instances, only a minority belongs to components I. Concerning *capitalists I* and *managers I*, an actual fusion occurred under neoliberalism, the *big capitalist owners-top managers* compact, or new ruling class. Components II are embedded within neoliberalism in the *neoliberal compromise*, in particular *managers II*. This fusion at the top, as observed in the US in the late 20th century, is not singular. An important historical precedent was the lasting transition between feudalism and capitalism, when: (1) the feudal rent took gradually capitalist features, as capitalist relations were increasingly governing economic mechanisms; (2) lords were engaging in business to raise their income, and (3) capitalists were acquiring estates and titles of nobility.

Income and social patterns in France

It is interesting to compare the fiscal data from the IRS to similar data in France: they do not show a restoration of the share of total income accruing to the better-off fractions of the population. We believe there are two reasons to this. First, as we will contend, the movement of wages was very different in France; second, the doubts manifested earlier concerning the declaration of financial income in the US, are fully confirmed in the case of France. The ratio of capital income declared to the fiscal authority, to that identified within French national accounting, displays a significant downward trend during the recent decades, signaling a growing trend towards under-declaration.[7] Overall, the fraction of capital income which appears in income statements is very low, estimated at an average of 18% during the 1990s!

As for the US fiscal data on wages, it is fraught with less uncertainty. Figure 10.3 also plots the relative wage of the top percentile in France. During the pre-war years, the ratios are similar to those observed in the US. A first striking observation is the difference in levels between the two countries, from World War II to the 1970s. In the US, the plateau, in Figure 10.3, was around 5: in France, the ratio was 9 or 10. Thus, the wage hierarchy in the upper fractions of wage-earners appears very strong in post-war France. It is impossible to determine to what extent this access to high wages was dependent on the ownership of capital or not, but the overall low levels of capital income and other features of the French society suggest that these high wages were basically an expression of the status conferred on top management. Despite the Keynesian compromise, this 'managerial' society was very unequal. Another dramatic divergence between the two countries is, however, observed during the later decades. In France, from the late 1960s onward, wage inequality was reduced. This observation probably echoes the new regulatory framework in which the determination of wages was embedded after 1968, in particular in the *Accords de Grenelle*. New rules were fixed for the determination of the minimum wage, and the determination of the levels of remunerations of managers is somewhat constrained. Thus, an important difference between the two countries is that, under neoliberalism, wage inequality rose strongly in the US, but not in France. A major consequence is that the new configuration of class relations suggested by the study of neoliberalism in the US, does not seem to apply to the French society, or to a quite lower degree.

This important finding points to other well-known differences: although the same common basic features were observed in both countries (in particular the rise of financial income), neither the Keynesian compromise nor neoliberalism, nor the trajectories of class struggle, were identical in the US and France. History is at issue.

History on the move

This section first recalls the main features of neoliberalism in the US and France. The focus is on similarities and differences, and these observations echo the income profiles identified earlier. The second section is devoted to class struggle in the US during the 20th century. This is where trajectories are determined, and this analysis provides important insights on the somewhat diverging paths followed by US and French societies.

Mimetism and idiosyncrasy

There are, in the two countries, many common facets to the difference between neoliberalism and the earlier Keynesian compromise:

1. A first element is the transformation of management or 'corporate governance'. It is now widely acknowledged that neoliberalism imposed a new management of corporations in which the interests of shareholders come first. This corporate governance under neoliberalism is also an expression of the return of the stock market central stage. The 'creation of value' for shareholders defines the new objectives of managers of big corporations. Symmetrically, the identification of these trends – managers dedicated to the new ruling class – implies, or should imply, the recognition that the behaviour of managers during the decades of the Keynesian compromise had distinct objectives: the assertion that managers are more dedicated to the interests of owners in neoliberalism, is equivalent to the proposition that they were less so during the previous decades. This is equivalent to saying that managers had developed sectional behaviours, in line with their position within class patterns, whose main feature was a lesser concern for shareholders. Besides profitability, the emphasis was on growth and technological change.

These managerial trends were well understood. It is not coincidental that the theories of *managerial capitalism* bloomed in the US in the 1960s and 1970s.[8]

2. As is well known, the decades of the Keynesian compromise were also specific in terms of policies, in particular macropolicies. After World War II, in France, the tolerance to inflation was large, and policy was targeted to growth and full employment. In the US, the 1960s marked the heyday of Keynesian macroeconomics, though the stimulation of the macroeconomy remained on the agenda to the end of the 1970s, up to the 1979 coup. The compromise leading to the definition of such policies was expressed in, and framed by, the existing political bodies, assemblies and governments, and technically enforced by officials. Considering these decades from the view point of capitalists, and keeping in mind that the officials in charge of the implementation of these policies were also part of the managerial class in the broad sense of the term, these policies testified to a type of 'sectional' behaviour similar to that identified for private management.

3. In relation to regulatory frameworks and property relations, the relationship between the financial and non-financial sectors was also at issue. In France after World War II, the financial sector was actually dedicated to the cheap financing of the economy in the context of high inflation rates. A calculation of the profit rate of financial corporations leads to negative profit rates! As shown in an earlier work,[9] such a difference in favour of the non-financial sector was also manifest in the US from the mid-1960s to the end of the 1980s, but returns were not negative.

4. Another common element, in which differences in degrees are at issue, is social protection, or welfare. In the US such frameworks emerged well before World War II, and can be traced back to the Progressive era, at the beginning of the 20th century. It is, however, true that the new social order after the Great Depression and World War II saw major accomplishments in terms of social protection. In France, in particular from the *Front populaire*, between the two world wars, to the *liberation* after World War II, a very broad framework of social protection was established.

5. As is well known, in both countries, in addition to social protection, state intervention after World War II was prominent in research, education, and industrial policy, but this was even more so in France, where part of the economy (non-financial and financial) was nationalised. These new trends were not only specific to the early post-war years. The *Programme commun de gouvernement* of 1972 between the socialist and communist parties (and the *Radicaux de gauche*) planned the extension of this public sector. When François Mitterand was elected in 1981, a short attempt was made at implementing such radical reforms. This ephemeral revival illustrates the strength of such trends, in this conflicting configuration.

There is an international facet to these mechanisms, in which the situation of France was distinct from that of the US. France drew a considerable benefit from the framework of Bretton Woods. It allowed the large degree of tolerance to inflation, with recurrent devaluations of the franc *vis-à-vis* the dollar, and the succession of periods of strengthening and relaxation of exchange controls. Rates of exchange were low. Inflation was a crucial factor in the financial repression of the capitalist class. In spite of the existing limitations to capital mobility, the country received large flows of US direct investment. In the context of the edification of the European community, and given this favorable international environment, France gradually bridged the technological gap with the US. In spite of this relative advantage conferred on less advanced countries, the framework of Bretton Woods was not damaging for the US; rather it perpetuated the hegemony of this country, at least until the dollar crisis of the early 1970s. Then, after a period of uncertainty during the structural crisis of the 1970s, the assertion of neoliberalism strengthened this hegemony to even higher degrees.

But the singularities between the two countries are particularly evident in the features of the new neoliberal phase, with important political implications: first, in the two countries, policies were dramatically altered with neoliberalism, in particular, for France within the European Union. Since the early 1980s, however, the macroeconomics of the US economy are quite specific. Demand is stimulated by a bold credit policy boosting the consumption of households; an important share of demand is directed toward the rest of the world, with a large deficit of foreign trade, and a small inflationary impact on the domestic economy; large flows of financing come from the rest of the world. (Note that this trajectory would be impossible if macropolicy was also targeted to the equilibrium of trade.)

Thus, concerning policy, the difference between the US and France is not so much one of 'liberalism', but of comparative position in the world economy. The US benefits from its global domination, and this makes neoliberalism less devastating for significant segments of the population, among middle classes. This context of growth and spending in the US played, we believe, a central role in the formation of the neoliberal compromise, since upper classes in general engaged in a consumption spree.[10] Secondly, concerning social protection the difference between France and the US was one of degree as stated earlier; but, what is an issue here is, above all, the fate of social protection under neoliberalism, which proved more resilient in France than could have been expected.

Thus, after 25 years of neoliberalism, two crucial differences are apparent between the two countries. The course of the macroeconomy remained more favorable in the US, and the managerial class was associated, though in an inferior position, to the neoliberal prosperity, benefiting mainly the members of the new ruling class. The French economy, and society in general, is deeply transformed, but a difference between the US and France is that many of the institutions of the post-war decades are still there. In particular, many of the features of the Keynesian compromise in terms of social protection were maintained, thanks to popular resistance and, probably, the adherence of large segments of management to these social arrangements. Actually, the contrast is very strong between the coexisting old (Keynesian) and new (neoliberal) aspects. Due to the simultaneous existence of these two facets, contemporary French society is sometimes called *social-liberal*.

Overall, in the two countries, the relationship between the capitalist and managerial classes was similar in many respects but also significantly distinct in others, both during the Keynesian compromise and neoliberalism: (1) The managerial features of the French society were particularly strong; (2) Financial interests were not only 'contained' but 'repressed'; (3) The intervention of the state was larger; and later, (4) The resistance to the neoliberal offensive was stronger. The differences listed above during the Keynesian compromise can be viewed as harbingers of this distinct social trajectory under neoliberalism, with strong idiosyncrasies. Note that these diverging social trajectories do not explain the comparative performances of the US during the second half of the 1990s, relative to France or Europe in general. Distinct positions in imperialist hierarchies are at issue.

Which circumstances may account for these divergences? The historical features of ownership probably play a role here, with an alleged significant attachment to '*bourgeois*' traditions in France. (But it is also true that a growing fraction of large French corporations is now held by international institutional investors such as US pension funds, who certainly do not act along such lines.) Management, in France is also marked by specific historical traits, such as a rather tight relation to the state, strengthened by the characters of the French system of education, with a tradition of attachment to centralisation and state intervention. To some extent, management is viewed in France as 'social' organisation, rather than profit maximising. In spite of permanent propaganda, the managerial class in France is, also 'to some extent', attached to the system of social institutions of the post-war decades. The role this class played in the history of social confrontation in France (its inclination towards 'socialism', be it, in the past, revolutionary or, up to the 1970s, reformist) remains present in a sense. Overall, the 'love affair' at the top, US style, between upper classes in neoliberalism was not achieved in France, neither, to a lesser extent, was the neoliberal compromise. This is where the observations made concerning income patterns, on the one hand, and specific economic and social features, on the other, converge.

In these complex mechanisms can we assert any direction of causation? It is obviously not that income trends caused the set of differences recalled above. At issue are distinct trajectories of class struggle, given their historical determinants.

Class patterns and struggle

Whatever the importance of technical change and profitability trends, the relevance of institutions, and so on, the evolution of class patterns and struggle is central in the interpretation of social trajectories. This section does not actually compare the dynamics of class struggle in the US and France; the perspective is rather strictly limited to the US. The purpose of the analysis is to show how the crucial role of class struggle should be concretely understood in relation to the transformation of class relations introduced in the previous sections.

Finance, as we define it, did not always exist. It was the historical product of the sharp transformation of the institutional framework of capitalism at the transition between the 19th and 20th centuries, when the separation between ownership and management was achieved and the new financial sector was shaped: capitalist owners, on the one hand, large and powerful financial institutions, on the other. From the establishment of this configuration onwards, financial institutions appeared as a prominent actor, acting on behalf of capitalist interests. The merger wave at the turn of the century occurred under the sway of the large financial institutions, with the emblematic figures of Morgan or Rockefeller. It is sometimes contended that the new financial capitalists took over industrial capital (and the concept of *financial capital* was certainly relevant in those years).[11] The new configuration was, anyhow, established, with the main contradiction located not between financial and industrial capitalists, but between the owners of the new financial or non-financial corporations, and the capitalists of the traditional sector.

In the following decades, a central issue was the control of the macroeconomy. A major objective was the stability of prices, assessed in those days in terms of gold instead of a broad bundle of commodities as in a price index. The large banks of New York and Chicago acted as *de facto* central institutions, since they were the banks of other banks.[12] This embryonic monetary policy was not very efficient, and crises were rather frequent with a wide financial component (windows were closed, banks failed). Clearing houses, as collective institutions, were used in order to attempt to check crises. Overall, large financial institutions opposed the creation of a central bank, as they were afraid of losing the control of monetary mechanisms. However, the crisis of 1907 created new conditions, and initiated the process which led to the establishment of the Federal Reserve in 1913.

Finance

The view that neoliberalism must be interpreted as the restoration of the power and income of a 'social entity' is now rather widespread. The emphasis is placed either on *financial institutions*, typically banks and pension funds, or *capitalists*. To account for the dual character of this social entity, the phrase 'financial capital' has much appeal because it is reminiscent of the work of Rudolf Hilferding and Lenin (as well as Marx in some translations).[13] Note that the phrase 'financial capitalists' would be more appropriate, since the world is not governed by such abstractions as capital, but by classes. It is, however, clear that neoliberalism cannot be described as the pre-eminence over industrial or commercial capitalists, or capitalists whose property would be concentrated in financial corporations: (1) The capitalist class, whatever its managerial traits, and financial institutions, for example funds, own *the entire economy* or, more accurately, its most advanced sectors, whether financial or non-financial corporations; (2) This does not mean that this distinction is totally irrelevant. Lower in the hierarchy of corporations, non-financial corporations and their owners may suffer from the power of finance (for example, high interest rates). To avoid such ambiguities, we coined the concept of 'finance', in the quite specific sense of the upper fraction of the capitalist class and its financial institutions.

The fact that it seems now more adequate to point, in the US, to a 'new ruling class' does not question the framework of analysis of *finance*, theoretically and empirically. With the emergence of neoliberalism, the capitalist facet of the new ruling class is so strong that financial institutions conserved their privileged functions.

This reluctance to create central monetary mechanisms and institutions capable of confronting the mounting tendency towards macro instability[14] – in an economy, in addition, fraught with considerable heterogeneity – ended in the Great Depression. Financial institutions were held responsible for the crisis, and the New Deal and post-war framework of 'contention' was implemented, a significant set back for the capitalist class. After the war, financial interests, in concert with business leaders, advocated the return to a free-market economy, that is unconstrained capitalism. The new compromise was struck, symbolically expressed in the Employment Act in 1946, which made full employment a duty for the state.[15] During the negotiations of Bretton Woods, the financiers in control of New York's big banks straightforwardly opposed the plan,[16] that, they contended, would prove inflationary. They, instead, put forward their *key currency* plan, which would preserve their central position in the control of international monetary mechanisms. They were defeated, although the agreements also reflected the same compromise mix typical of the new Keynesian frame-work. Capital movements were, anyhow, limited.[17] In the assertion of the second financial hegemony in neoliberalism, financial institutions acted, again, as the agent of the capitalist class in the class struggle, in particular from the new, deregulated, stronghold of Eurobanking. This has been well documented.[18] In a similar manner, the 1979 coup of Paul Volcker was directly encouraged by big banks, if not fully initiated.[19]

As is well known, in contemporary capitalism, mutual and pension funds play a central role in the disciplining of management in favour of share-holders. US financial institutions are extremely powerful, nationally and internationally. They are a central actor in the extension of the neoliberal order throughout the planet. The same is true of international monetary institutions such as the International Monetary Fund, the World Bank, and the Bank for International Settlements. Their role in the extension of neoliberalism, that is the progress of capitalist interests everywhere, has often been discussed (opening of commercial and capital frontiers in the wake of the debt crisis and the recurrent crises of the 1990s, imposition of stabilisation plans, primary budget surplus, and neoliberal reforms). Overall, financial institutions are a central actor in history, acting on behalf of the capitalist class. When this class lost the control of financial institutions, to whatever degree, its domination was weakened and its fate as the ruling class threatened. It was so during the Keynesian compromise.

The managerial class was symmetrically involved in all of the above con-troversies since its own emergence as an historical actor, though without the violence of capitalist or popular classes. Which social forces were backing the creation of the Federal Reserve? Who made the New Deal? And so on. Like the new urban classes of the 19th century, of which it is an off-spring (and whose function in the revolutions of the late 19th and early 20th centuries has been amply documented by historians), we believe it played a stubborn, though unobtrusive, role in the ongoing process of social transformation. Much work remains to be done to assess this place in history. Parenthetically, it is interesting to note that the managerial class finds in government institutions an opportunity to express its organ-isational capabilities. This is obvious concerning its public component, but it is also true of tasks which, under other circumstances, correspond to private management, as in a public corporation. And the weight of history was probably determinant in this respect, in particular in France, given the long practice of state interventionism. But, if their historical relation to the state had a possible impact on the formation of the class, as in France, managers are not intrinsically 'statist'. The property of the means of production does not have to be transferred to the state to limit or suppress the power of owners. This is clearly illustrated in the course of managerial corporate governance during the Keynesian compromise, in France, outside of the public sector. The case of Germany, where households held very few stock shares (as shares were held by other corporations), demonstrates that other configurations were also possible. Non-profit institutions, such as universities or hospitals in the US, are not necessarily owned by the state (federal government, states, or cities), and are handled by staffs of managers. Macropolicies are as 'statist' or 'para-statist' under neoliberalism as during the Keynesian compromise, because they must be performed centrally; the fact that their objectives were modified in neoliberalism is irrelevant to their statute. The example of the autonomy of central banks illustrates this duality.

The pressure from popular classes is present in our interpretation of history in various junctures in the US, beginning in the late 19th century and early 20th centuries. This period was one of strong class struggle on the part of industrial workers.[20] It saw the formation of a Socialist party (in 1901). But World War I provided the political circumstances conducive to the elimination of radical trends. These developments played a crucial role in the definition of the new framework of social protection.[21] The entire pattern of class struggle was, however, rather complex, since these decades were those of the emergence of the institutions of modern capitalism. A major contradiction was apparent among upper classes who opposed the capitalists of the traditional sector and aligned themselves with the new corporations backed by the financial sector. The tensions were also strong with farmers, pitted against big business. The managers of the new corporations initiated a process of collaboration with unions, and promoted the new reforms (accidents, housing, health, retirement programmes). The larger and rising profitability of large corporations allowed them to do so, contrary to the traditional sector.

Another historical juncture is the situation prevailing after World War II. It was created by the triple shock of: (1) the Great Depression; (2) the war itself; and (3) the emergence of USSR, after the war, as a major power. The labour movement was everywhere gathering momentum. The reply was simultaneously, as is generally the case, repression and compromise. The survival of capitalism was at issue. We will not document here what we mean by repression: McCarthyism in the US, physical elimination of communists everywhere. Only the social threat on the part of popular classes created the conditions for the Keynesian compromise. It was so domestically (social protection) and internationally (tolerance to, or encouragement of, development models in the context of the Cold War). Already, during the New Deal and the war, managers and officials had played a prominent role. Their intermediate position and their inherent capability to organise made them the inescapable linchpin of the new social arrangement. It was also an opportunity for them to assert their autonomy.

The 1970s illustrates negatively the centrality of popular struggle. In the context of the structural crisis, popular forces were defeated, and this defeat allowed for the new financial hegemony in neoliberalism. The same favorable juncture, for upper classes, explains how the top of the managerial class finally chose to merge with the upper fractions of the capitalist class, and how the rest of the class engaged in the neoliberal compromise, away from its alliance with broader social categories. It is also clear that popular resistance to the dismantling of the institutions of the Keynesian compromise, with respect to the institutions of social protection, is not specific to France. This resistance also exists in the US, but the commitment of the state was not as far-reaching as in France. One difference is that, in France, to date, the managerial class never rejected these institutions. This is one aspect of the distinct pattern of alliances in France, whose main feature is the absence – or immature form – of what we call the neoliberal compromise. These episodes provide interesting examples of the impact of popular struggles, and illustrate the interaction between these struggles and the diverging interests of the various components of the upper classes. Class struggle on the part of workers actually provides the social energy required to stimulate the changing configuration of social relations, the pre-eminence of the social order to come. To use a phrase in fashion, upper classes 'surf on the wave' of popular struggle, and the objective of each component is to lead.

There is a lot in common between popular struggle in France and the US. In particular, the same threats were posed by class struggle to capitalist societies, at the beginning of the century and after World War II. The same post-war shocks were felt in the major capitalist countries. It is, however, also the case that – from the French revolution, through the class struggles in France that Marx analysed, to the struggle during the interwar years which led to the popular front – social strife, in France, was always marked by radical traits. The situation after World War II, with a strong Communist party, was tense, and the necessity to compromise was acute. Paradoxically enough, neoliberalism was imposed in the context of the 'socialist' episode after 1981, another expression of the same radical trends. Again, popular resistance to the dismantling of social protection prevented the thorough adjustment of France to neoliberalism in all its components. In each of these successive episodes, the inclination of the managerial class towards social reformism played an important role.

Conclusion: Two historical trajectories?

A basic characteristic of contemporary capitalism is the coexistence of two upper classes, capitalist and managerial, potentially ruling. The managerial class stepped on the social stage at the transition between the 19th and 20th centuries. In this sense, it is recent. From the late 19th century to the Great Depression, the capitalist class occupied an hegemonic position. Note that at issue here are not the actual tasks in organisation, but power, that is the capability to impose its rule and secure its income. After the depression and World War II, capitalism lived in the Keynesian compromise, a very specific period, in which the autonomy of the managerial class, of its private and public components, was increased. This was made possible by the compromise with both popular classes and capitalist classes. Instead of labeling these two facets 'downward' and 'upward', along a social ladder, in a vocabulary which might be judged pejorative for popular classes, we will use the terms 'left' and 'right', which actually account rather adequately for the political spectrum. It might well be the unique manner of linking the polarisation left/right to class patterns.

In a country like Japan, it was certainly possible to refer to a managerial hegemony, since capitalist interests were very weak; in the US, this would be an exaggeration; in Europe, the situation can be deemed as 'intermediate'. With neoliberalism, the power and interests of the capitalist class were restored, and the position of financial institutions was strengthened, both dramatically. Managers were subjected to a new discipline. It was not only that their autonomy was plainly and neutrally diminished, but that their action was targeted toward capitalist interests. In this process, they were obviously not passive agents, but social actors – depending on groups (upper and lower) and countries. Thus, the imposition of this new discipline was made politically acceptable by the 'standard' managerial class by the neoliberal compromise, while top management fused with the upper fraction of the capitalist class – give and take.

This is where the story becomes quite telling concerning the future of our societies:

1. In France, although social compromises shifted to the right under neoliberalism, the distance between the two classes remained considerable, in terms of income and politics. Managers were first constrained to the left by the dynamics toward lesser wage inequality at the end of the 1960s, and, in neoliberalism, traditional income channels remained rather impervious. In neoliberalism, management was actually 'disciplined' by capital.
2. In the US the capitalist class learned from the Keynesian compromise and the structural crisis of the 1970s. When profit rates were depressed, and capital incomes low, wages 'appeared' as a privileged channel in the appropriation of the surplus. From the 1970s onwards, at the top of the managerial hierarchy, wages began their hike. Capitalist owners jumped onto the bandwagon, possibly set it in motion. A split occurred in the managerial class, with an upper fraction gradually coalescing with large capitalist owners in a hybrid class. The rest of the class, whose fate was already improving relative to the bulk of wage earners since the war, did not suffer from this fusion at the top, and was associated with capitalist prosperity through pension funds in this two-tier capital hierarchy,

where standard capital incomes are partly 'trivialised'. Far more than in France, this class arrangement shifted the centre of gravity of US society to the right. It is not coincidental that this social deal was struck in the country which dominates the world economy, with the subsequent movement towards renewed imperialism.

Overall, these configurations define the contemporary world alternative: (1) a new deal to the left, or (2) the continuation of the *big capital-top management* 'love story' in the new ruling class US style. One should not conclude straightforwardly that the diagnostic on the present situation of French society implies a return to the left; neither is it obvious that such a turn is unthinkable in the US. History is more complex, and the future of these trajectories will depend on economic conditions and class struggle, since, as Marx wrote, human beings make their own history, but under given [economic] circumstances.

Notes

* This paper has been prepared for the conference After Deregulation: The Financial System in the 21st Century, organised by The Centre for Global Political Economy, University of Sussex, May 26–28 2005
+ MODEM-CNRS, Université de Paris X-Nanterre 200, av. de la République, 92000 Nanterre, France. Email: gerard.dumenil@u-paris10.fr.
++ CEPREMAP-ENS, 48, bd Jourdan, 75014 Paris, France. Email: dominique.levy@ens.fr.
1. The paper builds on the foundations laid in G. Duménil, D. Lévy 2004a.
2. We will not discuss here the interpretation of these transformations in relation to Marx's analysis (G. Duménil, D. Lévy 1998; G. Duménil, D. Lévy 2004b).
3. G. Duménil, D. Lévy 2004c.
4. The data are from T. Piketty, E. Saez 2003.
5. G. Duménil, D. Lévy 2004c.
6. T. Veblen 1899; T. Veblen 1924.
7. There are three sources: (1) fraud, (2) exemption, and (3) withholding.
8. J.K. Galbraith 1967; A.D. Chandler 1977. It is interesting to cite here the book written, in 1963, by a French manager, typical of the men who led the economy after the war: François Bloch-Lainé (1963). The cover states: 'The enterprise is a community of interests, impossible to reduce uniquely to its owners. [...] Within an enterprise, as within the Republic, there are the governors (managers) and the governed (capital and personnel)'.
9. G. Duménil, D. Lévy 2004a, Figures 15.2 for France and 15.3 for the US.
10. The saving rates of upper classes shrank to incredibly low levels (D. Maki, M. Palumbo 2001).
11. W.G. Roy 1997.
12. O.M.W. Sprague 1910.
13. R. Hilferding 1910; V.I. Lenin 1916; G. Duménil, D. Lévy 2005: section 2.1.1.
14. The progress of private management, the development of exchanges, and monetary mechanisms results in a trend toward growing macro instability (the recurrence of overheatings and recessions). This tendency must be constantly

checked by the progress of policies. This is what we call 'the tendential instability thesis' (G. Duménil, D. Lévy, 1993: section 18.4).

15. In the framework of analysis in this paper, there is nothing like an autonomous state, and the dynamics of social transformation cannot be addressed in terms of a confrontation between the state and the market. (The reference to the 'market' hides the freedom of capitalist initiative.) This prominent role conferred on the state was the expression of the new class compromise.
16. G.W. Domhoff 1990.
17. A key element in the road to serfdom of von Hayek (1980).
18. E. Helleiner 1994.
19. W. Greider 1987.
20. One can cite here the example of the Colorado Coal Strike of 1913–1914, and the Ludlow Massacre, where workers and capitalists waged an actual war.
21. As shown in J. Weinstein 1968.

Part III
Embedding Deregulated Finance

The concluding part of this volume examines the historical and contemporary construction of the often-uneasy relationship between regulatory efforts and policies, and the institutional reproduction of financial dynamics. Our aim here is to unpack the inner organisation and mechanics of deregulated market-based financial systems, to examine their evolution and reproduction in various historical and spatial contexts, and to probe the efficacy of the emerging global paradigm of financial regulation. The essays presented here address these tasks in a two-fold manner. First, studies by M. Konings, K. Haiduk, R. Palan and R. Murphy probe the historic volition and significance of deregulated finance across different political-economic realms. Second, M. de Goede, A. Persaud and J. Nugée discuss the efficacy of the emerging paradigm of global financial governance, revealing the limitations in the currently dominant risk-centred approach, and analysing alternative policy options.

Martijn Konings explores the meaning of the monetarist revolution in the US, by setting it in its historical context. Challenging the conventional monetarist understanding of capital market-based model of American finance, his analysis regards institutions and markets as not necessarily distinctly different entities with inherently different logics of operation. On the contrary, he illustrates persuasively that social and political institutions are crucial not only in the containment but also in the creation and expansion of market dynamics.

Continuing the analysis of national institutional reproductions of deregulated finance, Kirill Haiduk addresses the complex phenomenon of post-Soviet capital flight. His paper unpacks the 'external' and 'internal' dimensions of post-Soviet capital mobility. Introducing the notion of 'domestic offshore' and positioning it in the context of the transformation of state authority in Russia, Haiduk explains the underlying structural causes of 'domestic offshorisation', the dynamics of its emergence and proliferation.

Taking corporate entities as a basis unit of critique, Ronen Palan and Richard Murphy reveal the phenomenon of 'creative accounting' which, they argue, lies at the heart of the new politics of numbers. Specifically, they focus on some of the factors that complicate the meaning of numbers and profits in capitalism. While in the popular image of the economy, profits and prices are the 'hard' indicators emanating directly from the accounts and are the indicators around which the entire system hinged, they find the experience of corporate life rather different. As Palan and Murphy show, declared corporate profit is subjected to a whole set of calculations that tends to obscure the issue.

The two concluding essays of this book critically analyse the currently shaping global paradigm of financial governance, focusing in particular on the risk component of many reform measures. Marieke de Goede, reflecting upon the meaning and form of financial regulation in the context of the war on terror, argues that the emerging regulatory regime of finance is historically specific: it aims to reconcile new regulation with continuing globalising markets, through a risk-based approach. In this process, the contingent set of laws and practices has effects on financial exclusion and economic citizenship. These effects suggest that the war on terrorist finance needs to be approached critically, and that the reregulation emerging in its name – while clearly drawing on earlier initiatives – is particular to the 21st century.

Finally, Avinash Persaud and John Nugée take the analysis of today's financial governance forward, scrutinising the current 'bottom-up' policy approach to financial regulation. Revealing flaws and systemic dangers contained in the currently dominant regime of regulation, they advocate instead an alternative, 'top-down' approach. This alternative, they explain, would encourage a macro-prudential management of risks in the financial system to reduce systemic risk – a systemic-sensitive approach – and a risk-classification approach to protect average consumers, based more on results than process. As they conclude, once you have made systems safe and protected average consumers, you do not need such detailed supervision of individual institutions, thus reducing the burden of supervision on the economy and consumers. Under such a regime, individual institutions may not be as 'safe', and there may be more failures for us to learn from, but crucially, the system and consumers would be safer than they are at present.

11
Monetarism in the US: The Development of New Forms of Institutional Control Over Banks and Financial Markets

Martijn Konings

Introduction

This essay explores the meaning of the monetarist revolution in the US by setting it in its historical context. From a neoliberal point of view, monetarism represents the financial side of the broader victory of markets over states and their regulatory institutions. It involves the acknowledgement that attempts to impose a framework of substantive regulation on financial markets are doomed to failure and that the aims of monetary policy ought to be limited to ensuring a fixed growth in the supply of money, leaving the market to determine its price. Any other use of monetary policy is likely to engender inflation and end up distorting market processes.

Aspects of this understanding of monetarism are shared by many authors who do not subscribe to a neoliberal understanding of the relations between state and market. In the discipline of comparative political economy (which tends to be dominated by institutionalist authors (for example, Hall and Soskice 2001), for instance, it is widely understood that markets are not natural phenomena and that it is not only economic logic but rather the configuration of economic and political interests and institutions that determines the precise relations between state and economy at any given time. But even though the turn to monetarism and neoliberalism is analysed in terms of the political response to the problems of the Keynesian policy regime of the post-war order, the rise of monetarism and neoliberalism is still conceptualised in terms of the traditional opposition of markets and institutions, that is, as the disembedding of markets from their institutional environment.

Institutionalist typologies of capitalist economies usually distinguish between a capital market-based model associated with a weak, decentralised system of regulatory governance and a bank-based model characterised by strong institutional capacities (Zysman 1983). Whereas Britain and the US are examples of the former, Japan and Germany are examples of the latter. The American economy, unfettered by the remnants of a feudal past, has always closely approximated the ideal of *laissez-faire* capitalism. That is particularly evident in its financial system, which is highly securitised and characterised by a very weak and fragmented system of regulation. Thus, in the case of the US, monetarist policies and deregulation are usually seen to represent a 'return to form', the final break with a system of New Deal regulation that was itself already a weak version of the more comprehensive Keynesian regime of regulation that characterised European states during the post-war period.

This essay will suggest that such interpretations of the American financial system are very one-sided. The US financial system is certainly highly marketised, but banks and institutions have played a crucial role in this process of marketisation. Similarly, the market-based US system is in its own way highly institutionalised. The Fed has gained a degree of policy leverage that is unavailable to any other central bank, and banks continue to play an essential role both in the further securitisation of the system and as the Fed's transmission channel to the financial markets. Such considerations point to a perspective in which institutions and markets do not necessarily appear as distinctly different entities with inherently different logics of operation. Of course a central part of the institutionalist case is that markets are always institutionally embedded, but in making this argument institutionalists seem to implicitly attribute certain inherent qualities to markets themselves. Markets are still seen as characterised by a logic of expansion and disembedding that needs to be contained and embedded by institutions; they are not seen as *themselves* institutional fabrications. A more thorough-going institution-based approach, however, would not put such a crucial aspect of socio-economic life beyond the reach of political choice and contestation. A perspective is needed in which institutions and markets do not necessarily appear as distinctly different entities with inherently different logics of operation. The view adopted in this paper does not attribute any such primordial qualities to markets and sees social and political institutions as crucial *not only in the containment but also in the creation and expansion* of markets.[1]

Foundations of American finance

The origins of modern banking and finance are to be found in late 17th century England. Rapid commercial development had spawned an inland market in short-term bills of exchange (the so-called discount market) whose value was secured by both the underlying transaction and the endorsements. Banks discounted these bills by issuing notes, and due to the liquid nature of their asset base thus accumulated they generally experienced few problems redeeming bank notes. Commercial banking, understood as the practice of taking deposits and issuing notes, became a viable undertaking in England because of the presence of a discount market.

The financial development of America differed from the English pattern in fundamental ways. Most of the new additions to the population settled in the West, and the first half of the 19th century witnessed not so much the industrialisation and commercialisation as the agrarianisation of the American economy (Van Fenstermaker 1965). Farmers did not primarily need short-term trade financing but rather long-term credit with which they could buy land and farms. In addition, trans-Atlantic merchants financed their trade through bills on London. And the domestic commercial networks that did exist relied heavily on informal bookkeeping credits (Williamson 1951: 232). Consequently, the US did not develop a substantial domestic discount market and the main American credit instrument became the promissory note, which was longer-term and not secured by the value of a commercial transaction (Myers 1931).

Farmers made their influence felt not only on a strictly economic level but also through political channels, that is, by imposing on the American financial system a regulatory framework that reflected their fears concerning the possibility of English-style commercial development that would jeopardise their existence as independent farmers (De Cecco 1984). Banks were not allowed to establish branches and were prohibited from endorsing bills of exchange. Farmers also opposed federal bank charters. Until the Civil War, the federal government only chartered three banks. One of these, the Second Bank of the United States, was in many ways an early central bank (Hammond 1957): it attempted to unify the American banking and currency system and to create an American discount market by replacing existing credit instruments with bills of exchange. It was fairly successful in doing so, but under popular pressure its charter was revoked. In other words, the decentralised, fragmented character of the American financial system is very much the result of attempts to impose a specific kind of regulation, not an indication of its absence.

Due to the absence of a discount market, American banks were forced to invest a large part of their funds in commercial paper and stock, assets that were longer-term and unsecured. As a result, American banks consistently experienced serious liquidity problems: while their note and deposit liabilities were redeemable on demand, their asset portfolio was comparatively illiquid (Hedges 1938). The pressure on banks to obtain liquid assets intensified from the 1840s due to the concentration of so-called bankers' balances (demand deposits held by one bank with another) in the hands of New York bankers as a consequence of the growing commercial connections between New York and the countryside.

What came to the banks' rescue was the market for call loans, that is, short-term loans made by banks to brokers on the basis of stock collateral (Myers 1931). The American stock market was prohibited from instituting its own clearing system (as existed in the London stock market), precisely because of populist concerns about the meshing of credit and speculative activities (Michie 1986). The result was that stock brokers had a very high need for outside liquidity. The call loan market grew from the 1840s, in large part owing to the expansion of the stock market consequent on the westward expansion of the railroads.

Even though Civil War financial legislation established a system of federal bank charters, it bore the direct imprint of agrarian and populist influence. The prohibition on branch banking remained in place, and strict limits were placed on the size of loans that banks were allowed to make to any single borrower. Nor did the National Bank Acts make it any more difficult for states to charter banks. Since calls for a central reserve association had foundered on populist resistance, a system of reserve balances was established whereby country banks held funds with city banks and city banks with New York banks. This 'pyramidal' system essentially formalised and extended the existing, voluntary system of correspondent banking (James 1978). It concentrated large amounts of funds in the hands of New York banks, exacerbating their liquidity problems and the pressure to find liquid, short-term assets.

The years preceding the Civil War had seen the tentative emergence of a discount market, but the war had aborted this development and subsequent developments gave a boost to the use of promissory notes. However, the latter differed from antebellum notes. The high rates of post-war inflation meant that merchants became concerned about lengthy credit terms. Therefore, instead of drawing a bill, merchants increasingly made use of open-book accounts and they encouraged debtors to settle in cash as soon as possible by offering them a large discount (Myers 1951: 572). The discount made it very tempting for debtors to borrow money from banks in order to immediately settle their debts – the rate on the bank credit being less than that on the original debt. To this end they issued their own promissory notes and offered them for discount to banks. Whereas antebellum promissory notes had usually borne the name of an endorser in addition to that of the promisor, the new notes were single-name, that is, not endorsed (Myers 1931: 317). And it was this kind of single-name promissory note that would become the basis of the specifically American institution of the American commercial paper market (Greef 1938; James 1995).

The introduction of the single-name promissory note made it considerably easier to issue financial obligations. It is important to appreciate the historical novelty of this practice. Hitherto, directly issuing and selling debt on the basis of nothing other than their creditworthiness was a privilege reserved for states or publicly chartered corporations – which could issue long-term bonds. Any private person or enterprise wanting access to credit needed to either borrow directly from a bank or get involved with the complicated mechanisms of bills and notes. Single-name promissory notes made the direct, unmediated access to credit more widely available. The significance of this development is hard to overestimate, as it laid the basis for what has come to be known as disintermediation, the bypassing of traditional financial intermediaries in favour of direct borrowing or lending in financial markets.

This was especially significant given the constraints placed on American banks. Disintermediation became pronounced when, from the 1880s, postbellum economic growth began to strain against the limits on loan size imposed on banks. Initially, borrowers tried to obtain loans from several banks at the same time, but as the postbellum economy took off many corporations and large enterprises outgrew banks' lending capacity to such an extent that this became highly impractical. Instead, they chose to raise funds directly in the commercial paper market (Foulke 1980 [1931]; James 1995).

With their ability to make direct loans under pressure, banks turned to the money and stock markets in order to fill up their asset portfolio. In other words, banks securitised their assets in response to disintermediation tendencies. In response to the advent of the single-name promissory note, banks had already begun to develop methods for gathering and evaluating information concerning the creditworthiness of commercial paper issuers (White 1998). Aided by the new methods, banks increased their purchases of commercial paper. Nevertheless, commercial paper was still unsecured, unendorsed, longer term, and without a secondary market. Banks therefore poured ever larger amounts of funds into the call loan market. Banks also began to get themselves more directly involved in the securities business through securities affiliates. The result was an ever more tightly connected network of connections between banks and financial markets – what was known as the New York Money Trust. Thus, banks' investment strategies fuelled speculative tendencies in a market that was already growing exponentially and was, due to the instabilities in the railroad sector, structurally unstable. The involvement of large New York banks with speculative financial markets was further driven on by the intense competition they experienced from less regulated state banks and almost completely unregulated trust funds (De Cecco 1984). The formation of a market in industrial securities that followed the incorporation of American industry around the turn of the century (Roy 1997) gave a further boost to the call loan market, financial innovation and speculative activities.

The Federal Reserve System in its early years

The Federal Reserve System was founded in response to the instability that pervaded the American financial system and culminated in the crisis of

1907. Ostensibly, its task was to stabilise the American financial system not only by standing by as a lender of last resort, but also by forcing banks to adopt more prudent investment practices. The Federal Reserve Act was created against the background of the investigations of the Pujo Committee into the practices of the New York financial establishment, characterised by a great deal of corruption and collusion. As a result, the Federal Reserve System was founded on fairly traditional and conservative notions of banking (West 1973). However, what New York financial elites realised, at least on an intuitive level, was that traditional notions of commercial banking – which prescribed the acquisition by banks of 'self-liquidating' bills of exchange – would in practice be increasingly irrelevant, given that the large money centre banks were loaded up with commercial paper, call loans and stock. Any centralised reserve institution would have little choice but to conform itself to existing practices if it wanted to be of any use. Thus, even though many aspects of the Federal Reserve Act reflected the influence of populist antipathy towards the New York financial establishment (Sanders 1999), the Act did little to undermine the power basis of the New York Money Trust, that is, the high degree of integration of banks, the money market and the stock market. The Fed's lender-of-last-resort function would soon come to trump the attempt to impose more conservative banking practices – a development accelerated by the war circumstances, which required the Fed to stand by to discount a wide variety of non-standard, that is, longer-term and poorly secured, bank assets. Thus, the practical effect of the foundation of the Fed was to embolden banks: the presence of a lender of last resort made them more, rather than less, willing to engage in risky investment strategies (Cleveland and Huertas 1985).

The first years after the war saw a growth in corporate finance and direct bank loans. However, soon the credit needs of corporations outgrew the financing capacity of American banks and they turned towards the stock market. Consequently, banks, which were highly liquid due to the Fed's liberal discounting practices, grew ever more willing to exploit the opportunities offered by their close ties to a highly integrated system of financial markets. That is, banks once again responded to disintermediation with the securitisation of their assets. It served to push banks further in the direction of a market-oriented conception of liquidity that was more concerned with an asset's saleability than with its underlying characteristics (Cleveland and Huertas 1985).

The liquidity effects of the bank's lender-of-last-resort function were reinforced by the passive policy orientation of the Fed (Wheelock 1991). It is important to realise that, strictly speaking, the Fed was born with a mandate not for monetary policy but for credit policy (Chandler 1971: 10–1): it saw its main task as accommodating the demand for credit as this expressed itself in the money market. The Fed was primarily a bankers' bank, an institution responsible for keeping the banking system liquid. That is not to say that the Fed was unconcerned with the state of the economy as a whole, but rather that such trends were interpreted through the demand for credit as expressed in the money market and that a full conceptualisation of the financial system as a transmission belt between government policy and the real economy remained absent.

More concretely, the so-called 'real bills' doctrine prescribed passive accommodation of banks' demand for credit in the money market (Degen 1987). While this principle may seem innocent enough, upon closer inspection it is rather contrary to what are nowadays considered to be the basic principles of monetary management. For its effects were procyclical. During an economic upturn, banks tried to meet the increased demand for credit; this translated into an increased demand for bank reserves, which the Fed perceived as an indication of monetary tightness that it would seek to loosen by discounting the assets offered by the banks; and vice versa. Thus, during an upturn the Fed would pursue expansionary policies and credit would be liberally available, and during a recession it would restrict credit expansion and it was hard to obtain credit for any purpose. This was all the more problematic given the fact that much of the excess credit generated during upturns was used for speculation.

The perverse effects of these Fed policies promoted the emergence of a partial and inchoate awareness of the need for a more countercyclical policy orientation (Wheelock 1991). It was, however, still a far cry from modern monetary policy, as the Fed still took its cue from the demand for credit as expressed in the money market (albeit now inversely). Moreover, while in principle the newly invented policy instrument of open market operations allowed for more active interventions than the passive instrument of the discount window, the former had fallen into the hands of the Federal Reserve Bank of New York, which was more concerned with the international interests of New York financiers than domestic monetary management (Greider 1987). The speculative activity culminated in the crash of 1929.

After the crash and the depression, New Deal legislation cut the American banking system down to size. Commercial banks were prohibited from involving themselves with the securities business. Interest rate ceilings were imposed to prevent excessive competition between banks for deposits – which, it was hoped, would eliminate the pressure on banks to invest their funds in risky assets. At the same time, federal deposit insurance was introduced, diminishing the Fed's responsibility for the lender of last resort function and freeing its hands for the more active use of monetary policy for the management of the economy as a whole. The Fed also became a more centralised institution and was given a range of new powers.

Contradictions of American finance during the post-World War II period

The American financial system as a whole was under political tutelage from the Depression until the aftermath of World War II. The 1950s initially saw an expansion of commercial and industrial lending. However, as in the past, this was followed by disintermediation trends. As the Fed withdrew its support for the market in government debt, market interest rates rose. Since the rates that banks could pay on deposits were capped, it became attractive for large depositors to invest their funds in short-term securities instead of holding them as deposits with banks. The dwindling supply of funds forced banks to cut down on their corporate lending and corporations turned to the money market for their borrowing requirements as well. The funding crisis had set in train a vicious spiral, and reversing this dynamic was crucial. However, the most obvious ways for a bank to obtain funds – paying for deposits and establishing branches – were forbidden by law.

During the next years banks invented a range of financial instruments allowing them to circumvent these restrictions by raising funds in the money market (Battilossi 2002). The most important of these was the negotiable certificate of deposit (CD), a time deposit for which the banks created a secondary market (Sylla 2002). Such innovations signified a shift from asset management to liability management strategies. Traditionally, banks had a fairly passive approach to their sources of funds. The profession of banking was primarily about managing assets on the basis of a given structure of deposit liabilities. The new approach that emerged turned this traditional approach to banking upside down. Instead of managing assets on the basis of a given liability structure, the burden of securing a bank's liquidity and profitability now shifted towards the management of its liabilities (Chernow 1990: 54). This meant that a bank would first set a target for the growth of its assets, extend credit accordingly, and then go after the funds needed to match these assets. Whereas in the traditional approach to banking the money market was a place where banks *bought* financial assets, in the new approach it started to function as a market where banks *sold* obligations and 'bought money'. Liability management essentially meant the further securitisation of traditional financial relations (Wojnilower 1987; Harrington 1987).

From the mid-1960s the Fed became more concerned about inflation and began to actively resist banks' liability management strategies. The banks' response was to look for ways to raise funds that would escape Federal Reserve control. Consequently, from the second half of the 1960s many of the financial instruments being developed in the US were introduced in the Euromarket, the market in non-resident dollar holdings that had grown up over the course of the post-World War II period. Thus, while the relation of US banks to the Euromarket is often understood in terms of their exit from the American regulatory system, it is important to realise that exit was so crucial in part because it allowed American banks to secure funding for *domestic* operations (Huertas 1990: 254). Moreover, once outside American borders, US commercial banks were no longer subject to any of the New Deal regulations. They took on securities business (Battilossi 2000: 169–70), developed sophisticated techniques for liquidity and risk management (which entailed an ever more integrated marketised approach to both sides of a bank's balance sheet) and provided a wide range of financial services.

Banks' ability to raise funds in the Euromarkets did much to complicate the Fed's management of the domestic credit and money situation. Fundamentally, the problem was that the Fed's operating procedures were ill-equipped to deal with the financial innovations and changing bank strategies, and even less equipped to deal with the application of these techniques in an offshore market outside the Fed's jurisdiction.

Although at this point in time the Fed was aware of its role in macroeconomic stabilisation, as its policies targeted the relation between interest rates and free reserves in the federal funds market they were still based on money market indicators (Bach 1971). The Federal Open Market Committee (FOMC) sought to raise or lower the federal funds rate by setting a target for the banks' net free reserves, which the Open Market Desk then sought to hit by pumping liquidity into or taking it out of the system through open market operations.

However, the financial innovations of the 1960s rendered these policies less effective (Degen 1987: 140). For to target a desired *free* reserves position gave no guarantees concerning the *total* level of reserves in the banking system. Free reserves reflect the reserves that banks have available over and above the reserves they are required to hold to satisfy the Fed's reserve requirements. In a situation where banks are passive receivers of deposits, controlling free reserves and controlling total reserves amounts to the same thing. However, in a situation where banks actively acquire reserve funds, this relation no longer holds. Fed control over the creation of credit and money rests on reserve requirements as a real constraint on bank behaviour, and it was precisely the banks' liability management strategies that loosened this constraint.

The contradictions of monetary management were intensified and ultimately came to a head during the 1970s. Due to higher market interest rates (Cargill and Garcia 1985), the flight out of bank deposits towards money market instruments and institutions became even more serious. The disintermediation trend was reinforced by the financialisation of economic life. Due to the economic downturn, corporations began channeling large amounts of funds into the financial sphere (Arrighi 2003). Money market mutual funds attracted funds that would normally be held as savings deposits and grew at an astounding rate (Edwards 1996). Banks responded to these developments by intensifying their efforts to access new sources of funds and the development of new financial techniques. In a growing Euromarket banks took on investment banking functions, stepped up their off-balance sheet activities, and gave a huge boost to derivatives and foreign exchange markets (Harrington 1987).

During the early 1970s the Fed actively tried to contain inflation by working within and shoring up the existing system of regulation. However, contractionary policies in the context of interest rate ceilings fuelled disintermediation, which then encouraged banks to intensify their liability management strategies. In other words, Fed policies ended up fuelling the growth of non-bank intermediaries and financial markets, and had little impact on inflation. Thus, during the 1970s the contradictions of the Fed's money market strategy became even more pronounced. The Fed's policies were further constrained by the fact that restrictive policies posed a serious threat to the position of the thrifts, which were unable to engage in liability management strategies given that their assets consisted largely of long-term and often fixed-rate assets such as mortgages. In addition, the Fed's monetary control was eroded by banks' ability to exit the System and continue operations under a state charter.

As the 1970s progressed, it became clear that monetary policy needed to be adapted in essential respects. This led to a heightened concern with monetary aggregates. However, the 'money supply' as such is not an operational target: central banks have some leverage over the mechanisms through which it is created, but no direct control over the money supply. Thus, while the target had changed, the operating procedures remained oriented towards money market indicators, that is, the federal funds rate and free reserves (Degen 1987: 157). But while the practical significance of the focus on monetary aggregates remained limited, what had happened in terms of the growth of financial consciousness is not to be underestimated. The concept of 'money stock' had first appeared in a Federal Reserve annual in 1948 (Degen 1987: 157). During the 1950s and 1960s the concept would pop up every now and then, but it never informed policy decisions to any meaningful degree and Fed policy remained concentrated on the price and availability of credit.

Monetarism and after

In October 1979 the Fed announced a change in operating procedures. The Fed would no longer target free reserves and interest rates in the federal funds market but instead total reserves and the money supply (Meulendyke 1988). This shift represented a dramatic departure from the money market approach to monetary policy. The new chairman Volcker felt monetarism offered the right policy prescriptions at the right moment. Whereas the relation between interest rates and the money supply was indirect and tenuous, that between total reserves and the money supply was direct

(Volcker 2002). In an important sense, the adoption of monetarism was also a public relations strategy. For the Fed now declared that it was targeting total reserves and no longer concerned itself with conditions in the federal funds market. How eager banks were to obtain additional reserves and how high they drove up interest rates in bidding for them was none of the Fed's business anymore (Krippner 2003; Rude 2004).

However, as we have seen, in the past restrictive policies had not only been ineffective but also given rise to a range of unpleasant side effects – such as the shrinkage of the banking system, problems in the thrift sector, and exit from the Federal Reserve System. It is crucial to realise that the monetarist revolution occurred in the context of a broader program of financial deregulation being in the works (on which the Fed successfully seized to press for more comprehensive authority over depository institutions). With their uses and sources of funds expanded, banks and thrifts were more competitive *vis-à-vis* mutual funds and financial markets and the danger of disintermediation was reduced. Also, the extension of Federal Reserve authority over all depository institutions meant that it no longer needed to worry about the exit threat. As a result, the negative side effects of the Volcker shock remained limited.

What turned out to be much more problematic were the workings of the principal economic mechanisms postulated by monetarism. Inflation came down, but monetarist policies functioned in very different ways than is normally assumed. Far from coming to a halt, the creation of money and credit exploded. The reason behind this was of course that despite the sudden squeeze on liquidity banks were able to get the needed reserves elsewhere, notably in the Euromarket (Greider 1987). Monetarism, predicated as it is on the notion that money is created as if it were dropped from an airplane, straight into the real economy, abstracts from the intervening mechanism through which money is produced. And it was of course precisely in those mechanisms that the real problems of monetary management were to be found. Even though the Fed had now correctly identified total reserves instead of federal funds market conditions as the key indicator, this did not mean that the Fed was actually capable of controlling total reserve and the money supply. In fact, deregulation had given bank strategies of financial innovation and liability management free rein.

Thus, the explanation for the success of monetarism in combating inflation must be sought elsewhere. Since the idea of controlling the quantity of money holds no special magic, it must be concluded that it was still interest rates doing the real work. However, they did not function in the traditional sense, that is, by making money more expensive and so limiting the creation of credit. In fact, due to deregulation the Fed was even less able to control the creation of credit than during the 1960s and 1970s. However, high interest rates served to depress manufacturing activity and suck large amounts of funds into the financial sector; that is, little of the additional credit found its way into the real economy. The high interest rates functioned both to contain inflation and to stimulate financial activity, that is, to keep consumer price inflation down while promoting asset inflation.

It soon became clear to policy makers that the real significance of the monetarist shock lay not so much in the targeting of monetary aggregates but rather in enhanced control over market interest rates (Rude 2004). Consequently, monetarism in its pure form was abandoned in 1982 – only three years after its adoption. Thus, considered on its intellectual merits as a doctrine of monetary management, monetarism is of limited importance. Monetarism was very much a one-off shock that had the remarkable effect of setting the American financial system on a new track. Its real significance lies in the fact that it ushered in a transition to a high interest rate regime that had a lasting transformative impact on American finance. The manufacturing sector was dealt a huge blow, and the financial sphere became a much better place to put one's money than the real economy (Krippner 2003). The high interest rate regime accelerated innovation and securitisation and gave a boost to processes of financialisation (Simpson 1992; Rude 2004). It drew in large flows of capital and so promoted the expansion of American financial markets (Arrighi 2003). The capital inflows also pushed up the exchange rate of the dollar, thereby reinforcing the economic recession and fuelling financialisation.

These processes of financialisation essentially represented a massive inflation of asset prices – not, however, an inflation that represented a dysfunctional aberration incompatible with the structures and institutions in place to organise economic activity, but precisely a kind of inflation that was embedded in institutions and policies bestowing on financial strategies a degree of systemic viability and coherence. Financialisation thus differed fundamentally from the highly dysfunctional price inflation of the previous decade. In fact, they should fundamentally be seen as different sides of the same coin. For it was the high interest rates spawned by the Volcker shock that stood at the basis of both.

The heightened degree of financial activity generated considerable instability, culminating in the crash of 1987. The crisis was followed by attempts to put in place a framework of market-friendly regulation, both on the domestic and international level. The most important elements of this were the construction of a domestic and international capital standards regime,[2] the Treasury's assumption of a higher degree of responsibility for the soundness of the American financial system through repeated interventions as well as the expectations that such interventions created for the future, and a buffering up of the public resources available for public intervention. Thus, by the early 1990s, the US had put in place regulations and institutions that did much to stabilise the vast and highly securitised American financial system. This laid the foundations for further deregulation (especially the gradual abolition of the separation of commercial and investment banking), which created the context in which depository institutions could further marketise their operations and non-bank intermediaries and financial markets could continue to grow.

New forms of Federal Reserve control

However, financial expansion in combination with the formation of a regime of market-friendly regulation and intervention does not by itself explain the financial aspects of the 1990s. Speculative financial flows had grown to enormous magnitude and they could have easily trumped any capital standards or public financial guarantees if monetary authorities had not also acquired some more substantive control over the direction of these flows. Over the course of the 1990s, the Fed acquired an uncanny ability to steer financial markets in particular directions with minimum effort, that is, it learned to 'talk' markets up or down.

In 1982 the Fed had reintroduced a partial focus on interest rates (Meulendyke 1988: 15), thus shifting 'away from monetarism toward eclecticism' (Degen 1987: 191). The eclectic policies came to an end with the crash of 1987, which forced the Fed to abandon any ambiguity and make clear its interest rate policy intentions (Krippner 2003: 143). Thus, 'In the weeks following the crash, the Federal Reserve reverted to direct interest rate targeting, conducting whatever volume of open market operations needed to maintain the federal funds rate within a narrow band' (Krippner 2003: 143–4).

In a sense, this returned the Fed to the time before the Volcker shock (Friedman 2000). But circumstances had changed. Its control over depository institutions was more comprehensive, and it no longer needed to be so concerned with the harmful side effects of its policies as the bulk of New Deal legislation and regulations had been dismantled. Moreover, the Fed now operated in a massively expanded and fully securitised financial system. The Fed did have ambitions to return to a policy regime based on the determination of interest rates by financial markets, but it was precisely the size, liquidity and potential volatility of deregulated financial markets that asked for more policy clarity (Krippner 2003: 148).

However, it was the very same phenomenon that would set the Fed on the road towards a new policy regime. For what had previously been a major liability – the tight connections between banks and financial markets, allowing banks ample opportunities to find ways around Fed policies – was now emerging as a point of great leverage. The Fed still did not control credit creation, but it did control the cost of reserves in the federal funds market; and owing to the high degree of integration between banks and financial markets, this gave the Fed effective control over market interest rates. The growth of market sise and liquidity and the consequent improvement in market arbitrage meant that changes in the federal funds rate were almost instantly transmitted to other financial markets (Phillips 1996). And since deregulation had stripped bank strategies in financial markets of their perverse effects, the federal funds market now appeared as a perfect transmission channel for monetary policy. But this was not a transmission channel in the traditional sense, that is, one that allowed for control over the creation of money and credit. Rather, the financial system *as a whole* had become more sensitive to Federal Reserve policies. And it was through controlling financial markets that the Fed was able to prevent the undiminished creation of liquidity from spilling over into the real economy and cause inflation. Thus, at the same time as financial markets were expanding at an unprecedented rate and becoming ever more fluid, the Fed's ability to regulate these markets increased because of its control over the cost of bank funds in a relatively small segment of that market, that is, the federal funds market. The securitisation and marketisation of American finance have ultimately served to enhance the Fed's control.

Subsequently the Fed's governance capacities evolved even further. In the early 1990s the Fed occasionally started announcing changes in federal funds rate targets. It did so because it was concerned that the markets would miss subtle policy changes, but also because it had come under serious political pressure to practice more openness. The Fed itself was surprised to see the reaction to these announcements: financial actors responded by adjusting their behaviour in the desired direction prior to the Fed undertaking any open market operations (Krippner 2003: 151–4). In other words, the Fed has acquired the capacity to 'talk' financial markets up or down. This phenomenon of the pre-emptive adjustment of the financial system to the announced policy changes of the Fed has received the label of 'open mouth operations' (for example, Taylor 2001). In a sense, the Fed has become an extremely powerful, 'performative' Walrasian auctioneer overseeing a set of highly liquid, institutionalised and largely predictable markets.

Conclusion

The conventional explanations for the extraordinarily high sensitivity of financial markets to Fed policies are highly problematic. The financial press has typically credited the Fed's chairman Alan Greenspan with super-human powers, and the explanations advanced by Federal Reserve economists are invariably couched in the terms of mainstream economics (for instance, Poole and Rasche 2000). However, the idea of Greenspan's magic is too voluntarist, and the timeless logic of economic choice too determinist, to serve as satisfactory explanations for what is fundamentally a social and historical phenomenon.

This article has tried to suggest a historically grounded understanding of the degree to which the American financial system is simultaneously marketised and institutionalised. The market-based nature of the American financial system cannot be understood except in terms of the interaction of banks and other actors with a range of financial institutions. Similarly, the development of US finance cannot be understood as the progressive emancipation of financial markets from their institutional context but is better seen in terms of the institutionalisation of market processes. Such a perspective casts the turn to monetarism in a new light. Rather than liberating markets, it reconfigured the relations between markets and institutions in such a way as to not only expand financial markets but also increase their sensitivity to institutional parameters. At least in American finance, the neoliberal era has not been about the victory of markets over institutions but rather about the development of new forms of institutional control over market processes.

Notes

1. For a theoretical elaboration of a non-institutionalist approach to studying institutions, see Konings 2005a and 2005b.
2. The emphasis on the ratio of capital to assets rather than the traditional ratio of reserves to liabilities meant an implicit acknowledgement of the fact that reserve requirements no longer constituted a significant constraint on bank strategies.

12
The Political Economy of Post-Soviet Offshorisation

Kirill Haiduk[1]

Introduction

Stories about the *nouveau riche* make frequent appearance in the media. One from the club, Mr. Roman Abramovich, an oil trader raised in the Soviet Union, came to own more than the Duke of Westminster by the age of 37. But only a fraction of his funds are held in Russia: most of the money is being held in offshore jurisdictions. The tendency to shift capital offshore, away from official tax rules, is not only the habit of wealthy individuals; many corporations have also 'gone offshore'. For instance, about one-quarter of the shares of the major Russian electricity producer and supplier[2] are owned by a faceless offshore company (Kabir 2003: 6–8). Even state-managed finance has been transferred abroad and (not always) back. The money of the International Monetary Fund, lent to the Russian government in 1993, had been channelled to a secret firm registered on the Island of Jersey (*The Washington Post* 23 March 1999). Notably, capital has not only been relocated abroad: inside the economies of the former Soviet Union, ordinary citizens prefer to keep their savings in foreign cash, preferably US dollars.

Alongside of the growth of a parallel, dollar-denominated monetary system, Russia and other republics of the former USSR saw the emergence of differential tax regimes. Yet the problem of the proliferation of the so-called 'low-tax regions', a domestic equivalent of offshore havens in the global political economy, has not been adequately addressed so far. Since the mid-1990s, a number of regions of the Russian Federation have been able to obtain tax preferences and capitalise on fiscal semi-autonomy. Some regions have been even advertising themselves as territories with 'special' federal regulations. As a result of these developments, budget-financed organisations and employees across Russia have come to face continuous financial distress. This paper aims to unpack the 'external' and 'internal' dimensions of post-Soviet capital mobility, emphasising in particular the internal forces at work. The first section provides an empirical overview of Russia's 'offshorisation'. The second part introduces the notion of 'domestic offshore' and explores its evolution and significance, while the final part unpacks the underlying structural causes of its emergence and proliferation.

Dimensions of capital mobility: capital flight, dollarisation and 'domestic' tax havens

Massive capital flight has been a notorious fact of Russia's transformation. According to the IMF, between 1994 and 1999, some US$15–20 billion[3] left Russia every year (Loungani and Mauro 2000: 4). The Office for Public Prosecutor and the Ministry of Interior jointly blame the Russian capitalists for moving as much as US$400 billion between 1994 and 2003, while the Ministry of Trade and Economic Development considers such an estimate an exaggeration and expects a decrease in the volume of capital flight to US$5–7 billion in 2005 (*Agenstvo Finansovyih Novostei* 17 June 2005). The Central Bank of Russia refers not to capital flight, but calculates annual outflow of private sector capital, which amounted to US$162.3 billion between 1994 and 2004 (Central Bank of Russia 2005). This implies that funds have not been used for luxury consumption, but were allocated to investment projects abroad. As early as in 1994, the Bank of France claimed that the volume of foreign investment made by Russian companies across 30 countries equalled US$50 billion. Of these, Cyprus and Switzerland seem to be the most attractive destinations (*Komsomolskaya Pravda* 25 August 2003).

Intriguingly, runaway capital does come back, typically dressed as 'investment of foreign origin'. For instance, in 2001, up to 50% of the investment in the black metallurgy came from the Antilles (*Kommersant-Dengi* 25 July 2001, No. 29: 8). Taken together, Cyprus, the British Virgin Islands, Luxembourg, and Switzerland account for 31% of investment; the Netherlands could also be added to this list because of its well-designed double taxation agreements (Kashin 1998).

While Russian companies prefer to mediate their domestic business by the services offered by the global offshore industry, ordinary citizens have designed their own wealth-protecting strategies akin to those practised by business. Commonly referred to as 'dollarisation' these practices imply using hard currency (typically US dollars) as a store of value, a unit of account and even as a medium of exchange (especially for highly-priced durables). When in the early 1990s price liberalisation unleashed hyperinflation, the anti-inflationary measures included, among others, the freezing of rouble deposit accounts in the Savings Bank. It is unsurprising, therefore, that the population lost confidence in the national currency. Relying on foreign currency has led to the transfer of purchasing power over time and the recovery of a certain 'privacy' in the chaos of transformation

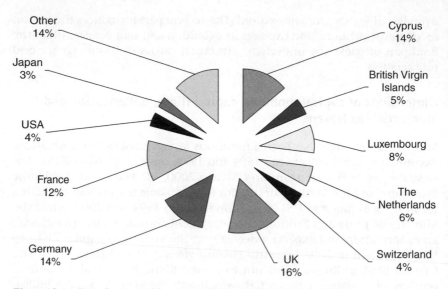

Figure 12.1 Distribution of Foreign Investment in Russia in 2003
Source: State Statistical Committee of Russia

Table 12.1 **Deposit Dollarisation Ratio in selected CIS countries, 1993–2001**

Country	1993	1994	1995	1996	1997	1998	1999	2000	2001
Russia	29.5	28.8	20.0	19.4	18.5	29.9	29.2	26.9	24.5
Belarus	37.7	56.5	23.5	24.2	27.3	55.6	43.7	58.7	52.0
Moldova	15.2	10.3	11.0	9.9	9.5	22.7	27.7	28.4	27.6
Ukraine	19.4	32.0	22.8	18.3	13.3	21.3	25.1	23.2	18.7

Source: Havrylyshyn and Beddies 2003: 8 (data are taken from IMF European II Department database)

(Cortbridge and Thrift 1994). This has been the case not only in Russia, but across the post-Soviet terrain.

Economists use a range of indicators to 'to measure the degree of...disquietude' to national money (Keynes 1937: 216). An often-used term is the ratio of foreign currency deposits to broad money. According to this benchmark, Russia and Belarus belong to the group of countries with a high degree of dollarisation (see Table 12.1). If the existence of large foreign currency savings is taken into consideration, the degree of dollarisation appears to be much higher (Feige and Dean 2002). The distrust of domestic banks and the existence of the shadow economy, where the US dollar remains indispensable for its economic agents (cf. Sosic and Faulend 2002), reinforce the process of dollarisation.

According to a survey by American Express at the end of 2002, US$-denominated cash circulating in Russia amounted to at least US$13.5 billion. At the same time, once individuals are taken into account, this figure goes up to US$18 billion (Semenov 2003). In 2004 about 59% of Russians held savings in foreign cash; and more than half of these savings were denominated in US dollars for the 'store of value' purposes (*Kommersant-Dengi* 18 July 2005, No. 28: 96). According to the Central Bank of Russia, in the first half of 2005 individuals were buying about US$2 billion per month, thus spending between 5% and 10% of income (*Izvestia* 20 July 2005: 3).

Offshore accounts – both inside the country, in the form of US$-denominated cash held in foreign banks – imply that credit supply in a given economy is made scarce. Since banks have to compete with the almighty dollar to attract deposits and to prevent capital flight (Ize and Parrado 2002), countries with weak currencies tend to have high real interest rates. Accordingly, enterprises are forced to pay more to lending institutions than their employees. This creates a situation which is characterised 'by a very unequal distribution between the remuneration of labour and capital', which is particularly visible in a dollarised economy like Belarus (Haiduk *et al.* 2004: 88).

Where do the dollars come from? An educated guess would suggests that the second wave of Jewish emigration to the US in the 1970s played an important role in making the US dollar, and not the deutschmark, a currency substitute for the Soviet rouble. Since the 1970s, contacts between Soviet and foreign societies had been growing beyond the formal world informed by détente. When state socialism collapsed, these relations began to mature into a network of interests that has bound certain commercial and social groups to others, especially when privatisation of the Soviet economy started (Mukhin 2003). Some of the émigrés became part of a network of intermediary agents providing 'assistance' in exports of oil products, non-ferrous metals, chemicals and cotton in the early 1990s.

The bifurcation of the national economy into 'offshore' and 'onshore' domains does not only lead to a loss of seigniorage and hamper domestic monetary management (Berg and Borensztein 2000). It also reduces the tax base, undermining the ability of the fiscal authority to command real resources from the private sector. In many post-Soviet republics this trend has been sustained by the emergence and spread of low-tax regions and special economic zones, offering fiscal sweeteners for foreign and domestic entrepreneurs. In Russia in particular, a range of regions, including Kalmykia, Ingushetia and Altai offered reduced tax rates for companies residing in their territories. The shaky federal architecture of post-Soviet Russia has opened the way towards interregional tax competition. This experience reflects a new spatiality of post-Soviet capitalism, which seems to be congruous to the logic of the offshore world of the global political economy (see Palan 2003).

The rise and decline of the domestic offshore in Russia

The story of 'inland offshore' in Russia goes back to the late 1980s, when the Soviet government experimented with reforms to enhance competitiveness and growth. In particular, several regions of the USSR were presented with 'simplified' tax and import duties, to attract export-oriented entrepreneurs from abroad. The Jewish autonomous region and Sakhalin were used as experimental fields with tax holidays. However, somewhat meaningful activity began only after the collapse of the Soviet Union, but involved corruption and abuse of eased regulations, forcing the permanent amendment of the law between 1992 and 1993 (*Ekonomika I Sziszn* January 2002, No. 3).

The experimentation carried on after the demise of the USSR, this time with the so-called 'enclosed administrative territories' and 'satellite cities' (commonly known as ZATO). Once centres for high-tech research and excellence, these formations had experienced a drastic cut of funding. The first post-Soviet government of Russia allowed them to keep their profit tax revenues, while ZATOs' administrations were allowed to set up tax rates to encourage companies to continue R&D activity, especially with the help of foreign capital. But instead of a scientific, these measures produced a rational-capitalist innovation. One example highlights a broader trend. In 1992 in Krasnoznamensk (a military and industrial research centre near Moscow) 136 enterprises were set up and registered in one dormitory. But neither their owners nor employees showed up in person. No investment came to run the laboratories and enterprises. Companies registered continued to extract gold or oil, make vodka or conduct financial operations. Similarly, the administration of Sarov[4] granted tax preferences of 30 billion Russian roubles to companies that had not even formally employed a single scientist in the field.

Russia is certainly not alone in experimenting with zonal differentiation of economic activity. Virtually all countries of Central, East and Southeast Europe either attempted to establish or created 'special economic zones'. Authorities of Poland, Bulgaria and Ukraine found the idea attractive. Ukraine in particular set up 11 'free economic zones' and nine 'priority zones', but all of them failed to attract foreign direct investment or foster economic growth (Vaknin 2003). In May 2001 UkInform reported, referring to Ukrainian President Kuchma, that about one-fifth of all meat sold in Ukraine was in fact smuggled through the 'free economic zones'. As a result, the country's budget lost about US$56 million (UkInform-News 21 May 2001). The Belarusian government founded four 'free economic zones' in Brest, Minsk, Gomel and Vitebsk, to attract foreign investment, promote high-tech manufacturing and increase economic diversification. The zones have not only attracted several hundred million US$ of investment but also shady industrialists and financiers who set up 'fronts' for parallel imports of shoddy or counterfeit goods. Recently, the Belarusian government confessed that special economic zones were not as successful as it was initially envisaged (www.tut.by 17 November 2005).[5] Kazakhstan also attempted to set up similar zones, but it conflicted with its international obligations under the WTO membership (Danko and Okrut 1998).

All these zones were set up to stimulate manufacturing, but for a number of reasons failed to do so. In the mid-1990s, a distinctly new type of zone, more akin to offshore tax havens, began to grow in Russia (Ushakov 2001). A range of regions, including Kalmykia, Ingushetia, Altai, Buryatia, Evenkia, Mordovia, Chuvashiya, the cities of Uglich, Kursk, and Smolensk, chose to base their development strategy on low-tax policies (Samoylenko 2004). Quite simply, the authorities of these regions and cities offered exemptions from regional and local taxes and duties[6] and sheltered certain companies from federal inspections (Slider 1997).

At that time, income tax in Russia was 35%, distributed in the following way: 11% was appropriated by the federal budget, 19% stayed at the disposal of the region's authorities, and 5% was given to the local budget. Kalmykia, for instance, initially offered a reduced regional tax rate down to 2%, and then replaced its portion of the income tax with a fixed fee denominated in US dollars (US$6,800) (*Korporatsiya* 1998, No. 6). To maximise revenues, as many businesses as possible had to be attracted. 'Administrative building' No. 249 on Lenina-Street in Elista hosted as many as 145 companies of various profiles, including branches of 'Lukoil', 'Apatit Trading' (one of the major companies of YuKOS), and 'Sibneft' (*Vedomosti* 22 August 2002). As for logistics, special 'secretary' companies were dealing with regional and local authorities that maintained secrecy and conducted infrequent and 'business-friendly' audit and tax inspections. When one tax loophole was closed, another one could offer similar service. For instance, when the Ingush free economic zone was closed in 1999, the BIN bank shifted companies it served to Buryatia where they were granted individual preferences on VAT and excise taxes (*Kompaniya* 5 April 1999, No. 12). On the top of that, 'domestic' offshore territories were used as transhipment points for sending capital abroad to 'genuine' offshore jurisdictions. According to a very modest estimate, at least US$2 billion per year have been transferred abroad *via* 'free economic zones' of various stripe since the mid-1990s (Kabir 2003).

Along with tax breaks, regional authorities sometimes encouraged the spread of the informal sector and the non-monetary arrangements such as barter to 'cement [clandestine] deals' with particular companies, making it more difficult for the federal centre to monitor their behaviour (Shleifer and Treisman 2000). In 40% of cases, companies registered in low-tax jurisdictions were physically located in Moscow or the Moscow region, specialising in the areas of housing construction, banking, oil and gas trading, and investment.

Despite the adverse impact on the fiscal situation in Russia, the government began to raise serious concerns only in 1999. Prior to that, the Primakov Cabinet of 1998 developed a comprehensive plan to eliminate domestic tax havens and discourage capital flight. The plan included monitoring of all correspondent account transactions made in tax havens by the special department of the Central Bank of Russia. The very limited term of the Cabinet did not allow these propositions to come into force. Only in 2004, the Duma approved a law that forbids regional and local authorities to grant selective tax preferences. The new Tax Code of 2004 has constrained the operation of the tax haven economy. Nevertheless, some loopholes survived like tax returns or subsidies to the arguably 'best' tax payers.

Post-Soviet state and the production of offshore

How can the phenomenon of 'domestic offshore' be better understood? International political economy literature tends to stress the particular international context of the post-Soviet transformation (Gowan 1999; Holman 1998; Laux 2000). Accordingly, domestic developments were significantly, if not decisively, impacted by the international setting, characterised by 'a worldwide coalescence of varied transnational processes and domestic structures, allowing the economy, politics, and ideology of one culture to penetrate another' (Mittelman 1996: 3). As latecomers, post-Soviet states are hardly in a position to initiate actions on their own; instead they are forced to react to worldwide economic forces. As a result, national development strategies have become reconfigured around a much narrower set of options (Radice 1998). More specifically, the outcome of cross-border competition between currencies and the process of their deterritorialisation have left countries with poor inflation records with no option but to subordinate the monetary authority to a stronger foreign currency with sound inflation records (Cohen 2000). Moreover, by decentralising the fiscal system, or changing the 'political economies of scale' (Cerny 1995), countries could avoid monetisation of budget deficit and a growing debt burden, thus attaining sound macroeconomic fundamentals that move it up the ladder of the global financial hierarchy.

Therefore, the instabilities of the first years of transition have produced local 'substitutes' for global economy structures; these 'domesticated versions' were partly configured to retain capital at home. Thus the emergence and spread of domestic tax havens appear to be a rational way to cope with the process of globalisation (Hülsemeyer 2000). To prevent capital outflow, the federal government tolerated (if not promoted) tax differentiation within Russia. In the words of one of the top managers of a leading Russian oil-exporting company, some members of the Russian government even asked companies to register their oil trading branches in the Kalmyk offshore because otherwise the government would lose much more in terms of tax revenues (www.gazeta.ru 10 December 2002). With this in mind, deregulatory enterprise could be interpreted as intention to tighten exit channels by 'fighting fire with fire'. Fiscal decentralisation became the chosen policy response to a severe lack of funds in the federal budget. As a result, regional administrations were granted a substantial degree of fiscal autonomy, which was often used to shelter selected companies by giving them tax preferences. But the emergence of offshorisation was not confined to the internal dimension only.

The internationalisation of the Russian economy proceeded not only in terms of trade and capital liberalisation, causing the disappearance of some industries, decline of real wages and rise of unemployment (Menshikov 2004); it also required a reconfiguration of the domestic institutional encasements, including the federal law. Institutional change was initiated and carried out through domestic political structures and actions of concrete agents, driven not just by plain 'market idealism', but also by sheer pragmatism (Sassen 1999). As a result, countries of the former Soviet Union, Russia included, were doomed to experience a reproduction of the contradictions of the global political economy internally.

One of these contradictions is between capital's necessary dependence on territory and its space-annihilating tendencies (Brenner 1998: 460). Accordingly, a series of combined processes of internationalisation and adjustment divided 'the sovereign corporate space of the nation' into 'virtual territories' characterised by 'different degrees of autonomy, regulation and control' (Palan 2003: 20). However, the 'offshorisation' of Russia is hardly a product of the adjustment to global tendencies. Domestic restructuring always entails the agency carrying out this task. According to Michel Aglietta (1979), economic logic alone could hardly be applied to understanding the formation and consequences of the economic policy, since the historical developments in the state and society are premised on dialectical unity and specific political, economic, and cultural conditions, which all have their roots in a more distant past. As such, this chapter argues, the development of the domestic offshore economy has to be traced to the late Soviet attempts to modernise the late socialist economy.

For Soviet planners, the Chinese experience of the creation of export processing zones looked promising. The development of small and medium-sized enterprises and the creation of new joint ventures were considered as key means of breathing new life into the technologically obsolete Soviet industry (Lavigne 1999). Since most advanced facilities that seemed easier to undergo modernisation were based in the ZATOs, the central government assumed that liberalisation of entrepreneurial activity and tax reductions would speed up the process of restructuring and enhancing of competitiveness.

The demise of the USSR opened up possibilities for further experimentation: approximately 150 regions requested approval to become 'free' or 'special economic zones'. Often this was considered as the only legitimate strategy to compensate for the lack of federal funding and also a tool to promote political independence (Semenov 1995).

But instead of experiencing an investment boom, those territories were left behind in growth terms, or were included into 'tax optimisation schemes' orchestrated by large companies. Initially, there were no strict benchmarks concerning employment and production, and tax payers were granted privileges as soon as they set up a company. Most of the entities were in fact 'shell' affiliates through which parent companies channelled their receipts. Only in 1999 were location and employment requirements modified so that companies could apply for tax benefits, yet only if they based at least 90% of their fixed assets in a low-tax jurisdiction, and if at least 70% of the employees were permanent residents of a given territory.

The outcome of the late-Soviet and early post-Soviet experimentation hardly came as a surprise. If the scope of the 'parallel economy' in the USSR and the underground commercial and social networks are considered, the abuse of the fiscal system is nothing but expected. François Seurot (1996) points to the existence of several 'exit options' that helped to resolve the contradictions of the Soviet system, but in the end contributed to its demise. The major exits were the shadow economy, which allowed the accumulation of illicit wealth in private hands, and the growth of informal, managerial-bureaucratic and political networks within the official hierarchies beyond the official structures of planning, administration, and control. These horizontal ties were strengthening at the expense of the formal vertical ties (Grossman 1998). Interregional inequalities and ethnic repressions aggravated the centrifugal tendencies in the Soviet Union and thus contributed to its collapse (Lapidus 1999). Soon after it, regional elites resorted to imagery of the past to mobilise the support of its constituents in favour of gaining autonomy from the federal centre. Between October 1991 and October 1993, the republics became especially vociferous in their demands. In the absence of a new Federal Constitution, many of the ethnic republics firstly unilaterally proclaimed a whole series or rights and privileges that was made legal in the 1992 Federal Treaties (Ross 2000).

Therefore, it is impossible to understand the development of Russia's domestic offshore economy without considering the profound domestic political developments of the early 1990s. At that time, democratisation had not only led to decentralisation, but also to a dramatic increase in 'the regional governments' sphere of activity' (Stoner-Weiss 1997: 88). Famously, President Yeltsin once proclaimed that 'regions should take as much freedom as they could stand.' To a great extent, this message was informed by the centre's financial distress. An OECD report reveals that much local expenditure 'took the form of a simple refusal by the federal government to finance certain expenditure categories', leaving them to pick up these expenditures, typically without any explicit source of finance (OECD 2000: 129).

In 1992, 21 ethnic republics were granted considerable control over their natural resources, the rights of secession (or autonomy), citizenship and sovereignty. In the climate of heightened capital mobility, this process of localisation redefined the coordinates of local, regional and national development. As a result, a number of regions had withdrawn themselves from the legal and economic orbit of the federation and became *de facto* autonomous islands within the Russian state (Ross 2000). The Ministry of Justice of the Russian Federation once estimated that of the 44,000 regional acts adopted over the period of 1995–97, almost half were in violation of the Constitution of the Russian Federation and federal legislation (Parish 1996). The growth of regional political autonomy has been reconciled with the development of the informal system of budgeting and taxation. By the mid-1990s, what had emerged in the remains of the 'Russian Soviet Federal Socialist Republic' of the USSR was then called 'an asymmetric federalism' (Solnick 1998).

Yet this type of federalism was not a product of institutional flaws, running in contrast to the well-composed 'theory of competitive liberalism' (Buchanan 1995, 96). In reality, a tiebout-like competition for capital has led to a race to the bottom in local taxes, welfare provision, and supply of consumer-oriented local public goods (cf. Keen and Marchand 1997). Interregional competition for capital encouraged the regional governments of Russia to act in ways that corrode the capacities of the central state (Cai and Treisman 2004) by appropriating a portion of the central government revenues, promoting tax evasion and exacerbating the federal political conflict.

By 1997–99, a zenith of 'offshorisation', regional governments had forged or promoted the formation of social alliances between transnationalised capital and locally constituted actors. The process of 'regionalisation' proceeded in combination with heightened global capital mobility, so the policies of sub-national states have gone far beyond the regional and even national economic milieu (Paul 2002). Clearly, messages about the structure of opportunities and constraints of the world economy open to individuals, companies and states have been taken into consideration by the regional elites of Russia. But the development of the inland offshore economy was hardly predetermined; neither did it result from an agency-level action. The structural properties of both the world and domestic political economy produced certain 'spaces of action' (Picciotto 1999), while the technical aspects of the design of the domestic tax havens have to be attributed to juridical and spatial coordinates of political power. It is therefore through a range of ostensibly autonomous developments and processes, beginning from the late Soviet developmental experiments, through democratisation and deregulation, that Russia's internal offshore economy became functionally tied to neoliberal policies 'that are simultaneously (sub-) national, international and global, [that is] take place within, across, and beyond national borders' (Overbeek 2000: 182).

Conclusion

This chapter analysed one of the most striking, but rarely reflected upon features of post-Soviet transformation: the division of sovereign monetary and fiscal spaces into distinct offshore and onshore parts. Such partition has been intrinsic not only to the behaviour of banks and firms that have gone 'offshore', but also of citizens who used US dollars alongside national currencies. Regional governments of Russia have designed 'domestic' tax havens within jurisdictions they have governed. But the capacity of international currency and domestic 'tax competition' as viable solutions to the problems of regional and national development is questionable. The dual bifurcation of sovereign space makes macroeconomic regulation an extremely complex enterprise, and has negative repercussions for the process of post-Soviet nation-building. The spatial reconfiguration of the post-Soviet space entails not just a disintegration of the former Soviet Union in terms of new states, but also a reshaping of national spaces 'from within', by goal-oriented praxis informed by constraints and opportunities of the world market. However, the unfinished story of the development of the domestic offshore in Russia shows that this outcome has neither been predetermined nor happened accidentally. It is hard to distinguish a political-economic infrastructure that has determined political, institutional and legal configurations of the post-Soviet states. Instead, as this chapter has analysed, there is a historical interrelation of political, economic, and spatial factors that produced the phenomenon of 'offshorisation'.

Notes

1. I am indebted to Prof. Kees van der Pijl, Prof. Hansjorg Herr and Prof. Jan Priewe for invaluable ideational support. Special thanks to Anastasia Nesvetailova for detailed comments on earlier drafts of this article. I am also thankful to the Centre for Policy Studies in Budapest for making me feel financially secure in the course of making research. I'm also grateful to my ILO colleagues committed to assist the solution of pressing social problems with which trade unionists are dealing with, and whose daily experience with the hardships of transition stimulates the research activity.
2. Currently managed by the father of Russian privatisation, Mr Anatoly Chubais.
3. US$15 billion, according to the so-called 'broad money' measure; US$20 billion according to 'hot money' measure.
4. Also known as Arzamas-16, a town with a high concentration of nuclear research facilities.
5. The Brest zone alone attracted US$120 million of investment, while 5,000 jobs were created
6. But not the federal ones.

13
Tax, Subsidies and Profits: Business and the Modern State

Ronen Palan and Richard Murphy[1]

Introduction

In all those civilised countries where the price system has gone into effect, observes Veblen, 'men count their wealth and money-values. So much so that by settled habit, induced by long and close application to the pursuit of net gain in terms of price, men have come to the conviction that money-values are more real and substantial than any of the material facts in this transitory world' (Veblen 1924: 88). Indeed, he notes, 'in the business world the price of things is a more substantial fact than the things themselves' (Veblen 1924: 89). According to Karl Marx, not only was the capitalist system organised on numerical principles through the price mechanism, but interpersonal relationships had become numerical in capitalist society. In Marx's words:

> The power, which each individual exercises over the activity of others or over social wealth, exists in him as the owner of exchange value, of money. The individual carries his social power, as well as his bond with society, in his pocket (1973: 165).

Numbers and statistics have become, in fact, closely associated with the rise of the modern state. They are considered not only the key indicators of financial solvency and business acumen, but they are also treated increasingly as objective instruments for measuring the health and well-being of our society. Numbers are arguably the principal instruments of organisation and control in modern society.

But if politics is as David Easton (1953) says, about resource allocation, then it follows that any societal instrument for organisation and control must become a political issue. Numbers are becoming the subject of politics not only in the conventionally understood sense that politicians and governments would try to manipulate statistics to their advantage, but in a more profound manner. One of us has argued (Palan 2006), that social

177

norms and institutions are best viewed less as delineating spaces of acceptable behaviour, and more as boundaries that structure areas of possibilities.
Any types of rules and norms, whether explicit or implicit, serve simultaneously to restrict and prescribe behaviour as conventional institutionalists
argue, but they also serve at the same time as pointers for transgression,
change and evolution. Institutions and norms account, in other words not
only for what is not allowed, but they also, crucially, stimulate through
prohibition, patterns of transgression and change, and so point to new
possibilities and new worlds. Change takes place, therefore, not only
within the boundaries of institutional path-dependency, but also crucially,
by reimagining these very boundaries, moulding and transgressing them.

This is exactly what has taken place in the politics of numbers. The maze
of contradictory regulations, accounting standards, and state subsidies, all of
which emerged originally within the context of a strong territorial state
organisation, have created a 'perverse' price mechanism. So while the convention is that numbers never lie, in the economy they certainly do; a point
very well understood by the main users of numbers, the accountants, if not,
unfortunately, by many other professions. As Professor Michael Bromwich
argued when delivering *The ACCA/BAA Distinguished Academic 1999 Lecture:*

> Only a few accounting items have an existence in the real world. These
> do include cash, some sales transactions, some historical cost values, tax-
> ation paid and market prices. In contrast, accounting depreciation, the
> values of non-tradable brands accruals and matched items and, of
> course, profits are illustrations of accounting items that do not have an
> empirical existence. This lack of an empirical base plagues choices
> between accounting systems (1999).

While in the popular image of the economy, profits and prices are the
'hard' indicators which emanate directly from the accounts and are the
indicators around which the entire system hinged (and even bureaucracies
are now encouraged to emulate the system by creating real or proxy
numerical principles of exchange) the experience of corporate life appears
to be rather different. Declared corporate profit is subjected to a whole set
of calculations that tends to confuse the issue.

This chapter discusses some of the factors that complicate the meaning
of numbers and profits in the economy, leading to the phenomenon of
'creative accounting' which is at the heart of the new politics of numbers.

Business, intangible property and dealmaking

It is rarely appreciated that the legal definition of contractual relationships and
private property had been revolutionised towards the end of the 19th century.
The modern politics of numbers is a by-product of that revolution.

Older concepts of property consisted of two types of items: corporeal property, the material things owned, and incorporeal property, contracts, debts, and so on. But as argued by John Commons, in the light of the development of business culture, the US Courts moved by the end of the 19th century towards acceptance of a third dimension of property, the principle of 'intangible property' (Commons 1959 [1924]: 3). Crucially, he argues, the concept of intangible property assigns pecuniary value not only to intangibles such as trademark and patents, but also, more generally, to 'goodwill'.

A key historical moment in the development of the legal definition of property relationship occurred, according to Commons, in the process that led to the formation of the US Steel Trust by Andrew Carnegie in the early 1880s. Carnegie called upon J. Pierpont Morgan and Company to construct a huge holding company which integrated corporations in and around Pittsburgh to form the Trust. The new combination had to buy all of Carnegie's interests, whose value, writes Commons,

> As corporeal property was estimated on the basis of reconstruction cost at about 75 million dollars. But, owing to Carnegie's threatening position in the markets, he was able to command 300 million dollars in gold bonds. This difference of 225 million dollars could not be ascribed, on the traditional theory of economics, as the value of the corporeal property. Nor was it incorporeal property since it was not a debt owed to Carnegie. The only other name that could be given to it was 'intangible property' the name given by the financial magnates themselves (Commons 1959 [1924]: 649–50).

Carnegie described the difference of US$225 million as his contribution to the enterprise as 'goodwill'. The case was taken to court and Carnegie won, establishing in effect the principle.

But how is the value of intangible property measured? How did Carnegie reach the figure of US$225 million? The valuation of Carnegie's holding, Commons argues, 'arose solely from the need of all competitors to remove Carnegie from the price-cutting competition which it was known he would initiate' (Commons 1959 [1924]: 650). The value of such intangible properties as 'goodwill' is in fact entirely 'subjective' in a sense that it can be measured only in terms of the potential or anticipated future earnings that may accrue to the owner. In other words, the value of Carnegie's 'goodwill' was an agreement of the loss in future earnings to his competitors if he remained a competitor. His 'value' was measured, therefore, ultimately in his ability to make business unprofitable for others, an ability which in itself obtains a pecuniary value.

In time, the value of intangible property has settled on the principle of what the market anticipates its future profit potential to be, and capital becomes under the new regime, primarily (but not exclusively, according to Commons) the anticipation of future profits:

> It is the market-value expected to be obtained in exchange for the thing in any of the markets where the thing can or might be sold. In the course of time this exchange-value has come to be known as 'intangible property' (Commons 1959 [1924]: 19).

How is this potential for future profits assessed? The critical point is that intangible property is 'the kind of property whose value depends upon right of access to a commodity market, a labour market, a money market, and so on' (Commons 1959 [1924]: 19). By definition, this requires there to be an imperfect market, to use the language of positive economics. The 'imperfect market' reaches conclusions about value by assessing the ability of the possessor to exact monopolistic access, whichever way the possessor of such property achieves such monopolistic access. It is the ability and acumen of the possessor of property titles to make deals, manipulate or 'disturb' and 'sabotage', as Veblen calls it, any of these markets, which become a source of enormous profit. For example, in today's economy, the ability of companies such as Microsoft to place their product strategically as the market standard is considered the main source of their profit and hence, the main factor determining their market valuation. Bill Gate's strategic handling of the Microsoft 'brand' will tend to have a tangible impact on its perceived value – and in that sense it may be argued that Bill Gates adds 'value' to the company. Brand name, advertisement, corporate alliances, formal and informal 'deals', government regulations, and so on, are all typical methods for obtaining such monopolistic access and hence play a role in the valuation of anticipated future earnings.

The advent of this twin phenomenon of the hierarchical corporation and intangible property rights in the late 19th century had almost instantaneous effect in the rise of what Marxists call 'monopoly capital' and Commons calls 'bankers capitalism'. But the problem with the theory of monopoly capital is that it effectively collapses the two sets of developments into one. The theory fails to grasp that once the *de facto* business practices of the day, the principles of intangible property became enshrined in law, the economy is organised on business or pecuniary principles (Veblen 1961). And hence, it is not a matter of simple change from the so-called competitive capitalism to oligopolistic competition, but a more fundamental change towards a system geared towards anticipated future earnings. Paralleling these important developments in the legal definition of property, businessmen immediately set about organising their holdings in such way as to augment anticipated future earnings. Dealmaking by the 'captains of industry' is aimed ultimately at reorganising business and the economy in such way as to augment the 'market' perception of the future earnings of their business in the light of the deal.

So, for instance, when British Airways proposed few years ago the merge with American Airlines, the idea behind the deal was not to increase efficiency and service to the customer, as the two airlines claimed, nor to extract additional surplus-value from the employees of the two companies, but rather, the idea behind the combination was that the two airlines between them have would have access to nearly 75% of the landing slots in Heathrow, and hence could effectively control the prices of their tickets. The deal itself would indicate to the 'market' a possible augmentation in anticipated future earnings of the combined company, which would translate immediately to higher stock price and greater ability to borrow in the markets. In fact, once the deal is 'capitalised' through these markets, the absentee owners of the merged corporations are equally likely to abandon their company in search of a new deal as much as remain holder of the company. It is the deal that is of interest to them, not the actual running of this or that airline. This behaviour might in itself contribute to the perception, endorsed by international accountants KPMG, that 50% of all corporate mergers do in fact fail to deliver the anticipated benefits.[2] This will not be of significance to those who simply seek to profit from the deal itself.

It is this principle of dealmaking and business making in the age of intangible property, where 'deals' are conceived with an eye for anticipated future earnings which is a central feature of the development of the relationship between business and state. The modern capitalist system is run according to business principles, that is, the principles of bargaining, dealmaking, alliances and sabotage. As a general proposition, we can assume that business people are likely to use the state, or indeed, any other social institution (family, sovereignty, the church, 'human rights', democracy, and so on), to advance their parochial business dealings in whatever way they can. Everything that in fact can be used to further one's business will be used. How these institutions are used in business deals is ultimately down to the imagination of the businessman and woman.

Tax and profits

It is in light of the above that we need to rethink the relationship between state and capital. The European State system, which has now colonised the entire world, developed complex and varied systems of taxation in order to finance military expenditures and its leaders' conspicuous consumption. But once business taxation was introduced towards the end of the 19th century, this unsurprisingly gave an almost instantaneous fillip to an otherwise rather mundane and minor aspect of business society, the phenomenon of the accounting profession, with the aim of rearranging corporate accounts in such way as to minimise taxation. In other words, business taxation offered corporations opportunities for differential advantages since the ones who innovated systems of avoidance could reap enormous benefits in competition with others.

Accountants, with enthusiastic help from lawyers and finance departments, began to develop schemes for reducing declared corporate profits to ensure minimal business taxation. The introduction of personal taxation and in particular heavy inheritance tax similarly stimulated interest in ways of avoiding paying tax. In the US, some small states like Delaware and New Jersey responded to the new taxation by drafting 'liberal' incorporation laws so that companies (or wealthy individuals forming family trusts) could shift their residences to these states to take advantage of low taxation. Switzerland, followed soon by Liechtenstein, then adopted similar schemes in Europe. With the formation of trust corporations located in zero or near zero corporate tax regimes, companies (and wealthy families) also began to innovate with the system of transfer pricing ensuring that profits flowed, and still flow, from subsidiaries located in high-tax countries to those located in low-tax regimes. In fact, so large is the business of re-arranging accounts for tax purposes that an entire economy, the offshore world, that contains approximately 70 tax havens and through which an estimated half of the global stock of money traverses, has emerged (Palan 2003). Such are the benefits that one of us was able to contribute to an analysis in the Wall Street Journal of the actions of Microsoft in reporting almost all its European profits in Ireland (a state with a nominal 12.5% corporation tax rate in comparison to the current OECD norm of about 30%), from which action it is estimated to have benefited by approximately US$500 million in 2004 (*Wall Street Journal,* 7 November 2005).

The advent of business taxation, combined with the rise of personal taxation gave great incentive to corporations and high-net individuals (the very rich) to find ways for reducing their declared profits. Estimates of the size of the phenomenon of tax dodging are notoriously difficult. Murphy (2005) estimates that high net worth individuals might hold US$11.5 trillion offshore with a resulting cost to their governments by way of lost taxation revenues of US$255 billion per annum.[3] The politics of numbers discussed in this article suggest, of course, that these figures are only rough approximation. This estimate excludes all taxation lost as a result of corporate tax planning but such is the extent of this activity by individuals there must, by implication, be real risk that actual declared corporate profits considerably underestimate the actual profits of corporations.

It is a fair assumption to make that without the advent of the system of intangible property, declared corporate profits would have reached a very minimal level indeed. But capital formation and accumulation, as we mentioned above, is geared towards anticipated future profits. And this means, in turn, that corporations are pulled also in the opposite direction. They have great incentive to exaggerate their profits margins so that by doing so, they are able to raise the value of their stocks and increase their borrowing capacity and use this increased leverage for 'dealmaking' and sabotage that will augment their value of their holdings even further.

They have two mechanisms for doing this. The first has been to seek to declare profits that have not been subject to tax, or have been subject to low rates of tax. Such profits include non-taxable revaluations of assets, capital gains, which frequently attract low rates of tax, or profits which have been located in low-tax territories but which can be claimed by the reporting parent company as its own and which boost earnings whilst not requiring tax to be paid. The offshore world contributes to this activity by providing the means to locate profits in this way. There is evidence that this trend is increasing.

The second mechanism also uses the offshore world. In fact, so great is the incentive to embellish and overstate profits that the very offshore world that was believed for so long to serve as means for reducing declared profits, appears now to have been used on occasion in order to 'bury' debts and generate 'virtual' profits. This is exactly what companies like Enron or Parmalat did. These companies employed a maze of subsidiaries in tax havens in order to hide away their failed business and to take liabilities off their balance sheets to appear far more profitable than they were in consequence. The result was entirely fictional accounts of their profits. Although Enron and Parmalat are clearly cases of frauds they alert us to the possibilities of employing the offshore world not only for tax avoidance, but also to generate fictional profit.

The above discussion suggests that corporate declared profits and profit margins are not as straightforward as we tend to think. Indeed, rather than representing 'hard' numbers, published figures are as likely to represent the outcome of a balancing act, perpetrated by management with their lawyers, accountants, financiers and tax experts, in which 'real' profits are subject to conflicting incentives determined ultimately by each individual company.

Profits and subsidies

The situation is further complicated once we introduce another dimension of the relationship between state and business. In light of apparent or real danger of capital flight, states are increasingly adopting measures to ensure that capital invests in their territories and stays there (Palan 1998). In fact, a whole system of incentives has developed whereby states support business by offering tax holidays, grants, cheap loans, infrastructural support and other sweeteners in order to attract capital to their territories. There is not much international comparative research done on the subject, but the little available suggests that the phenomenon is far larger than suspected. Writing in the early 1990s, Ford estimates that the subsidy paid out as a percentage of sectoral value added tended to rise in most OECD countries through the 1970s, but then stabilised in the 1980s at around 2 to 3.5% of GDP (1990: 6). He calculates that support averaged almost 9% of industrial value added in the ten European countries he investigated. Gonenç (1990) however believes that 'these figures under-state the true rate of support. In a comparative study of 21 OECD coun-tries, he comes to the conclusion that there had been in fact a slight increase in state support during the 1980s.

These are considerable sums of money. Anecdotal evidence suggests that the figures are even higher. For Intel's research facility in Israel, at an esti-mated cost of US$1.6 billion, the Israeli government paid US$600 million, or 38%. In addition Intel demanded and received ten years worth of tax holiday (Palan 1998). The Mercedes plant in Alabama is reported to have attracted a US$253 million gift box of tax incentives and other sweeteners. And that was for a relatively small plant forecast to offer direct employ-ment to only 1500 workers in an area which enjoys little unemployment. Siemens investment on Tyneside, UK, which will create 1500 jobs is esti-mated to have attracted 200 million pounds, or over 100,000 pounds per worker. As a rule, foreign direct investment in the former communist coun-tries ensures nowadays at least five years of total tax holiday, while in remote countries like Mongolia or Albania companies demand and get at least ten years of tax holidays. It is not therefore beyond reason to suspect that host governments nowadays pay for, about 40% to 50% of 'genuine' Foreign Direct Investment (FDIs) in one way or another (Palan 1998).

The US government's own study taken in the early 1980s suggests that the scale of the phenomenon might be much higher. An Urban Institute's research paper (Levinson 1992) maintains that US Federal incentives to industry amounted at that time to US$303.7 billion or 13.9% of GNP in 1980! During the first two years of the Reagan Administration this figure increased by US$44 billion: 'in 1982 US$86.5 billion or 24% of the US$361 billion raised in credit markets was diverted to federal clients through loans or loan guarantee' (Graham 1992: 175). These are gross figures with no attempt to differentiate between types of subsidies. Nevertheless they are indicative of the significance of the state in generat-ing profit. Furthermore, as Graham points out, the US government was not aware of the amount of subsidy and support it provided and could not have planned any strategy.

It is, therefore, not unreasonable to assume that government subsidies to industry, which in effect are funds transferred from tax payers to share-holders, amount to between 4 to 13% of GDP in advanced industrialised countries. In fact, even the lower estimate of about 4% of GDP of transfers in OECD countries yields a figure considerably higher then the aggregate declared profits of the Fortune 500 in either the US or Europe!

We may reach two conclusions from the above. First, whether through taxation, regulations, contractual laws or subsidies and sweeteners, the state is deeply implicated in every aspect of profit making in the economy. But the state's role is not one sided, or even generalisable. So we cannot even assume that the relationship between state and business would tend, on the whole, towards either exaggerated or alternatively understated rates of declared profits. On the contrary, the relationship between state and business creates a complex system of penalties and rewards which leads to a great variety in responses by business. Second, the relationship is so deep and intimate that we have simply no way of telling what profits are or could be in some abstract world – which unfortunately is all too real for economists and political scientists – in which states and markets are two separate and independent systems of resource allocation.

The accounting profession and declared profits

The accounting profession is very much aware of some, if not all the difficulties associated with notional profits. We have already quoted Michael Bromwich in the introduction saying that 'only a few accounting items have an existence in the real world'. He continues:

> This lack of an empirical base plagues choices between accounting systems. It is difficult if not impossible to resolve such debates by looking at the presently available empirical evidence partly because there may be no possibility of obtaining any empirical evidence with regard to some issues and also because many favoured systems are being debated before implementation and the competing systems are not run in parallel (1999).

Bromwich hits the nail on the head here in his own distinctive way with astounding clarity rarely found elsewhere. This problem is in fact exacerbated by changes in accounting theory. To understand this one has to look, primarily, at thinking in the UK, which, to complicate matters, is rather different from development in accounting standards in the US. Bromwich again has that to say 'The UK Accounting Standards Board has been brave in developing a theory and seeking to stick to it, although not always successfully. In comparison, the Financial Accounting Standards Board (FASB) in the US, in my view, tends to tackle more pragmatically immediate concerns without much reference to its conceptual framework.'

It is the development of that framework which demonstrates the capacity of business to adapt its methods for the benefit of engrossment. The UK's approach to accounting standards arose over three distinct periods, pre-1970, 1970 to 1999 and post-1999. The first era can be described as that of pure historic cost accounting. It was a simple time. Assets were valued on balance sheets at the price paid for them less, if appropriate, provisions for diminution in value such as depreciation, stock reserves and bad debts whilst liabilities were recorded as the sum anticipated to be paid, irrespective of timing. Capital was, in consequence, the aggregate of assets less liabilities and the more complex economic concepts of valuation were not known. As a result profit was said to be revenue less costs and the movement between one balance sheet and the next was profit less distributions.

The problem of this era was the failure to recognise that prices, whilst determined by cash, were not a good measure of value, certainly since the advent of intangible property whereby the principal assets are capitalised future earnings. The accounts that resulted bore little or no relationship to that intangible value, sometimes seriously understating the market worth of some companies and providing opportunities for the era of the assets strippers, such as Slater Walker or Jim Goldsmith, while other times overestimating the value of companies. Goldsmith, for instance, had discovered in 1985 that the Bridgestone Tyre Company of Akron Ohio, maintained a savings account of US US$2 billion for R&D purposes. Since that savings account was not reflected in the stock valuation of the company, he organised a syndicate of 60 banks to buy the company's stock, divide it into its parts, sell the pieces independently and share the US$2 billion loot among the 60 banks. The state of Ohio changed the laws three times to save Bridgestone, and although it maintained its independence, Goldsmith walked of with a US$70 million payoff and Bridgestone quickly liquidated its savings.

Conversely, these accounting rules did on occasion attribute value to assets that had no future income generation potential. This was case with Rolls Royce which failed in 1971 despite being apparently profitable because all its costs of development of a new engine had been capitalised as an intangible asset which proved to be of little worth when it failed to achieve safety certification. The conflict between price and value had become apparent.

The ASB era (which started as the Accounting Standards Committee and is now part of the Financial Reporting Council) started in 1970 in the UK and developed rapidly in response to the failure of Rolls Royce. The conflict between intangible assets and the limited empirical certainty of accounting data had now become apparent. In response the ASC/ASB realised that there was a need for a consistent basis of decision making to reconcile this disparity and declared in Statement of Standard Accounting Practice 2 that there were four accounting concepts:

- Going concern
- Accruals/matching
- Consistency
- Prudence

The approach was, however, flawed. The new accounting principles were aimed at the accounts production process – that is, it was drafted by, and for, accountants to protect themselves. The new principles were in effect a defence mechanism set by the accounting profession to hide behind 'best practice' accounting with the objective of limiting their liability in the event of claims arising. The new principles did not seek to deal with concepts of value, except by implying that when in doubt accounts should understate rather then over-state worth. And, with the notable exception of the short-lived attempt to introduce inflation accounting in the UK during the late 1970s and early 1980s, issues of valuation were largely avoided by generally seeking to limit the use of valuations other than cost, or by restricting their use to readily mar-ketable assets such as land and quoted securities with one remarkable excep-tion. That exception, which accords fully with Veblen's view of the focus of business activity was to allow revaluation of assets acquired when taking over another business, such revaluation being allowed to be either upward or down-ward. The resulting possibility of creating untaxable profits was not lost on business and fuelled the takeover boom that has been a continuing theme of corporate life since the 1970s and which has seen the number of quoted com-panies in the UK fall from over 4,000 in the 1960s to little over 1,300 in 2005.

The arrival of the next era of accounting, represented in the UK by the arrival of Financial Reporting Standard 18 on Accounting Policies, changed this 'accountant centric' approach by concentrating on the supposed needs of the users of accounts. That Standard says the key features of accounting policies should now be those that are:

- Relevant
- Reliable
- Comparable
- Understandable

These are external measures. They relate to financial reporting. Here, the crit-ical point was a shift in focus onto the user, not the producer of accounts.

This change reflected the UK's new Statement of Principles for Financial Reporting issued by the ASB in 1999 and closely linked to the International Accounting Standards Committee's (or IASC now Board – IASB) Framework for the Preparation and Presentation of Financial Statements issued in 1989 but of little importance until the IASC became the IASB with this Framework being adopted in 2001. This framework has moved accounting away from its historic cost basis to a fair value basis. This means that the definitions of the key elements in a balance sheet have changed so that they now have the following meanings:

- Asset. An asset is a resource controlled by the enterprise as a result of past events and from which future economic benefits are expected to flow to the enterprise. [F.49(a)]

- Liability. A liability is a present obligation of the enterprise arising from past events, the settlement of which is expected to result in an outflow from the enterprise of resources embodying economic benefits. [F.49(b)]
- Equity. Equity is the residual interest in the assets of the enterprise after deducting all its liabilities. [F.49(c)]

Definitions of the elements relating to performance are now:

- Income. Income is increase in economic benefits during the accounting period in the form of inflows or enhancements of assets or decreases of liabilities that result in increases in equity, other than those relating to contributions from equity participants. [F.70]
- Expense. Expenses are decreases in economic benefits during the accounting period in the form of outflows or depletions of assets or incurrences of liabilities that result in decreases in equity, other than those relating to distributions to equity participants. [F.70][4]

As a result of these changes, income is not just sales, but can now also be derived from the enhancement in value of an asset. An asset, in turn, is a future benefit stream, not an unexpired past cost. This opens, of course, the possibility for some assets and some liabilities at least to be valued on the basis of future discounted cash flow as an economist might, with all the associated subjectivity. In other words, the concept of value that Veblen and Commons recognised already in the beginning of the 20th century is now incorporated into the accounting framework wherever the remit of the IASB Board applies, as it does throughout the EU and in over 30 other states, at least with regard to publicly quoted companies.

The problem is that at this point the concept of profit becomes confused. If fair value is dominant, and the value of capital on the balance sheet is the most significant factor in accounting, then the dynamic of this model has changed. Profit is no longer cost less revenues. It is the movement in the value of capital worth of the enterprises adjusted only by the (relatively objective) measure of cash withdrawn for shareholder rewards. It then follows that the conventional relationship between the enterprise and the state, most commonly expressed through the payment of tax, becomes open to the risk of significant misinterpretation.

Now, taxation has traditionally recognised a capital/revenue split. The former may or may not be taxed under capital gains tax, the latter almost always under an income tax or equivalent for corporations. But accounts now contain both within the income statement and measure performance on this basis. This leads to massive problems:

(a) If a state has no capital gains charge or (as is common) charges gains at lower rates then the ability to misrepresent income as gain gives rise to innumerable tax-saving possibilities. In other words, multinational companies have great incentive now, to represent income stream as 'capital gain' and shift those towards low or no capital gains tax regimes. In other words, more subtle forms of offshore and transfer pricing are emerging.

(b) Should the entity which no longer records transactions on the basis of cost be able to claim relief on cost? Or is subjective value substituted? Does accounting have meaning any more for these purposes in fact?

These problems exacerbate the existing problems already inherent in historic cost accounting, even in its modified form as used until the introduction of International Financial Reporting Standards (IFRS). It has been commonplace for the accounting convention of dividing capital and revenue to be broken down for example, depreciation is normally provided at relatively modest rates in corporate accounts to reflect the likely lives of assets. For instance, Vodafone's 2003 accounts assume asset lives shown in Table 13.1.

Many of these assets in the UK will be assumed to have lives of no more than 4 years for tax, whilst some assets, such as office buildings, get no relief at all. Until 1987 most assets however got relief of 100% when acquired. In contrast, R&D is now provided with tax relief at more than 100% of cost incurred in the UK! These factors alone can lead to substantial differences between the tax profit of a corporation and the reported accounting profits. This is why in the US, where special reliefs are common that the following proportion of US corporate tax filings were for nil tax in the years in question.[5] See Table 13.2.

Enron is, of course, the prime example of a corporation declaring profits which did not pay tax. But do not be fooled by Enron's fraudulent accounts, most US corporations do not pay tax!

In the UK the proportion of corporations not paying tax is lower but PriceWaterhouseCoopers undertook a survey of 70 heads of tax in large UK companies in April 2005 (36 of them members of the FTSE 100), and found that 26% were not paying UK tax either because of losses (whether purely for taxation purposes or otherwise) or because of the interaction of international taxes. Most of these companies appeared however not to be reporting losses to their shareholders.[6] What this confirms is the very real difference between declared and taxable profits.

Table 13.1   Asset life assumption in Vodafone's 2003 accounts

Freehold buildings 25–50 years	
Leasehold premises	the term of the lease
Motor vehicles	4 years
Computers and software	3–5 years
Equipment, Fixtures and fittings	5–10 years

Table 13.2   US companies with nil tax bills

Companies with a tax bill of zero		
Tax year	Foreign returns	U.S. returns
1996	46,791 (67.7%)	1,360,566 (60.3%)
1977	50,625 (71.7%)	1,331,638 (60.9%)
1998	50,671 (71.8%)	1,335,000 (61.0%)
1999	50,149 (72.3.%)	1,310,280 (61.2%)
2000	50,688 (73.3%)	1,332,239 (63.0%)

Source: General Accounting Office

It is however important to recognise that another (and rarely noticed) misconception of profit and of the corporation itself is hidden within this data. This is the difference between declared profits in the accounts of consolidated groups of companies and fiscal liabilities due by the differing member entities. CEOs manage group profit. That is the glossy report they produce each year. But tax is never paid on the basis of the declared results in that glossy report. Tax is paid on the results of each of the individual member companies, which may number into the hundreds, each with its own home state and differing tax rules. In addition, whilst the consolidated accounts include only third party transactions, those of each member company include intergroup transactions, on which tax is both paid and deduction claimed in the recipient entity. The taxation rules of each state may differ of course, the result being that attempts are often made to get a sale in one territory tax free matched by a taxable deduction in another (a trick called 'double dipping'). Therefore there is a remove between the accounts on which the group reports and the underlying accounts. The result is that the stock exchange accounts are in every sense a fiction which tell only half a story. The OECD says that 60% of all world trade is intergroup that is, sales from one group subsidiary to another group subsidiary.[7] This trade 'disappears' on consolidation of the accounts of conglomerates and may well not be publicly reported anywhere. This is despite the fact that these sales are real and do take place, in contrast to the accounts that are published which are, in fact, for a fictional entity that does not exist.

If we look at the resulting possibilities we can see how the situation is much worse than Bromwich (1999) suggests when he says only a few accounting entries have an existence in the real world. Take the four bases of profit referred to below and we have the following possibilities. (Table 13.3).

These possibilities pose real questions for the numerical world:

- Who understands this in the 21st century, or is there a problem of people being divided by an apparently common language of accounting?
- How big are the differences between these possibilities?

Table 13.3   Accounting conventions

Description	Basis	Consequence
Historic cost	Cost	Misrepresentation of objectivity
Fair value	Value	Misunderstanding of result
Tax	Legislation	Underpayment
Consolidated	Fiction	Manipulation

We know, for example, that fair value is having a big impact. For example, Vodafone's results for the six months to 31 September 2004 improved by £6.8 billion as a result of the adoption of fair value accounting under IFRS rules.[8] One of us has also estimated that the average UK corporation tax paid in 2003 by the top 25 FTSE companies was 25.2% against a rate declared in their accounts of 30.9%. The difference amounted to over £4 billion for those companies alone in that year.[9]

Conclusion

The above discussion suggests that it is not only in the offshore world that there is suppression of data and hidden spaces in which transactions take place, apparently extra territorially in pursuit of the creation of a numerical existence. That exercise is paralleled in the world of accounting where the apparent territorial limit of the conglomerate corporation, as defined by its published accounts, includes numerous, and maybe extensive, hidden spaces between subsidiary companies where transactions take place entirely out of sight to facilitate the presentation of the required management view of this numerical entity. The accounting used for these hidden spaces can be to any standard that management require. Most will, at the end of the day, be only known to them.

We come, therefore, full circle to our opening question: although numbers are clearly becoming the principal organising mechanism of modern society, and even the state is in transition to a numerical basis, the numbers do not provide the sort of 'hard' and objective information that is hoped for. On the contrary, the shift towards numerical principles of organisation stimulates, as Veblen or Commons would have predicted, a new political economy as the numbers are manipulated to the full extent possible within rule-bound spaces (the institutional 'habits of thought' of accounting and tax principles) to achieve business aims. If territorial principles of organisation are likely to generate 'counter-territories' (offshore) for engrossment purposes, numerical principles are generating their own counter virtual numerical spaces, courtesy of the accounting profession, for engrossment purposes.

Notes

1. This paper was presented first at the international University Bremen in May 2005. We are grateful to Anastasia Nesvetailova for providing us with detailed comments.
2. http://news.bbc.co.uk/1/hi/business/542163.stm.
3. http://www.taxjustice.net/e/press/Price_of_Offshore.pdf.
4. Paragraph numbers relate to the IASB Framework. Summaries are quoted from http://www.iasplus.com/standard/framewk.htm published by Deloitte Touche Tohmatsu 2005.
5. http://moneycentral.msn.com/content/Taxes/P80242.asp based on a report by the General Accounting Office presented to the US Senate.
6. Total Tax Contribution Framework, PWC, London, April 2005.
7. John Neighbour, OECD Centre for Tax Policy and Administration, Quoted in OECD Observer April 2002.
8. http://213.219.8.102/pdfs/vodafone/ifrs_2005/press_release.pdf.
9. Richard Murphy, unpublished research on the UK Tax Gap, 2005.

14
Financial Regulation and the War on Terror

Marieke de Goede

Introduction

It is possible to argue that September 11 2001 spelt the end of financial globalisation as we know it. In the context of the war on terror, far-reaching new regulation of financial institutions and transactions is being put in place in order to detect and prevent the financing of terrorism and money laundering more generally. This new regulation, enacted by national governments and international institutions alike, could be seen to run counter to the course of financial globalisation and liberalisation that dominated the 1980s and 1990s (Langley 2002; Germain 1997). Only days after 9/11, Stephen Roach (2001) argued in the *Financial Times* that the 9/11 attacks could spell the end of globalisation: 'Terrorism puts sand in the gears of cross-border connectivity and the result threatens the increasingly frictionless world of globalisation. The events of 11 September have, in effect, levied a new tax on such flows. The security of national borders will now have to be tightened'. Some, like Thomas J. Biersteker, cautiously welcomed unexpected political will to financial reregulation. According to Biersteker (2002: 83), 'the window of opportunity is...open' for multilateral coordinated global action against terrorist finance as well as tax havens and offshore finance more generally (see also Biersteker 2004).

This chapter reflects upon the meaning and form of financial regulation in the 21st century as it is taking shape through the war on terror. The chapter demonstrates a particular regulatory regime to be emerging that is intending to reconcile new regulation with continuing globalising markets, through a risk-based approach. This does not mean that I argue that neo-liberalism continues unhampered and is the main, totalising force in financial governance. Neither does it mean that I observe an unequivocal move 'back to borders' in post-9/11 financial practice. Instead, I argue that a complex set of laws and practices is contingently emerging through the risk-based approach, that has effects on financial exclusion and economic citizenship. This complex set of laws and practices is best understood through the lens of *biopolitics*, a diffuse form of power, conceptualised by Michel Foucault, that operates through definitions of normality and deviance. The effects of the war on terrorist finance on financial exclusion and economic citizenship suggest that it needs to be approached critically, and that the reregulation emerging in its name – while clearly drawing on earlier initiatives – is particular to the 21st century.

A window of opportunity?

The war on terrorist finance includes far-reaching domestic and international financial regulation. As early as 24 September 2001, the White House issued the 'Executive Order on Terrorist Financing' that dramatically enhances government powers to freeze assets of suspected terrorist individuals and organisations and that issues a blacklist of terrorist suspects. In the accompanying press release, President Bush said: 'We will starve the terrorists of funding, turn them against each other, rout them out of their safe hiding places, and bring them to justice'.[1] Title III of the USA Patriot Act that was signed one month later is called the 'International Counter-Money Laundering and Financial Anti-Terrorism Act,' and significantly strengthens existing Anti-Money Laundering (AML) legislation in the US and beyond. For example, the Act extends suspicious transactions reporting requirements to securities and derivatives brokers, including mutual funds and hedge funds. Title III prohibits US banks to maintain accounts with 'shell banks' and sharpens customer due diligence procedures in offshore jurisdictions. It moreover strengthens customer identification procedures for both new and existing customers of US banks and brokers, and requires customer identities to be checked against the Treasury's terrorist blacklist.

Among the most important international initiatives concerning terrorist finance is UN Security Council Resolution 1373 adopted in September 2001, which criminalises financial support of terrorism, obliges signatories to take measures against terrorist financing, and in effect globalises the US government's terrorist blacklist.[2] The resolution establishes reporting requirements for individual countries, which have to keep the UN updated on their implementation of anti-terror law and the (legal) steps they are taking to detect and prevent terrorist financing. UN Resolution 1377 moreover invites states to seek technical assistance in the implementation of anti-terror laws, thus giving the UN a considerable role in domestic legal practice (Biersteker 2004: 60–3). Another important international initiative is the list of Eight Special Recommendations on Terrorist Financing issued by the Financial Action Task Force (FATF), the OECD's anti-money laundering organisation, in October 2001 to supplement its 40 recommendations on money laundering.[3] The special recommendations include stipulations on suspicious transactions reporting, guidelines for regulating informal money transmitters, and, in cooperation with the World Bank, assessment procedures for non-compliant countries. Furthermore, the EU has developed the Third Money Laundering Directive that explicitly includes terrorist financing.[4] This directive extends customer identification procedures for all financial institutions and introduces regulatory requirements for money wiring businesses. It was approved by European Parliament in June 2005 and is expected to come into force in 2007. Finally, most governments have included financial provisions in their national anti-terrorism legislation, and best-practice guidelines on detecting terrorist financing are forthcoming from industry self-regulating bodies including the Wolfsberg Group[5] and the Bank for International Settlements.[6]

The Bush administration certainly made a remarkable turnaround with regard to financial regulation and money laundering policy. Before 9/11, it halted or hampered domestic and international initiatives in this area, including policy changes set in motion by the Clinton administration. For example, Phil Gramm, chairman of the Senate Banking Committee, early in 2001 'boasted that [he] killed the Clinton administration's anti-money laundering legislation' (*The Economist* 2001: 10). Moreover, only one month before the attacks, William Wechsler (2001: 55), advisor to the US Treasury under Clinton, expressed worry at the 'Bush backtrack' on multilateral anti-money laundering coordination. At the time, the US opposed OECD policy on the prevention of harmful tax competition, on the grounds that it is an 'affront to the sovereignty of jurisdictions and a form of regulatory "overreach" that has dire consequences for sovereignty at home' (Maurer 2005: 478). In contrast, in October 2001 Bush's Secretary of the Treasury Paul O'Neill delivered a fervent plea for the development of special anti-terrorist finance recommendations and stringent compliance monitoring before the extraordinary FATF session on terrorist finance. O'Neill (2001) said: 'Our goal must be nothing less than the disruption and elimination of the financial frameworks that support terrorism and its abhorrent acts. To achieve this end, we must commit to employing every influence both within FATF membership and throughout the world'.[7] Since 9/11, intervention in other countries' sovereignty in financial regulation seems no longer problematic to O'Neill, and countries are under great diplomatic pressure to comply with FATF and UN regulation.

Plenty of reason, then, to concur with Biersteker (2002: 83) that it is possible to welcome a 'sea change' in political will to fight terrorist financing as well as offshore finance more broadly. May 9/11 have offered a window of opportunity for significant financial reregulation, something that has been appealed for in the literature on global finance since the breakdown of Bretton Woods (for example, in Strange 1986; Helleiner 1994; Palan 2003)? May this be an unintended upside of the otherwise problematic return to borders since 9/11 (Andreas and Biersteker 2003)?

Regulation and risk

It is important, in this light, to examine the particular shape that post-9/11 financial regulation is taking, as well as the ways in which it is being implemented in practice. There are two main differences between pre-9/11 anti-money laundering policy and the current war on terrorist finance (c.f. Aninat, Hardy and Johnston 2002). First is the desire in the war on terrorist finance to trace transactions that are not in themselves illegal, but that may at some point in the *future* be used for illegal purposes. Second is its relevance for retail finance: because of the relatively small amounts of money used by the 9/11 hijackers, monitoring of everyday financial transactions for markers of suspicion is becoming a central feature of the war on terrorist finance. What is emerging at the heart of the policy constellation pursuing the war on terrorist finance to address these issues is a *risk-based approach* – which offers common ground to (inter)national public regulators and industry self-regulating bodies. This means that monitoring for suspicious (risky) transactions and customers is being required by regulation, but *also* that there is considerable flexibility in the ways in which banks implement these regulatory requirements. A 2003 discussion paper by British financial regulator Financial Services Authority (FSA) (2003: 7) sets out the centrality of the risk-based approach to current anti-money laundering regulation: 'A risk-based approach is not a soft option. It puts the responsibility on firms...to identify, assess, mitigate and monitor their money laundering risks on a considered and continuing basis'. The risk-based approach is not *new* to financial practice, but already existed, for example, in relation to the new Basle Capital Accord on reserve requirements (Basle II) that is based on banks' own risk-modelling. In the case of Basle II, the risk-based approach arguably leads to larger exposure and smaller reserves than percentage-based reserve requirements (de Goede 2004: 209; see also Izquierdo 2001; Tickell 2000).

Elsewhere I have argued that the risk-based approach to the war on terrorist finance entails a significant change of previous anti-money laundering regulation because of its emphasis on *prevention* and not just prosecution (Amoore and de Goede 2005: 151–3). Here, it is important to repeat the centrality of terrorist finance to the war on terror more broadly which is illustrated by this turn to prevention. As Robert O'Harrow (2005: 260) puts it in his critical assessment of electronic surveillance in the war on terror:

There is no overstating the value government investigators place on financial activity. It's considered almost like a fuel for their intelligence engine. Bank transfers, the ties among customers, the use of automated teller machines. Such records also contain a wealth of identity information. The FBI...believe that these details, coupled with data mining, amount to a new kind of weapon in the amorphous war on terrorism.

It is clear that the risk-based approach intends to reconcile these difficult demands of fighting terrorist financing and unearthing terrorist networks with the continuing existence of globalising financial markets. As Aufhauser (2003: 302) puts it, 'The world economy is a deliberately open and porous one, designed to encourage the free flow of capital, investment and economic development. To elect rules that intrude on that dynamic is to hand victory to the enemy'. Indeed, the question of the resurrection of state (regulatory) power in the midst of a globalising world post-9/11 is of central concern to scholars of IPE, who, according to Martin Coward, 'are...faced with reconciling the territorially based sovereignty evinced by American statecraft or the borders hardened to fight terrorism with the de-territorialising transversal forces that have shaped the post-Cold War era' (Coward 2006: 63). In other words, the war on terror is often regarded as entailing the return of sovereign power in a globalising world (for example, Cox 2001, 2004). However, as Coward (2006: 63) argues, 'neither American statecraft under George W. Bush, nor the borderless jihad envisioned...by al-Qaeda cells has undermined the various deterritorialising forces of capital'.

One way of understanding these seemingly contradictory developments is to analyse the invigorated (financial) sovereign power as a biopolitical mode of governing that operates through definitions of normality and deviance, and that entails complex networks of public/private authority. According to Jenny Edkins and Véronique Pin-Fat, 'the notion of sovereign power as opposed to sovereignty is crucial here'. So, although Edkins and Pin-Fat argue that 'sovereign power is far from dead', this should not be taken to mean that they observe 'the survival...of sovereign statehood' (2004: 3). Instead, it is important to explore the continuing grammars and relations of disciplinary and biopolitical power that use 'sovereignty' as their rationale, and how these are productive of 'particular forms of life (or lives lived)' (Edkins and Pin-Fat 2004: 4).

In IPE literature, much has been written about the increasing salience of private authority and global governance, for example, through the operation of commercial law, credit rating and auditing, at the expense of state regulatory capacity (Cutler *et al.* 1999; Hall and Biersteker 2003; Sinclair 2005). The war on terrorist finance, however, does not simply entail a shift back from private to public authority – as the 'back to borders' thesis would suggest – but entails more precisely the enduring and even enhanced power of particular state agencies, in close cooperation with industry self-regulating bodies and private risk assessment firms. In other words, the public-private distinction *itself* is becoming blurred through the risk-based practice of the war on terrorist finance. In the US context for example, private outsourcing of terrorist-related surveillance is sometimes seen as a way to *enhance* policy legitimacy, as US citizens are thought to be afraid of nothing as much as a 'big brother' government. As documented by

O'Harrow, governmental officials of the Transportation Security Administration (TSA) actively encourage private outsourcing in order to foster legitimacy. 'Instead of bringing massive amounts of information to the government,' O'Harrow (2005: 239) writes of TSA's air passenger risk management program, 'they would rely on subcontractors, companies that would verify individuals' identities by sifting through storehouses of commercial and public record information.'

A biopolitical understanding of this exercise of power in which subcontracting is actively sought and private (risk-assessment) firms acquire jurisdiction over (financial) access and opportunity is thus helpful. Biopolitics is a term developed by Michel Foucault to denote sovereign power over life itself, through the identification, compilation and statistical analysis of populations that can be seen to emerge in the second half of the 18th century in Western Europe.[8] Foucault posits that with the modern Western state and the imagination of its population as a coherent entity that undergoes periodic transformation through rates of fertility, mortality and disaster, a new form of power emerges: the power to monitor, regulate and manipulate the properties of the population. That power comes to be called biopower: 'a technology which brings together the mass effects characteristic of a population, which tries to control the series of random events that occur in a living mass, [and]...which tries to predict the probability of those events' (Foucault 2003: 249; see also Foucault 1991). Statistics and the normalising power of statistical regularities are at the heart of biopower and 'define its power's field of intervention in terms of the birth rate, the mortality rate, various biological disabilities' (Foucault 2003: 245).

Biopower, then, is to be understood as a technique of rule that does not emanate from a clear sovereign centre, but that is managed by state as well as non-state bodies and that operates through the imagination of statistical normalities and abnormalities in diverse areas of life. According to Michael Shapiro (2002, §10), 'the biopolitical aspect of war and peace arises in connection with an understanding of sovereignty that *exceeds its juridical dimensions*' (emphasis added). In other words, biopolitical power fights war in the name of the population, extending its power through the privatised practices of military subcontracting, airport security, and, most relevant to this chapter, financial middle-management (see also Butler 2004). It operates through the creation of subjectivities of the healthy, active and (financially) responsible citizen (for example, Amoore 2004; Dean 1999; O'Malley 2004).

While operating in the name of the general health and well-being of the population, Foucault forcefully demonstrates that biopower entails a logic of exclusion, political expulsion and racism, by 'creating caesuras within the biological continuum' (Foucault 2003: 255). It is precisely the statistical technique that necessarily introduces 'a *break* into the domain of life that is under power's control: the break between what must live and what must die' (Foucault 2003: 254, emphasis added). Making clear that he does not (just) mean this latter reference to death literally, but to include 'political death, expulsion, rejection' (p. 256), Foucault's point is to analyse statistical power as a way in which groups of the population are being separated out into normal and abnormal, viable and non-viable, legitimate and illegitimate. These seemingly technical decisions have vast political consequences, and suggest that close scrutiny of *what it is* that is deemed financially suspicious and devious is warranted.

Before I go on, in the next section, to look more closely at the risk models that are being developed to mine for suspicious financial behaviour, it is important to see that the analysis of the regularities and deviancies of given populations through computerised risk-assessment is becoming a central strategy of the war on terror more broadly (Lyon 2003). Initiatives by the Bush administration in the war on terror have included several versions of intensive datamining programmes that propose preventative screening to separate out the normal from the suspicious. For example, the US-VISIT programme, run by consulting firm Accenture, uses risk management techniques in order to police America's external borders. Accenture's 'smart border solution' collects and analyses traveller data in order to sort people into categories of riskiness (Amoore 2006). A logic of prevention and proactive intervention characterises this embrace of risk-management, according to Rens van Munster (2004: 147), which 'operates on the basis of permanent feelings of fear, anxiety and unease.'

Datamining and suspicious transactions

In the war on terrorist finance, a vision is projected of a secure world in which 'legitimate' global financial markets continue to operate unhampered, as 'illegitimate' transactions are automatically and painlessly filtered out through continuous and computerised transactions monitoring. This vision entails, in the words of Mariana Valverde and Michael Mopas (2004: 239), a 'dream [of a] "smart," specific, side-effects-free, information driven utopia of governance'. According to Aufhauser (2003: 304–5), these techniques have the ability to prevent terrorist acts through 'the real time production of electronic commerce to a central storage facility.' Says Aufhauser:

> If all such information was joined together and challenged with formulas intended to detect anomalies, it is conceivable that the two wire transfers to Dubai from a small town in the USA in Maryland by Mohammed Atta days before the 11th September attacks *would have set off a blinking yellow light* that said something is amiss – to be checked out before people lose their lives. (emphasis added)

Identifying risky and suspicious transactions relies on the prior construction of 'normal financial transactions', in order to identify those transactions that deviate from the norm which is believed to indicate terrorist behaviour. In this way, however, terrorist finance becomes classified as a problem particularly associated with migrants and the poor, and it may lead to financial exclusion of these groups. For example, US Treasury's *Terrorist Financing Rewards Program*, which offers rewards of up to US$5 million for information leading to the dismantling of terrorist organisations, implies quite clearly that terrorist money is *foreign* money. As Treasury Undersecretary Jimmy Gurulé (2002) stated at the inauguration of the program: 'Our strategy is simple: international terrorism is financed by money sent to terrorists *from sources around the world*; thus, we must disrupt and stop that flow of money. This program will help us gain new information and insights into how terrorist financiers are moving money for deadly purposes' (emphasis added). The rewards program has distributed posters and flyers with indications of 'what to look for', accompanied by images of Osama bin Laden, the falling World Trade Towers, and pictures of *foreign* cash (that is, no US dollars). Suspicious transactions include 'transactions involving a high volume of incoming or outgoing wire transfers', as well as 'transactions with no logical economic purpose'.[9]

By comparison, FATF's (2002: 7) identification of 'characteristics of financial transactions that may be a cause for increased scrutiny' moreover, seems to include almost any use of banking accounts that does *not* involve a regular income and expenditure (salary and mortgage, for example). FATF (2002: 7) regards as suspicious 'accounts that receive relevant periodical deposits and are dormant at other periods' and 'a dormant account containing a minimal sum [which] suddenly receives a deposit or series of deposits followed by daily cash withdrawals'. FATF further encourages banks to scrutinise cases where the 'stated occupation of the transactor is not commensurate with the level or type of activity' and regards as suspicious more specifically cases where 'a student or an unemployed individual...receives or sends large numbers of wire transfers'.

In banking practice, the new regulatory requirements issued by Treasury, FATF and other bodies partly materialise as investments into sophisticated technology for the detection of money laundering risk and suspicious behaviour, as well as increased requirements for documentation concerning the customer's identity (Garcia 2004: 332). Software providers that promise compliance through automated surveillance and algorithmic analysis of banking transactions are multiplying. For example, software company Mantas offers behaviour-detecting software as well as specialised Anti-Money Laundering Programmes which aim to fulfil regulatory requirements through 'the ability to automatically monitor and analyse customer, account, and transaction information across the entire organisation for a complete and accurate picture of behaviors of interest'.[10] Mantas (2002: 1–2) promises the ability to 'detect suspicious activity, money laundering schemes or customers *prior* to an event' through the monitoring of '*each* and *every* transaction' (original emphases). By comparison, financial datamining company Searchspace advises financial institutions to take a proactive approach, not so much in tracking terrorist finance, as in the demonstration of regulatory compliance, and has developed stringent account opening procedures that are 'customised to fit individual lines of business'. Thus it is possible to establish an account profile at the time of account opening, which includes 'expected activity; frequency of cash deposits and withdrawals; funds transfer activity and international activity' (Everhardt undated: 4). Searchspace technology claims to be able to discover, map, compare and predict patterns of account use and test them against a representative peer group. Clearly, these strategies depend upon prior modelling of 'financial normality' and good financial citizenship: anyone deviating from norms of regular income and expenditure becomes suspect in these classifications.

It should be understood that regulation issued in the war on terrorist finance is not so much *constraining* markets, as it is enabling and shaping them, and providing business opportunities (MacKenzie 2005a, b, c: 569; de Goede 2005: 121–5). According to financial consultant Virginia Garcia, banks and financial institutions should see compliance not as a necessary and expensive evil, but as a *competitive strategy* that enhances an institution's reputation and reduces its risk of legal costs and fines. In this way, compliance and business opportunity blend into each other seamlessly. Writes Garcia (2004: 334) in relation to the USA PATRIOT Act: 'consider intelligent systems for detecting suspicious behaviour. This technology will also be useful for furthering institutions' objective of getting to know their customers better for increasing cross-sell ratios and customer retention rates'. In other words, suspicious transactions mining may yield sales opportunities, and Know-Your-Customer requirements may be used to identify more and less desirable groups of customers to a bank or insurance company.

As in the war on terror more broadly then, where private subcontracting in military logistics and prison management are completely normalised (Avant 2005), commerce and compliance in the war on terrorist finance go hand-in-hand. This intimacy between governmental regulation and commercial data-mining can*not* be properly understood through identifying a reassertion of sovereign regulatory power in the field of finance. According to Julian Reid (2005: 243), 'critiques of the war on terror that buy into the regime's own account of it as a return to imperialism ignore the vital roles played in its conduct by agencies, practices and discourses of biopolitical form'. What is needed then, is a grasp of how in the war on terrorist finance biopower operates as a diffuse power which regulates and intervenes in the everyday life of global finance in the name of the health and well-being of the population while simultaneously creating caesuras and exclusions (Langley 2002).

Economic citizenship and financial exclusion

What is particularly problematic of the operation of biopower in the war on terror is the lack of transparency and accountability of decisions concerning access and opportunity by immigration officials, bureaucrats, financial middle-managers and *inside* software. I have argued that typologies used in the war on terrorist finance define and depend upon normalities of good financial citizenship and proper account use. A 2004 report by the US Technology and Privacy Advisory Committee (TPAC) outlines quite a number of problems associated with datamining programs, especially those in which private contractors were involved, including the frequent occurrence of data inaccuracies, the pressing problem of data security and false positives. The report expresses particular concern at what it calls the 'chilling effect', or the fact that 'people are likely to act differently if they know their conduct *could be* observed' (TPAC 2004: 35). The committee (2004: 35) concludes: 'The risk is not only that commercial and social activities are chilled, but that protected rights of expression, protest, association, and political participation are affected as well'. Similar fears are being expressed by the European civil liberties organisation Statewatch which points out that electronic monitoring enabled by anti-terrorist policy measures may also be used to target popular protest (for example, Bunyan 2002).

In order to produce the appearance of a continuing secure and legitimate world of global finance, risk is displaced and reallocated onto vulnerable populations, who experience increased surveillance and financial exclusion, and who may have money frozen. Evidence is emerging that financial exclusion is increasing since 9/11, particularly of migrants. For example, in Britain the 'Fighting Crime and Terrorism: We Need Your Help' campaign launched in mid-2003, requires high-street banks to step up security checks not just of new retail customers, but also of existing ones. The campaign leaflets compel banking clients to comply with the new identification requirements under the banner 'You can make life harder for terrorists', and lists the acceptable identification documents, including passport and proof of residency.[11] However, as a critical investigation in *The Guardian* points out, it is not uncommon for poorer population groups to have neither passport nor driver's licence, while tenants do not always have proof of residency in the form of utility or council tax bill. *The Guardian* reports:

> Many bank interpretations of the rules encourage financial exclusion because the poor cannot produce correct pieces of paper…Coming from

abroad also makes establishing identity tricky. It is difficult for someone living in bed and breakfast, or other temporary accommodation, to satisfy the residence rules. They will not have utility bills as they are either paying through a slot meter or an all-in amount with their rent (Levene 2003: 3).

Research of the London charity Services Against Financial Exclusion (SAFE) corroborates these findings and notes that AML identification requirements are the biggest barrier for low-income clients opening bank accounts (SAFE 2005: 43–4). The FSA is aware of this problem and in June 2005 FSA chairman Callum McCarthy said in a speech to the financial inclusion forum: 'A problem for the financially excluded is having few or none of the normal tokens for identity required for account opening...At a time when anti-terrorist concerns have led to an emphasis on documents for account opening...this has become a particularly acute obstacle'. McCarthy (2005) concludes that the FSA should encourage banks to be flexible on identity requirements. However, precisely the rigidity of software models as well as fear of financial institutions and counter staff of disciplinary action, makes flexible interpretation of rules difficult in practice.

Another way in which financial exclusion worsens under the war on terrorist finance is through the assumption that *cash itself* is suspect, which may hurt (undocumented) migrant workers and others who have no choice but to rely on cash for their daily lives.[12] The faith in technology displayed in the risk-based approach relies on 'the proposition that each movement or transaction...leaves a trail of electronic traces, which means that individuals cannot easily disappear' (Levi and Wall 2004: 206). In other words, money in electronic form – credit cards, account debits, ATM transactions – is registered and traceable, and thus police-able. However, this assumption criminalises cash use, and ignores the growth of the informal economy that is not associated with criminal activity but with neoliberal regimes of labour flexibility. If a sizeable informal economy was once seen as a sign of underdevelopment, it is now widely acknowledged that with neoliberal regimes of global competition and labour flexibility, the informal economy has grown in the centres of global capitalism. According to Sassen (1991: 286) the growth of the informal economy in New York, London and Tokyo 'represent[s] a downgrading of work connected to the dynamics of growth in leading sectors of the economy', and is inextricably connected to the exploitation of migrant labour (see also Peterson 2003: 84–112). A recent study of the US economy estimates that in California around 8 million illegal migrants work in the cash economy, and that in LA County about 28% of farm workers are paid in cash (Campbell 2003). Migrant labour and informal employment are at the core – not the margin – of the contemporary global economy, and criminalising the cash economy implicates migrant labour in money laundering and terrorist financing.[13]

The central issue in the politics of the risk society, according to Beck (2002: 41) is *'how to feign control over the uncontrollable'* (original emphasis). It is possible to argue that targeting vulnerable financial constituencies is one way in which control over terrorist financing is feigned, as relevant authorities are keen to be seen to tackle the problem. However, these policies rest upon problematic dichotomies between the licit and the illicit in finance, and do not recognise the complexity of the task of fighting money laundering (de Goede 2003; see also Amoore and Langley 2004: 108–10). At the same time, evidence of success in the war on terrorist finance is mixed at best. Although the US government maintains that the war on terrorist finance is having significant impact on the ability of terrorists to raise funds, a 2002 UN report concludes that al-Qaeda 'continues to have access to considerable financial and other economic resources' (UN Monitoring Group 2002; c.f. Levi 2003).

Conclusion: closing the window of opportunity?

If there was a window of opportunity in the wake of September 11 for significant financial reregulation, I argue that it is being closed down through the practical manifestation of the war on terrorist finance in the form of suspicious transactions datamining and intensified customer identification procedures. Biersteker (2004: 73) is certainly right that there is a 'sea change in the tolerance of financial reregulation across the globe'. However, the particular form of regulation that is emerging leads to large-scale transactions monitoring that attempts to weed out suspicious transactions on the basis of problematic definitions of financial normality and deviance, which disproportionally targets vulnerable financial constituencies. While migrant's remittances and individual client's identification documents have come to be at the forefront of the war on terrorist finance, targeting tax evasion and white collar crime seem to be much less so.

At the same time, the war on terrorist finance offers considerable business opportunity and leads to a booming industry in anti-money laundering education. International conferences such as the Annual International Anti-Money Laundering Conference in Miami, or the Annual European Money Laundering Conference that was held for the first time in Vienna in September 2004, are specifically designed for government officials and representatives of smaller financial institutions, and cost thousands of Euros to attend.[14] Still, this does not mean that neoliberalism continues to be the main totalising force in shaping the war on terrorist finance (c.f. Larner 2006). On the contrary, the financial industry is generally unhappy about new reporting requirements, and clearly there are business losers as well as winners in this new regulatory environment (Bailes 2004). Instead, what is emerging is a complex set of laws, practices and agencies through which biopolitical power is exercised over everyday financial life, by separating groups into normal and abnormal, viable and non-viable, legitimate and illegitimate. This set of practices emerged through contingent political struggle: in other words, there was no fixed or logical form that the war on terrorist finance should take under neoliberal capitalism.

According to Mark Pieth (2002: 375) 'money laundering' as a criminal concept is at risk of becoming an *'empty concept*, that is arbitrarily adapted' (emphasis added). In other words, potentially unlimited power may be exercised in the name of fighting terrorist financing, and 'conceptual technology gives the fight against money laundering a distinct emancipatory ring' (Pieth 2002: 375). However, the war on terrorist finance includes some of the most depoliticised but far-reaching measures of the war on terror more broadly. Financial regulation in the 21st century, then, is not to be unconditionally welcomed but should be subject to critical scrutiny of its democratic legitimacy, cultural assumptions and effects on financial exclusion.

Acknowledgements

Many thanks to the editors of this volume, Libby Assassi, Duncan Wigan and Anastasia Nesvetailova. Many thanks to Louise Amoore, Paul Langley and Erna Rijsdijk for their comments on earlier versions of this paper.

Notes

1. See, Fact Sheet on Terrorist Finance Executive Order, 24 September 2001, http://www.whitehouse.gov/news/releases/2001/09/20010924-2.html
2. Security Council, Press Release SC/7158, 'Security Council Adopts Wide-Ranging Anti-Terrorism Resolution,' http://www.un.org/News/Press/docs/2001/sc7158.doc.htm
3. In October 2004 a ninth recommendation was added. For the nine recommendations, see: http://www.fatf-gafi.org/document/9/0,2340,en_32250379_32236920_34032073_1_1_1_1,00.html
4. The provisional text of the Third Money Laundering Directive is available at http://europa.eu.int/comm/internal_market/company/docs/financial-crime/unoffical3dir_en.pdf
5. Wolfsberg Statement on the Suppression of the Financing of Terrorism, http://www.wolfsberg-principles.com/financing-terrorism.html
6. 'Initiatives by the BCBS, IAIS and IOSCO to Combat Money Laundering and the Financing of Terrorism,' http://www.bis.org/publ/joint05.htm. For overviews of anti-terrorist financing regulation implemented see: Navias (2002), Biersteker (2004) and Pieth (2002).
7. 'Remarks by Paul H. O'Neill before the Extraordinary Plenary Meeting of the Financial Action Task Force, 29 October 2001, http://www.ustreas.gov/press/releases/po735.htm
8. On the emergence of statistics and governmentality, see also de Goede (2005: 90–5). On biopolitics and the war on terror see, for example, Edkins, Pin-Fat and Shapiro (eds) (2004), Reid (2005), Coward (2006).
9. Download the posters at: http://www.ustreas.gov/rewards/. See also de Goede (2003: 525–6).
10. Mantas, 'Overview', http://www.mantas.com/Products/Index.html

11. Find the leaflet online at the British Banking Organisation's website: http://www.bba.org.uk/pdf/awareness2.pdf
12. The objective of reducing cash use is not new, and the FATF's 40 Anti-Money Laundering Recommendations, published in 1990, include the stipulation that 'Countries should...encourage...the development of modern and secure techniques of money management, including increased use of checks, payment cards, direct deposit of salary checks, and book entry recording of securities, as a means to encourage the replacement of cash transfers' (Recommendation 25, Forty Recommendations, FATF I, http://www.fatf-gafi.org/pdf/40Rec-1990_en.pdf). But the faith in technology displayed in the war on terrorist finance means that this targeted reduction of cash-use intensifies.
13. Another way in which migrant workers feel the consequences of the war on terrorist finance is through the targeting of informal remittance networks, which since 9/11 have made remittances more costly. See, for example, de Goede (2003), Horst and van Hear (2002), Passas (2005).
14. For the Miami conference, which costs US$1,985 to attend (excluding accommodation), see http://www.moneylaunderingconference.com/2006/default.aspx. For the European conference, which costs €1745 (excluding accommodation), see: http://www.moneylaundering.com/conferences/europe05/default.aspx

15
Redesigning Financial Regulation

Avinash Persaud and John Nugée[1]

Preface

In this article we explore the fact that the current policy approach to regulating risk in the financial system is 'bottom-up', that is starting from assessing and regulating the individual institution, with the aim being to make the financial system safe by making each institution safe. We endeavour to show that this is both damaging in itself (because it stifles product innovation and consumer choice) and does not work because regulators will merely end up chasing risk to places it cannot be seen – which is seldom the best place for it from either a macroprudential, or consumer protection perspective.

Further, we demonstrate that an 'institutions-based' bottom-up approach to regulation automatically forces regulators to treat very different institutions, with expertise in very different types of risk (for example, banks, insurance companies and pension funds) in a similar way, to avoid discrimination between individual firms, creating a homogeneity in the financial system that will misallocate risks and add to systemic risks. More fundamentally, risk-sensitive regulation of institutions, the holy grail of modern regulation, focuses on private risks, rather than the point of regulation, which is systemic risks, and the latter is not some multiple of the former.

We advocate a 'top-down' approach, which encourages a macroprudential management of risks in the financial system to reduce systemic risk – a systemic-sensitive approach – and a risk-classification approach to protect average consumers, based more on results than process. We conclude that once you have made systems safe and protected average consumers, you do not need such detailed supervision of individual institutions, thus reducing the burden of supervision on the economy and consumers. Individual institutions may not under such a regime be as 'safe', and there may be more failures for us to learn from, but the system and consumers would be safer.

Introduction

The supervision of financial institutions is a comparatively young industry. It is sometimes romantically assumed that the UK authorities' involvement in the financial health and soundness of the banks and other financial institutions in their markets started in the 19th century with the Bank of England's increasing oversight of the London banking system. But the Bank's intention was in fact largely to protect its own interests, and those of its stockholders, rather than to conduct supervision of the banks as a public good. The dominant rule of the day was very much *caveat emptor*, and it was not until the latter decades of the 20th century that the concept of the authorities' duty to provide financial stability took hold, and with it the role of formal supervision as a major factor in maintaining healthy financial systems. Domestic supervision was to some extent galvanised by international supervision, which in turn grew out of attempts to avoid a repeat of the adverse impact on international payments and settlements caused by the closure of a mid-sized German Bank, Herstatt Bank, in 1974.

For a young industry, though, supervision has shown enormous tenacity and strength, growing at great pace in its scope and reach, and in the process creating whole new armies of regulators and supervisors. In the US alone, there are around 26,000 financial regulators, and they cost £2.2 billion a year to maintain. In the UK the cost to the financial sector of financing the FSA's 2,300 regulators was a more modest £287 million per year in 2004, but it is interesting to note that just five years previously the FSA had just 200 employees, costing £10 million per year to maintain. It is not clear to the authors that the financial system was 20 times weaker than it is today. (To be fair to the FSA, its growth has partly been fuelled by taking on more responsibilities, though this process seems to have been independent of any real assessment as to whether the Authority has been a resounding success at anything, besides growth.) Few industries have made such relentless advances, to the extent that in many countries it can hardly keep up with itself: most regulatory bodies and their staff are under heavy workload pressure, the torrent of new regulations shows no sign of ceasing, and the burden placed on those being regulated appears only ever to increase.

The supervisory industry has seen great changes as it has grown. Some of these changes were almost universal as the scope and scale of supervisory oversight increased, for example the move from informal to more formal regulation, and from custom-based to a more rules-based approach. Other issues are more moot, for example whether it is better to adopt a sector-by-sector approach or establish a unified overarching regulator such as the UK's Financial Services Authority, and whether banking supervision in particular should be done from within the central bank or not. There are strongly-held views on this last point, and the movement is by no means all towards separating the regulatory function from the central bank: witness the creation of the Hong Kong Monetary Authority 12 years ago, which brought together under one roof Hong Kong's banking supervision and monetary policy activities for the first time,[2] or more recently the increasing supervisory roles of the central banks of the Netherlands[3] and the Republic of Ireland.[4]

One factor has however remained constant right from the start of supervision. The approach to supervision has always been and remains 'bottom-up': that is, supervision is conducted on an institution by institution basis, and relies overwhelmingly on the precept that by supervising and making safe individual institutions, the financial system as a whole is made safe. It is not conceptually obvious, given that private risks and systemic risks are quite different, that focusing on the individual risks run by institutions will sufficiently reduce systemic risk and yet it is an idea that has never seriously been tested. The evidence is increasing that this is at best an extremely costly way to promote systemic safety, and may actually be counterproductive.

The consequences of bottom-up supervision

In any regulated activity there is always a tension between those who are applying rules for the good of all, and those who – while accepting the general value of regulation in principle – seek to gain an advantage for themselves by bending those rules at the margin. Where regulatory capacity is weak this can lead to the worst form of supervision, in which institutions tick boxes to show they meet the letter of the law while seeking ways to evade its spirit. But even under the most sensitive supervisory regimes, there is always the temptation to push the rules as far as possible, and some of the brightest and well-remunerated minds in the financial sector spend many hours seeking out new ways of wringing advantage out of the system of rules and regulations.

This in itself is a challenge for supervisors, who face a never-ending battle closing loopholes and extending their reach to cover ever-wider fields. No sooner is one activity caught in their net, than innovative minds in the financial institutions design another, which in turn has to be researched, understood and regulated by underpaid and overworked supervisors. And so on. If the supervisors are not careful, the body of regulations required to control the ever-inventive minds of the market grows relentlessly and monotonically – indeed, it is almost impossible to avoid this happening however careful the supervisors are.

This in itself creates a large and growing overhead for the financial services industry. It is a commonplace that financial companies now employ many more compliance officers, and many more people to submit reports to their regulators, than they did 5, 10 or 15 years ago. In the US, for example, the total cost of compliance with financial regulation was estimated at 13% of the non-interest operating expenses of banks, and thus equivalent to around 50% of banks' net income, (Elliehausen 1998). As for incremental costs, the same study gives a range of between 1% and 6% of banks' ongoing non-interest expenses. In 2002, the FSA estimated that the costs of compliance with financial regulation added between 2% and 10% to operating costs (Financial Services Authority 2002), with the cost impact of compliance being considerably higher for smaller institutions.[5] (It should be noted that since 2002 the FSA and its costs have nearly doubled.)

In the laudable aim of increasing the resilience of financial systems, these costs are blithely assumed to be both inevitable and in a worthy cause. But ultimately they are a cost on society as a whole not just the institutions who initially bear them, whether through the lower returns for stockholders or through a sub-optimal growth in the provision of financial services for the general economy. At a micro-level, the recent desire of investors to consider largely unregulated, private equity or hedge fund investments, and of company bosses to consider de-listing their company from public exchanges is a revealed preference by sophisticated market participants for the risk-return trade-off of less regulated sectors. It is important to remember that the economic point of regulation is not to tax the financial system, but to create confidence that improves the risk-return trade-off of regulated activities and those related to it.

There are of course less visible social costs and externalities too of the regulatory burden. It is now necessary to ask whether the cost of this emphasis and expenditure on avoiding risks and losses is not now beginning to exceed the cost of the potential losses themselves. A risk-averse financial industry that has lost the will to innovate because of the expense involved, does not serve a modern economy well. It is noteworthy that the UK government's noble attempt to create low-cost 'stakeholder' pensions has been thwarted by the inability of the industry to deliver a commercially viable, low cost product, in no small part due to heavy compliance and regulatory costs.

But there is another serious consequence: as the body of regulations grows in both scope and complexity, it starts to form a significant barrier to entry for new institutions seeking to conduct financial business. Regulations are in general, size-intolerant. As we have seen, the burden on new entrants, who tend to be small in size, is therefore disproportionate. This further undermines innovation in the financial industry: it is neither in the incumbents' interests to innovate, nor in the supervisors' interest to promote innovation. Genuinely new ideas become expensive and time-consuming to bring to market, as regulatory approval has to be sought in advance for each new division or activity that a financial institution wants to introduce. And without the pressure of new entrants, established players will increasingly stick to what they have rather than seek out new ideas. In many regulatory jurisdictions today, in order to have the regulatory approval to be a fund manager you effectively have to be...a fund manager.

A second result of this institution-based supervision is a continual trend for business to move from regulated sectors to less regulated ones. This regulatory arbitrage, both between financial sectors and between financial systems or markets, occurs in many different forms; as an example, the two financial sectors booming at the moment, the hedge fund and private equity sectors are very lightly regulated. And the concern in the EU about the possible migration of banking business to, for example, Switzerland, is a clear indication that the authorities are not unaware of the potential for arbitrage between regulatory regimes.

As regulators chase risks from one sector to another, risks can also end up being pushed to where the regulators may not see it. Moreover, assuming that risk is homogenous and should be managed in common ways or not held, will push risk away from places where it may be well managed to places where it may not be. For example, one of the consequences of accounting and financial regulation is a switch from defined benefit pension plans to defined contribution plans, which is essentially a shift in risks from corporations, where risk is highly regulated, visible and managed by experts, to individuals, who are less able to understand and manage these risks. Institutions that do not require instant liquidity like insurance and pension funds should not be discouraged from holding assets that are less liquid through mark-to-market reporting requirements. Regulations of a different kind have led banks, which have much understanding and capacity for diversifying credit risk, to pass on credit risks to insurers, who may not.

Another related result of institution-based supervision is that the rules become so prescriptive that the number of business models that are both permissible and profitable is reduced. This results in system homogeneity, and this in turn can lead to system fragility. When all players in a market are viewing risks in the same way, there is no resilience due to diversity. The clearest example of this is the now almost ubiquitous[6] use of Value-at-Risk models to determine institutional risk appetites. As general risk levels in a market rise, institutions individually seek to reduce risk by reducing (that is, selling) their positions. This increases volatility and hence measured VaR risk, and leads to further pressure to reduce positions. In the end the market can be left with no-one willing to take on risk, because all players have concluded from their risk models that their individual optimal stance is to reduce risk.[7]

This is not just a hypothetical fear. There is quantitative evidence that the measure of this breakdown in the market's ability to clear – number of times and markets which encounter periods of positive feedback between prices and flows (price declines do not bring out bargain-hunters in a stabilising fashion, but more sellers in a destabilising fashion) – has increased over the past decade.[8] These periods of dislocation increase the demand on the authorities – usually central banks – to act as risk-takers of last resort, not so much through institutional bail outs, but investor bail outs *via* over-easy monetary policy. During Alan Greenspan's reign as Governor of the Federal Reserve Bank, he was forced on no less than three separate occasions to cut interest rates to below a rate consistent with economic activity as a result of a financial dislocation: Savings & Loans, LTCM, dot.com bubble. This is a perverse result to arise from the drive to make financial systems systemically safer!

At the heart of all of these conundrums is the single issue of whether the aim of supervision is to make systems safe or institutions safe. Does supervision aim to users and an aura of confidence in the system by the users of the financial system, or the institutions that provide those services? In concentrating supervision on institutions, in a bottom-up manner, regulators risk creating an environment of isolated safe institutions within a system where the risk migrates from the centre to the fringes, from the heavily regulated sectors to the less regulated, and from those most able to bear risk to those least able to.

An alternative approach

Rather than try to make institutions safe – a task which is both replete with moral hazard and literally an endless task, as there are always new activities to draw within the ever-widening net – it is our belief that regulators should concentrate solely on those actions which make consumers and systems safe. It is worth explaining why these two issues justify a degree of intervention in the financial markets that goes beyond government intervention in other markets.

Finance is characterised by two things that mark it out from most other industries. The first is the central role of time and uncertainty in financial operations, and the second, the degree of interconnectedness of agents. To illustrate the importance of time, we have to consider what generally makes a market self-policing. Markets work well when there is immediate consumption (of goods or services) and the prospect of repeat transactions. The feedback mechanism from a previous experience in the market to the next decision is clear and quick – one soon knows which fruit stall on the Northcote Road market in London to buy apples from and which to avoid, because the experience of buying apples and enjoying them is close in time and easy to identify. A seller of bad or expensive apples is soon identified, and the same is also true of service industries, such as for example barbers or hairdressers.

But most consumers make only a handful of large financial decisions in their life – for example, their mortgage, life insurance, car loan or pension provisions. And for these decisions they usually only find out whether they made the right decision or not very much later, and usually when it is too late to do anything about it. Consequently, consumers need more protection when they buy a pension than when buying apples: the average consumer cannot learn from, or indeed recover easily from, his or her own mistakes.

The interconnectedness of financial markets is the other main feature which distinguishes them from other service sectors. Economic activity, especially across national borders, necessitates a thick web of banks extending credit to other banks, and whether internationally or at the domestic level of a payments clearing system, there is a certain minimum level of trust and mutual cooperation between financial agents that is necessary for the system to operate at all. If one bank fails, it has reverberations across the entire financial system, and financial history is full of contagious 'runs', as fear of failure can increase its likelihood.

It is for this reason that the authorities are concerned with systemic risk. Put simply, the financial markets are almost alone in that a failure in one relatively small institution can spread rapidly through the system, and for sound institutions to lose the confidence of the public simply because their unsound peers have. (In many industries, a failure in one place, leads to more business in others.) As a result there is an enormous systemic benefit in having a financial system where people have confidence in every link in the chain, and this benefit goes beyond an individual bank's private benefit from being a safe bank. Left up to the markets alone, banks would under-invest in systemic safety – from the perspective of any individual institution, systemic issues are peripheral; they are concerned with their own safety, not that of the financial system in general. Consequently, if left unchecked, the chain will snap a few times and economic activity will be much reduced.

In summary, finance is one of the markets where the general public is least able to learn from their own experiences and mistakes,[9] and where systemic stability is a worthwhile common good for all but not an overriding objective for any one participant – a classic public good in the economic sense like city parks. These then are the arguments for regulation of the financial sector. This further highlights the odd placement of institutions at the centre of our current regulatory order. Rather than concentrating on the consumer (who needs help) and the system (which is nobody else's first priority), regulators expend their energy micromanaging institutions which have every incentive to be managing themselves anyway!

With this in mind, we propose a more parsimonious approach to regulation, bringing regulation directly to bear on to the points of market failure and removing all other distractions for the regulators. To this must be added a consideration of the economic cost of consumer and systemic safety. It is possible to make a financial system safe by transferring all the risks to the government and in turn the tax payer. Arguably the Soviet Union had a safe financial system in the sense that banks did not fail, but the consequences were lower economic activity as a result of government misallocation of credit. Deposit protection schemes in many countries mean that the tax payer is the ultimate guarantor of much of the banking system; the main consequence of this is moral hazard and the weakening of market discipline on poorly managed institutions that may actually lead to greater systemic risk. (An example of this risk exploding is the mass failure of the Savings & Loans industry at the start of the 1990s in the United States. To gauge the full cost of such events, it is important to note that some argue that the series of financial bubbles in the United States in the late 1990s relate to the Federal Reserve holding down interest rates for a long time in order to support the weakened financial system.) The objective of our redesign is to refocus on consumer protection and the avoidance of systemic risk, and to achieve these ends in a way that is low cost, encourages risks to end up where they are best managed and intervenes most where markets fail and not where they would otherwise be a source of healthy competition and innovation.

Protecting financial consumers

More classification and less regulation

If the issue is to protect the average consumer the first distinction to be made is between the retail consumer and the professional consumer of financial products. The latter needs no more protection than currently afforded by existing consumer protection and product liability law. The former needs more protection for the reasons cited earlier. But this can be done in a far more simple and less costly way. One useful but not exact analogy is with the British Board of Film Classification. Film directors and studios are not regulated; instead their output, their films, and the distributors of films are. The regulation is simple, clear and cheap. The Board classifies many hundreds of films per year, but employs just 50 people, only 13 of whom are examiners. Films are given a broad classification that is consumer-focused and simple to understand, such as U for universal, PG for parental guidance, 12 and 18 for teenagers and adults.

To obtain an U certificate for a financial instrument, the seller would have to show that the risk carried by the consumer is low – either directly *via* the characteristics of the instrument or indirectly *via* the likelihood that the seller/counter-party fails. Those counterparties that specialise in retail investors will require a low risk classification as well. Is this not another word for risk-sensitive regulation of institutions? There are similarities but there are also important differences.

An institution that has no systemic worry (see below) and is only selling instruments to professional investors, has no additional regulatory requirements than an ordinary company and no capital requirement. An institution that wants to sell instruments to retail investors will need a low risk classification. This will depend on two things: the proven risk profile of the company and the amount of capital it is running. Any institution can improve its risk classification by increasing its capital or improving its record of measuring and managing its risks. This is incentive compatible and is quite different from today where an institution with an unstellar record of managing its risk profile, can end up with a low amount of capital, because it is large enough to afford a complex credit process that is compliant with banking regulations. Our approach is results driven – which favours innovation – and not process driven – which favours size. New institutions would be disadvantaged from selling to retail investors but not discouraged from entering the industry. They would have to begin by focusing either on low risk instruments to be sold to retail investors or riskier instruments only sold to professional investors. In our proposed new order, the main device for consumer protection would not be the regulation of institutions, but the classification of products (classifications would have to be renewed regularly).

At first sight, the proposal that only professionals could purchase certain financial instruments may appear elitist, but only if it is elitist to limit who can represent others in Court or fly an aeroplane, or to ask market professionals to be the guinea pigs for new financial products. If new financial products prove popular and successful, product providers will be incentivised to develop versions that would carry a safer classification and would be open to a wider market. This arrangement achieves consumer protection at low cost while safeguarding and perhaps encouraging product innovation. Further, product development, financial advice and retail distribution would all become more independent of each other, maximising innovation and protection at the same time, rather than trading off each other.

Systemic risk

At any given time an individual institution may wrongly assess the risks it faces, and in doing so it puts its solvency and even survival at risk. But few failures of individual institutions lead to whole markets being at risk. Rather, whole markets are at risk when either a systemically important institution fails or collectively, they assess risk wrongly. These are the issues upon which capital charges should be centred. Let us deal with the former issue next and the latter issue afterwards.

It would seem to us that the most important activity of banking regulators ought to be assessing how systemically important an institution is – this being one of the two key activities of banking regulators. Sadly we do not think regulators have expended enough energy in this regard and as a consequence methodologies for assessing how systemic an institution is are not well-developed. Systemically important institutions should pay an insurance premium to the authorities which would act to compensate tax payers in the event that they have to bail out the institution and would create an incentive for the institution to find ways of reducing its systemic nature.[10] Regulators should develop an estimate of the short-term and long-term cost of an institution failing and charge a premium that relates to that risk. It is true that many of these risks are inherently qualitative such as issues of confidence and reputation, but focusing only on those risks that are easily quantifiable is a very risky endeavour. This is an institution-specific charge but it only relates to systemically important institutions. But it is not sufficient.

Which risks are markets most likely to collectively mis-assess? Of the two major risks that markets face – risks across institutions and risks across time – markets are better at assessing the former than the latter. Markets differentiate very successfully between the credit quality of General Motors and Union Bank of Switzerland or Argentina and Australia, and impose a restraining discipline on bad credits. But time-consistency of risk-assessment is more challenging: markets often under-estimate all risks during financial booms, and after crashes, they often overestimate them.[11]

The roots of systemic risks are therefore often found in the economic cycle.[12] Put simply, systemic risks are usually at their highest at the extremes of the cycle, and furthermore they usually only cover large institutions or sectors.[13] Outside the extremes of a cycle, or in the case of smaller institutions (for example, BCCI or Barings in the UK), the authorities usually decide to let companies fail without instigating a bail-out.[14]

If the cycle and the size of the institution under pressure are the key elements determining when risks become systemic, then counter-cyclical measures and extra restraints on large institutions should be at the heart of financial regulation. Yet, most often, the exact opposite is the case. Most regulatory measures, such as capital adequacy ratios or using external credit ratings to assess risk, are heavily pro-cyclical, and many measures such as the increasing use of technology and data intensive risk management systems, such as the IRB approach of the Basle Committee's Second Capital Adequacy Accord, favour larger institutions.[15]

We believe this is wrong. We believe that regulation should be explicitly counter-cyclical (in other words, tightened in good times, to offset the natural optimism that markets have that the good times will go on forever). Counter-cyclical measures need not be elaborate or complicated. For example, in the area of credit extension, it would be simple to require any institution that extends non-collateralised credit to pay a systemic risk charge, with the charge rising and falling with national credit growth. If this charge is set sufficiently high, it will act as a brake on credit cycles and the deterioration of loan quality often seen in a boom.[16] Just like systemic risks, booms and crashes, this measure does not differentiate between institutions but instead focuses on the market failure we are addressing, the positive feedback of markets which lead them to conjure up booms and crashes from the normal ups and downs of economic activity and technological progress.

A further protection against systemic risk hinted at throughout this article is diversity. It is probably sensible for a few market players to view risk as a function of a common measure of volatility of an instrument and to reduce risk when volatility or correlation rises. But if everyone does so, this will lead to systemic, self-feeding crashes. If however, we were to pursue our approach of risk-suitability, and the level, maturity and type of risk is matched to risk capacities, market behaviour will be less sensitive to short-term changes and there is the potential of more stabilising behaviour.

To encourage this an institution should be able to reduce its systemic risk rating and premium by convincing the regulator that they have reduced risks by good matching and diversification. To develop this approach regulators will have to learn to differentiate more between the three types of risks which exist: market, credit and liquidity. As an example, institutions can reduce their liquidity systemic risk by having assets with greater liquidity than their liabilities. In this way, insurance companies and pension funds with very long-term liabilities would be incentivised to invest in less liquid assets, but banks with short-term liabilities would not be and this would be the correct incentives and placement of liquidity risk. Institutions that are in a better position to diversify market and credit risks would be incentivised to do so. In this way, risks will go to where they are better managed. This critical feature of our proposed system reveals the bankruptcy of the so-called risk-sensitive approach. By considering risk and institutions in a homogenous way the current system removes the main avenues by which risk is reduced. By taxing risk the same way everywhere, it gets pushed away from experts and sources of risk-diversification towards those who have the least capacity to manage it: individuals.

Conclusion

Current regulation is costly and complicated and yet only half complete. It does not focus on systemic risks – one of two key purposes of regulation. In the name of safety it promotes systemic homogeneity, pro-cyclical lending practices and the pushing of risks from places where it may naturally sit to where we can no longer see it. In the name of consumer protection it reduces innovation and choice.

The behaviour of consumers, investors and company directors and of the regulated and unregulated industries does not tell us that 100,000 regulators and billions of dollars later, consumers feel safer and system-wide risk is lower.

We propose a simple system of regulation based on a classification of products and systemic activities. Light regulation is a modest end in itself, but the real merit of this system is that it is directly aligned with the market failures that justify regulation more directly than the current extravagant system of rules and regulations. Product providers and market professionals are given freedom to innovate, but consumers are protected. Standards are to be used, but not so much that homogeneity creates risk. Markets are to be relied upon, but not in gauging the economic cycle where failure is well-documented. Risk is not to be driven to dark corners where it is not easily seen or understood, but encouraged into places where it is better managed.

By being less centred on institutions, this new order is also less prone to regulatory arbitrage and regulatory capture, and less likely to require the endless updating that is such a characteristic of financial regulation today. Above all, it creates very clear and appropriate division of responsibilities. There is no hiding behind the rule book. Consumers are responsible for their decision to save or spend. Professional investors more so. The regulator is responsible for identifying sources of systemic and consumer risk. Where the current system delivers regulatory arbitrage, risk spillovers to pensioners and shareholders, and rigidity and high costs, this alternative delivers responsibility, diversity, competition and safety at a price the economy can afford.

Notes

1. We are indebted to a number of people who have discussed these ideas, encouraged us and stopped us making A3 many mistakes as we would otherwise have done, principally, Stephen Spratt, Anastasia Nesvetailova, Andrew Rozanov, Brandon Davies, Michael Mainelli, Peter Walker and Yarema Ronish.
2. The HKMA was formed on 1 April 1993 by the merger of the Office of the Commissioner of Banking (that is, the Hong Kong Government's banking supervisory body) and the Office of the Exchange Fund (that is, the manager of Hong Kong's reserves and linked exchange rate).
3. De Nederlandsche Bank, which assumed the duties of the Pensions and Insurance Supervisory Authority of the Netherlands (Pensioen- & Verzekeringskamer/PVK) on 30 October 2004.
4. The Central Bank and Financial Services Authority of Ireland, created in 2000 by incorporating the Irish Financial Services Regulatory Authority within the Central Bank of Ireland.
5. In 2005 the FSA has commissioned Deloitte and Touche to undertake an indepth study into the costs of compliance with financial regulation. The results are expected by the end of the year.
6. And soon to be institutionalised in the Basle II arrangements.
7. See Persaud (2000) for a fuller description of this phenomenon, and Nugée (2003) for an exposition of how it affects market participants in practice.
8. See Persaud (2004) for a description and measurement of these Liquidity Black Holes.

9. It is not unique in this; the health sector is another market where the general public can be faced with decisions which are both infrequent and irreversible, and where as a result they have no personal experience to go on and very limited ability to recover from a wrong decision.
10. Claudio Borio has also been thinking along similar lines, see Borio (2003).
11. This is an observed fact, though there is much less agreement in the literature as to <u>why</u> it happens. It probably relates to the asymmetry of risks that investors face between running with the herd and being a contrarian, though the short-termed nature of communal memory in markets, most obviously seen in a strong tendency to extrapolate the most recent trend, is also a factor, as stressed by proponents of behavioural finance amongst others.
12. This insight has long been of interest to economists, and was perhaps first formalised in the early 1930s by Irving Fisher (1933) in the context of the Wall Street Crash and the Great Depression.
13. Because financial 'bail-outs' of consumers create moral hazard and indiscipline, they are usually only considered when there are serious systemic concerns, so it is telling that (as well as mainly occurring when large institutions are at risk), most bail-outs occur in the aftermath of market crashes.
14. Indeed, the observation that some financial institutions may be seen as 'too big to fail' by the relevant authorities is viewed by some as a considerable source of moral hazard for these institutions. (See Price 1987, for an early perspective on this viewpoint, and Stern and Feldman 2004, for a more recent exposition).
15. As an example of an industry which is <u>not</u> heavily regulated, and in which innovation flourishes and smaller players compete aggressively, consider the asset management industry. A whole range of alternative investment styles (for example, but not limited to, the hedge fund phenomenon) has developed in the last decade, to the extent that established asset managers are being forced to reconsider their investment approaches. Entry (and exit) in the asset management industry is easy and the industry is – we think partly as a result – one of the more innovative parts of the financial sector.
16. Mortgage financiers already operate on this principle when granting mortgages to homebuyers. As house prices become more and more extended, both the size of loans and the percentage of the house purchase price that they are prepared to grant are cut back. This simple counter-cyclical measure curbs borrowing activities and eventually restrains the housing cycle, and also protects lenders when housing booms turn sour. There is no reason why a similar principle should not be applicable in the general regulation of bank lending.

Bibliography

Adult Financial Literacy Advisory Group (AdFlag) (2000) *Report to the Secretary of State for Education and Employment* (London: AdFlag).

Agenstvo Finansovyih Novostei [Agency of Financial News], Belarus (17 June 2005) *'MERT: Ottok kapitala iz RF v 2005 g. sostavit 5–7 mlrd. USD'* [Ministry of Trade and Economic Development of Russia: Capital outflow from Russia would amount to 5–7 billion USD in 2005], www.afn.by. Accessed 18 June 2005.

Aglietta, M. (1979) *A Theory of Capitalist Regulation: The US Experience*, London: Verso.

Aglietta, M. (1998) 'Capitalism at the turn of the century: Regulation theory and the challenge of social change', *New Left Review* I/232: 41–90.

Aglietta, M. (2000) 'Shareholder value and corporate governance: some tricky questions', *Economy and Society* 29(1): 146–59.

Aglietta, M., Breton, R. (2001) 'Financial systems, corporate control and capital accumulation', *Economy and Society* 30(4): 33–466.

Akbar, Y.H. and McBride, B.J. (2004) 'Multinational Enterprise Strategy, Foreign Direct Investment and Economic Development: the case of the Hungarian banking industry', *Journal of World Business* 39: 89–105.

Amoore, L. (2004) 'Risk, Reward and Discipline at Work', *Economy and Society* 33(2): 174–96.

Amoore, L. (2006) 'Biometric Borders: Governing Mobilities in the War on Terror', *Political Geography* 25(3): 336–51.

Amoore, L. (2006, forthcoming) 'Biometric Borders: Governing Mobilities in the War on Terror', *Political Geography*.

Amoore, L. and de Goede, M. (2005) 'Governance, Risk and Dataveillance in the War on Terror', *Crime, Law and Social Change* 43(2): 149–73.

Amoore, L. and Langley, P. (2004) 'Ambiguities of Global Civil Society', *Review of International Studies* 30(1): 89–110.

Andreas, P. and Biersteker, T.J. (eds) (2003) *The Rebordering of North America*, New York: Routledge.

Aninat, E., Hardy, D. and Johnston, R.B. (2002) 'Combating Money Laundering and the Financing of Terrorism', *Finance and Development* 39(3).

ANZ (2003) 'ANZ Survey of Adult Financial Literacy in Australia. Stage 3 In-Depth Interview Survey Report' (Melbourne: ANZ Banking Group, 2003), http://anz.com/australia/support/library/MediaRelease/MR20030502c.pdf> (accessed 2 January 2006).

Arrighi, G. (2003) 'The social and political economy of global turbulence', *New Left Review* II/20.

Aslanbeigui, N. and Summerfield, G. (2000) 'The Asian Crisis, Gender, and the International Financial Architecture', *Feminist Economics* 6(3): 81.

Aufhauser, D.D. (2003) 'Terrorist Financing: Foxes Run to Ground', *Journal of Money Laundering Control* 6(4): 301–05.

Avant, D. (2005) 'Private Security Companies', *New Political Economy* 10(1): 121–31.

Aybar, S. and Lapavitsas, C. (2001) 'Financial System Design and the Post-Washington Consensus', in Fine, B., Lapavitsas, C. and Pincus, J. (eds) *Development Policy in the Twenty-first Century*, London and New York: Routledge.

Bach, G.L. (1971) *Making Monetary and Fiscal Policy*, Washington, D.C.: Brookings Institution.

Backé, P. and Zumer, T. (2005) 'Developments in Credit to the Private Sector in Central and Eastern European EU Member States: Emerging from Financial Repression – A Comparative Overview', *OeNB working paper Focus On European Economic Integration Series*.

Bailes, A.J.K. (2004) 'Business and Security: Public-Private Sector Interface and Interdependence at the Turn of the 21st Century', in Bailes, A.J.K. and Frommelt, I. (eds) *Business and Security: Public-Private Relationships in a New Security Environment*, Oxford: Oxford University Press.

Bailey, J.J., Nofsinger, J.J. and Michelle O'Neill (2003) 'A Review of Major Influences on Employee Retirement Investment Decisions', *Journal of Financial Services Research* 23(2): 149.

Bajtelsmit, V.L. and Jianakoplos, N.A. (2000) 'Women and Pensions: A Decade of Progress?', Employee Benefit Research Institute (November).

Bajtelsmit, V.L., Bernasek, A. and Jianakoplos, N.A. (1999) 'Gender differences in defined contribution pension decisions', *Financial Services Review* 8(1).

Bakker, I. and Gill, S. (eds) (2003) *Power, Production and Social Reproduction*, Toronto: Palgrave Macmillan.

Bakker, I. (1996) 'Introduction: The Gendered Foundations of Restructuring in Canada', in Bakker, I. (ed.) *Rethinking Restructuring: Gender and Change in Canada'*, Toronto: University of Toronto Press.

Bank of England (2004) *Financial Stability Review* 2003, London: Bank of England, December.

Bank of England (2005) *Financial Stability Review* 2004, London: Bank of England, December.

Barisitz, S. (2005) 'Banking in Central and Eastern Europe since the Turn of the Millennium – An Overview of Structural Modernization in Ten Countries', *OeNB Focus on European Economic Integration Series*.

Bartram, S. and Dufey, G. (2001) 'International Portfolio Investment: Theory, Evidence, and Institutional Framework', *Financial Markets, Institutions and Instruments*, Vol. 10, No. 3.

Batten, J., Fetherstone, T.A. and Szilagyi, P.G. (2004) *European Fixed Income Markets*, Wiley, Finance Series, Chichester.

Battilossi, S. (2000) 'Financial Innovation and the Golden Ages of International Banking: 1890 to 1931 and 1958–81', *Financial History Review* 7: 141–75.

Battilossi, S. (2002) 'Banking with multinationals: British clearing banks and the Euromarkets' challenge, 1958–1976', in Battilossi, S. and Cassis, Y. (eds) *European*

Banks and the American Challenge. Competition and Cooperation in International Banking under Bretton Woods, Oxford: Oxford University Press.

Beck, U. (1992) *Risk Society: Towards a New Modernity*, London: Sage Publications.

Beck, T., Demirgüc-Kunt, A. and Levine, R. (1999) 'A New Database on Financial Development and Structure', *Policy Research Working Paper*, 2146, World Bank.

Beck, U. (2002) 'The Terrorist Threat: World Risk Society Revisited', *Theory, Culture and Society* 19(4): 39–55.

Bello, W., Malhotra, K., Bullard, N. and Mezzera, M. (2000) 'Notes on the Ascendancy and Regulation of Speculative Capital', in Bello, W., Malhotra, K. and Bullard, N. (eds) *Global Finance. New Thinking on Regulating Speculative Capital Markets*, London, New York: Zed Books.

Ben-Ami, D. (2001) *Cowardly Capitalism: The Myth of the Global Financial Casino*, Chichester, New York: John Wile and Sons.

Beneria, L. (2003) 'Economic Rationality and Globalization: A Feminist Perspective', in Ferber, M. and Nelson, J.A. (eds) *Feminist Economic Today: Beyond Economic Man*, Chicago: University of Chicago Press.

Berg, A. and Borensztein, E. (2000) 'The Pros and Cons of Full Dollarisation', *IMF Working Paper*, No. 00/50, Washington, DC: IMF.

Berger, A.N., Klapper, L.F. and Udell, G.F. (2001) 'The ability of banks to lend to internationally opaque small businesses', *Journal of Banking and Finance* 25: 2127–67.

Bergeron, V. (2001) 'Political Economy Discourses of Globalization and Feminist Politics', *Signs: Journal of Women in Culture and Society* 26: 983.

Beunza, D. and Stark, D. (2004) 'Tools of the Trade: The Socio-Technology of Arbitrage in a Wall Street Trading Room', *Industrial and Corporate Change* 13: 369–400.

Biersteker, T.J. (2002) 'Targeting Terrorist Finances: The New Challenges of Financial Market Globalisation', in Booth, K. and Dunne, T. (eds) *Worlds in Collision: Terror and the Future of Global Order*, Basingstoke: Palgrave.

Biersteker, T.J. (2004) 'Counter-Terrorism Measures Undertaken Under UN Security Council Auspices', in Bailes, A.J.K. and Frommelt, I. (eds) *Business and Security: Public-Private Relationships in a New Security Environment*, Oxford: Oxford University Press.

Blackburn, R. (2002) *Banking on Death or Investing in Life: The History and Future of Pensions*, New York: Verso.

Black, F. (1986) 'Noise', *Journal of Finance* 41: 529–43.

Black, F. and Scholes, M. (1973) 'The Pricing of Options and Corporate Liabilities', *Journal of Political Economy* 81: 637–54.

Blackburn, R. (2002) *Banking on Death or Investing in Life: The History and Future of Pensions*, New York: Verso.

Blake, D. (2003) 'The UK pension system: Key issues', *Pensions* 8(4): 330.

Bloch-Lainé, F. (1963) *Pour une réforme de l'entreprise*, Éditions du Seuil, Paris.

Bonner, W. and Wiggin, A. (2005) *Financial Reckoning Day. Surviving the Soft Depression of the 21st Century*, New York: John Wiley and Sons.

Borio, C. (2003) 'Towards a macroprudential framework for financial regulation and supervision?', BIS Working Paper No. 128.

Borowski, J. (2004) 'Costs and Benefits of Poland's EMU Accession: a Tentative Assessment', *Comparative Economic Studies* 46: 127–45.

Boyer, R. (2000) 'Is a finance-led growth regime a viable alternative to Fordism? A preliminary analysis', *Economy and Society* 29: 111–45.

Boyer, R. and Saillard, Y. (2002) *Regulation Theory: the State of the Art,* English translation by Shread, C., London: Routledge.

Brenner, N. (1998) 'Between Fixity and Motion: Accumulation, Territorial Organization and the Historical Geography of Spatial Scales', *Environment and Planning D: Society and Space* 16(5): 459–81.

Brenner, R. (1998) 'The economics of global turbulence', *New Left Review,* May/June.

Brenner, R. (2000) 'The Boom and the Bubble', *New Left Review,* No. 6, November/December.

Brenner, R. (2001) 'The world economy at the turn of the millennium toward boom or crisis?', *Review of International Political Economy* 8: 1.

Brenner, R. (2002) *The Boom and the Bubble: The US in the World Economy,* London, Verso.

Brenner, R. (2004) 'New Boom or New Bubble?', *New Left Review* 25: 57–102.

Brodie, J. (1997) 'Meso-Discourses, State Forms and the Gendering of Liberal-Democratic Citizenship', *Citizen Studies* 1: 223.

Bromwich, M. (1999) Angels and Trolls: *The ASB's Statement;* Academic Lecture. http://www.lse.ac.uk/collections/accountingAndFinance

Brown, S., Goetzmann, W. and Ibbotson, R. (1999) 'Offshore Hedge Funds: Survival and Performance, 1989–95', *Journal of Business* 72(1).

Bryan, D. and Rafferty, M. (2006) *Capitalism With Derivatives: A Political Economy of Financial Derivatives, Capital and Class,* Basingstoke: Palgrave Macmillan.

Bryan, D. (1995) *The Chase Across The Globe: International Accumulation and the Contradiction for Nation States,* Boulder: Westview Press.

Bryan, D. and Rafferty, M. (1999) *The Global Economy in Australia,* Sydney: Allen and Unwin.

Buchanan, J. (1995/96) 'Federalism and Individual Sovereignty', *The CATO Journal* 15(2–3), Fall/Winter 1995/96.

Bunyan, T. (2002) 'The War on Freedom and Democracy', *Statewatch Analysis* 13, http://www.statewatch.org/news/2002/sep/analy13.pdf.

Butler, J. (2004) *Precarious Life: The Powers of Mourning and Violence,* London: Verso.

Byrne, A. (2004) 'Employee Saving and Investment Decisions in Defined Contribution Pension Plans: Survey Evidence from the UK', Pensions Institute Discussion Paper PI-0412, London.

Cadbury, A. (1992) *Report of the Committee on the Financial Aspects of Corporate Governance,* London: Gee and Co.

Cai, H. and Treisman, D. (2004) 'State Corroding Federalism', *Journal of Public Economics,* No. 88: 819–43.

Callon, M. (ed.) (1998) *The Laws of the Markets*, Oxford: Blackwell.

Campbell, D. (2003) 'With Pot and Porn Stripping Corn, America's Black Economy is Flying High', *The Guardian*, 2 May: 3.

Campbell, J. and Bhatia, A. (2005) 'Offshore Financial Centres', in *The Handbook of World Stock, Derivative and Commodity Exchanges* available: http://www.exchange-handbook.co.uk/articles_story.cfm?id=5634

Cargill, T.F. and Garcia, G.G. (1985) *Financial Reform in the 1980s*, Stanford: Hoover Institutions Press.

Cassard, M. (1994) 'The Role of Offshore Centers in International Financial Intermediation', IMF Working Paper, WP/94/107, Washington DC: IMF.

Cassel, A. (2002) 'Why US Farm Subsidies are Bad for the World', *Philadelphia Enquirer*, 6 May.

Castells, M. (2000) *End of Millenium*, 2nd edn, Oxford: Blackwell.

Celarier, M. (1996) 'Plastics profits approach meltdown', *Euromoney*, 10–13.

Central Bank of Russia (2005) *Balance of Payments Statistics*, http://www.cbr.ru/eng/statistics/credit_statistics/print.asp?file=capital_e.htm. Accessed 19 September 2005.

Cerny, P. (1993) 'American decline and embedded financial orthodoxy', Cerny, P. (ed.) *Finance and World Politics: Finance, Regimes and States in the Post-Hegemonic Era*, Cheltenham: Edward Elgar.

Cerny, P. (1994) 'The infrastructure of infrastructure', in Palan, R. and Gills, B. (eds) *Transcending the State-Global Divide*, Boulder Co: Lynne Publishers.

Cerny, P. (1995) 'Globalisation and the Changing Logic of Collective Action', *International Organization* 49(4), Autumn 1995: 595–625.

Cetina, K.K. and Bruegger, U. (2002a) 'Global Microstructures: The Virtual Societies of Financial Markets', *American Journal of Sociology* 107: 905–51.

Cetina, K.K. and Bruegger, U. (2002b) 'Inhabiting Technology: The Global Lifeform of Financial Markets', *Current Sociology* 50: 389–405.

Chandler, A.D. (1977) *The Visible Hand. The Managerial Revolution in American Business*, Cambridge, MA, London: Harvard University Press.

Chandler, L.V. (1971) *American monetary policy 1928–1941*, New York: Harper & Row.

Charupat, N. and Deaves, R.V. (2004) 'How Behavioural Finance Can Assist Financial Professionals', *Journal of Personal Finance* 3(3): 41.

Chernow, R. (1990) *The House of Morgan: an American banking dynasty and the rise of modern finance*, New York: Atlantic Monthly Press.

Chicago Board of Trade, website: http://www.cbot.com/

Claessens, S., Demirgüc-Kunt, A. and Huizinga, H. (2001) 'How Does Foreign Entry Affect Domestic Banking Markets?', *Journal of Banking and Finance* 25, 891–911.

Clark, G.L. (2000) *Pension Fund Capitalism*, Oxford: Oxford University Press.

Clarke, G., Cull, R., Peria, M.S.M. and Sanchez, M.S. (2001) 'Foreign Bank Entry Experience, Implications for Developing Countries, and Agenda for Further Research', *World Bank Policy Research Working Paper No. 2698*, October 2001.

Clementi, D. (2004) *Financial Education*, presentation at the OECD Forum, May 2004 http://www.prudential.co.uk/prudentialplc/cr_home/library/fineducation.pdf (accessed 7 December 2005).

Cleveland, H. and Huertas, T.F. (1985) *Citibank 1812–1970*, Cambridge, Mass. London: Harvard University Press.

Coakley, J. (1992) 'London as an International Financial Centre', in Budd, L. and Whimster, S. (eds) *Global Finance and Urban Living*, London: Routledge.

Coates, N. (2003) 'Pensions funds and the internationalisation of insurance companies: An Australian example', in Lönnborg, M., Olsson, M., Rafferty, M. and Nalson, I. (eds) *Money and Finance in Transition – Research in Contemporary and Historical Finance*, Huddinge: Sodertorns Hogskola.

Coates, N., Rafferty, M. and Nicoletti, R. (2005) 'International Portfolio Investment Flows, Confusing Mess or Conceptual Confusion: A Case Study on the IMF Coordinated Portfolio Investment Survey', *AEGIS Working Paper*, November 2004, www.aegis.uws.edu.au.

Cohen, B. (2000) 'Money in a Globalised World', in Woods, N. (ed.) *The Political Economy of Globalisation*, Chapter 4, London: Macmillan.

Cohen, S. (1972) *Folk Devils and Moral Panics: Creation of Mods and Rockers*, London: MacGibbon and Kee.

Coleman, W.D. (1996) *Financial Services, Globalization and Domestic Policy Change*, London: Macmillan.

Commons, J. (1959 [1924]) *The Legal Foundation of Capitalism*, Madison, Wisconsin: The University of Wisconsin Press.

Condon, M. (2000) 'Limited by Law? Gender, Corporate Law and the Family Firm', in Lacombe, D. and Chunn, D. (eds) *Law as a Gendering Practice*, Toronto: Oxford University Press.

Condon, M. and Philipps, L. (2006) 'Transnational Market Governance and Economic Citizenship: New Frontiers for Feminist Legal Theory', *Thomas Jefferson Law Review*.

Condon, M. (2002) 'Privatizing Pension Risk: Gender, Law, and Financial Markets', in Cossman, B. and Fudge, J. (eds) *Privatization, Law, and the Challenge to Feminism*, Toronto: University of Toronto Press.

Cook, J. and Roberts, J. (2000) 'Towards a Gendered Political Economy', in Cook, J., Roberts, J. and Waylen, G. (eds) *Towards a Gendered Political Economy*, New York: St. Martin's Press, Inc.

Cook, J. (2000) 'Flexible Employment – Implications for a Gendered Political Economy of Citizenship', in Cook, J., Roberts, J. and Waylen, G. (eds) *Towards a Gendered Political Economy*, New York: St. Martin's Press, Inc.

Cortbridge, S. and Thrift, N. (1994) 'Money, Power and Space: Introduction and Overview', in Corbridge, S., Martin, R. and Thrift, N. (eds) *Money, Power and Space*, Oxford, UK: Blackwell.

Cossman, B. and Fudge, J. (eds) (2002) *Privatization, Law, and the Challenge to Feminism*, Toronto: University of Toronto Press.

Coward, M. (2006) 'Securing the Global (Bio)Political Economy: Empire, Poststructuralism and Political Economy', in de Goede, M. (ed.) *International Political Economy and Poststructural Politics*, London: Palgrave.

Cowen, M. and Shenton, B. (1996) *Doctrines of Development*, London: Routledge.

Cox, M. (2001) 'The Meanings of Victory: American Power after the Towers', in Booth, K. and Dunne, T. (eds) *Worlds in Collision: Terror and the Future of Global Order*, Basingstoke: Palgrave.

Cox, M. (2004) 'Empire, Imperialism and the Bush Doctrine', *Review of International Studies* 30(4): 585–608.

Cutler, C.A., Haufler, V. and Tony Porter (eds) (1999) *Private Authority and International Affairs*, Albany: State University of New York Press.

Cutler, T. and Waine, B. (2001) 'Social Insecurity and the Retreat from Social Democracy: Occupational Welfare in the Long Boom and Financialization', *Review of International Political Economy* 8: 96.

Danko, T. and Okrut, Z. (1998) *'Svobodnye Ekomicheskie Zony'* [Free Economic Zones], Moscow: Infra-M.

de Cecco, M. (1984) *Modes of Financial Development: American Banking Dynamics and World Financial Dynamics*, European University Institute Working Paper, No. 84/122.

de Goede, M. (2003) 'Hawala Discourses and the War on Terrorist Finance', *Environment and Planning D: Society and Space* 21(5): 513–32.

de Goede, M. (2004) 'Repoliticizing Financial Risk', *Economy and Society* 33(2): 197–217.

de Goede, M. (2005) *Virtue, Fortune and Faith: a Genealogy of Finance*, Minneapolis: University of Minnesota Press.

de Haas, R.T.A. (2002) 'Finance, Law and Growth during Transition: A Survey', *DNB Staff Reports* 74. The Netherlands Bank.

de Haas, R.T.A. and van Lelyveld, I.P.P. (2002) 'Foreign Bank Penetration and Bank Credit Stability in Central and Eastern Europe', *Research Series Supervision* 43, The Netherlands Bank.

de la Torre, Cris and Moon, K.P. (2004) 'H.R. 1000 and the Independent Financial Planner', *Journal of Personal Finance* 3: 58.

Deaves, R. (2005) 'Unravelling a Knotty Problem', *Canadian Investment Review* (Spring): 6.

Degen, R.A. (1987) *The American monetary system. A concise survey of its evolution since 1896*, Lexington, Massachusetts/Toronto: Lexington Books.

DeSear, E. (2004) 'The Evolution of Credit Card Structures: Are They Flexible Enough for Today's Challenges?', *Journal of Structured Finance* 10: 9.

Dixon, L. (2001) 'Financial Flows via Financial Centres as part of the International Financial System, *Financial Stability Review*, June, Bank of England.

Dodd, R. (2002) 'The Role of Derivatives in the East Asian Financial Crisis', in Eatwell, J. and Taylor, L. (eds) *International Capital Markets*, New York: Oxford University Press.

Dodd, R. (2005) 'The Virtues of Prudential Regulation', in Stiglitz and Ocampo (eds) *Capital Markets Liberalization and Macroeconomics Overview Book*, New York: Oxford University Press.

Domhoff, G.W. (1990) *The Power Elite and the State. How Policy is Made in America*, New York: Aldine de Gruyter.

Dooley, M. and Walsh, C. (1999) 'Academic Views of Capital Flows: An Expanding Universe', Reserve Bank of Australia Conference, download: http:www.rba.gov.au/new/

Dooley, M., Claessens, S. and Warner, A. (1995) 'Portfolio Capital Flows: Hot or Cool?' *The World Bank Economic Review* 9(1), (January) 153–74.

Drucker, P. (1986) 'The Changed World Economy', *Foreign Affairs*, Spring, 64: 4.

Dufey, G. and Bartram, S. (1997) 'The Impact of Financial Centres on International Capital Markets', *The International Executive*, Sept–Oct. 39: 5.

Duménil, G. and Lévy, D. (1993) *The Economics of the Profit Rate: Competition, Crises, and Historical Tendencies in Capitalism*, Aldershot, England: Edward Elgar.

Duménil, G. and Lévy, D. (1998) *Au-delà du capitalisme?*, Paris: Presses Universitaires de France.

Duménil, G. and Lévy, D. (2001) 'Costs and benefits of neoliberalism. A class analysis', *Review of International Political Economy* 8(4): 578–607.

Duménil, G. and Lévy, D. (2004a) *Capital Resurgent. Roots of the Neoliberal Revolution*, Harvard, Massachusetts: Harvard University Press.

Duménil, G. and Lévy, D. (2004b) 'Production and Management: Marx's Dual Theory of Labor, 137–157', in Westra, R., Zuege, A. Value and the World Economy Today: Production, Finance and Globalization, Basingstoke: Palgrave Macmillan.

Duménil, G. and Lévy, D. (2004c) 'Neoliberal Income Trends. Wealth, Class and Ownership in the USA', *New Left Review* 30: 105–33.

Duménil, G. and Lévy, D. (2005) La finance capitaliste: rapports de production et rapports de classe, Paris: *PSE, EconomiX*.

Dunbar, Nicholas (2000) '*Inventing Money: The Story of Long-Term Capital Management and the Legends Behind it*', Chichester, West Sussex: Wiley.

Dunbar, S., Johnston, B. and Zephirin, M. (2003) 'Assessing Offshore', *Finance and Development,* September.

Dwyer, T. (2000) 'Harmful Tax Competition and the Future of Offshore Financial Centres, Such as Vanuatu', *Pacific Economic Bulletin* 15(1): 48–69.

Dyker, D. (2000) 'The Dynamic Impact on the Central-East European Economies of Accession to the European Union' ESRC 'Oneurope or Several Programme', Working Paper June 2000.

Easton, D. (1953) *The Political System: An Enquiry into the State of Political Science,* N.Y.: Knopf.

Eatwell, J. (2004) 'Useful bubbles', *Contributions to Political Economy* 23(1): 35–47.

Eatwell, J. and Taylor, L. (2000) *Global Finance at Risk,* Oxford: Polity Press.

ECB Occasional Paper (2000) 'Structural Analysis of the EU Banking Sector', ECB.

ECB Working Paper Series (2005a) No. 547 November 2005, ECB.

ECB Monthly Bulletin (2005b) May 2005, ECB.

Edkins, J., Pin-Fat, V. and Shapiro, M.J. (eds) (2004) *Sovereign Lives: Power in Global Politics,* London: Routledge.

Edkins, J. and Pin-Fat, V. (2004) 'Introduction: Life, Power, Resistance', in Edkins, J., Pin-Fat, V. and Shapiro, M.J. (eds) *Sovereign Lives: Power in Global Politics*, London: Routledge.

Edwards, F. (1999) 'Hedge Funds and the Collapse of Long-Term Capital Management', *Journal of Economic Perspectives* 13(2), Spring, 189–210.

Edwards, F.R. (1996) *The New Finance. Regulation and Financial Stability*, Washington, D.C.: AEI Press.

Eichengreen, B. (1998) *Globalizing Capital: A History of the International Money System*, Princeton, NJ: Princeton University Press.

Eichengreen, B. and Iversen, T. (1999) 'Institutions and economic performance: evidence from the labour market', *Oxford Review of Economic Policy* 15(4): 121–38.

Eichengreen, B. and Mathieson, D. (1999) 'Hedge Funds: What do we Really Know?' *International Monetary Fund*, Washington, September.

Eichengreen, B. and Sussman, N. (2000) 'The international monetary system in the (very) long run', IMF Working Papers 00/43, Washington: International Monetary Fund.

Ekonomika I Sziszn, Russia, No. 3, January 2002.

Elliehausen, G. (1998) 'The Cost of Bank Regulation: A Review of the Evidence', *Board of Governors of the Federal Reserve System Staff Study 171*, April.

England, P. (2005) 'Separative and Soluble Selves: Dichotomous Thinking in Economics', in Fineman, M. (ed.) *Feminism Confronts Homo Economicus: Gender, Law, and Society*, New York: Cornell University Press.

Ericson, R. and Haggerty, K. (1997) *'Policing the Risk Society'*, Toronto: University of Toronto Press.

Erturk, I., Froud, J., Johal, S. and Williams, K. (2004) 'Corporate governance and disappointment', *Review of International Political Economy* 11: 677–713.

Erturk, I., Froud, J., Johal, S. and Williams, K. (2005a) 'Pay for performance or pay as social division', *Competition and Change* 9: 49–74.

Erturk, I., Froud, J. Johal, S., Leaver, A. and Williams, K. (2005b) 'The democratisation of finance? Promises, outcomes and conditions', *Working Paper no. 9*, University of Manchester: CRESC.

Everhardt, N.F. (undated) 'Meeting the AML Compliance Challenge', *Searchspace White Paper*, http://www.searchspace.com/files/PDF/nelson_aml_whitepaper.pdf

Everhardt, N.F. (undated) 'Meeting the AML Compliance Challenge', *Searchspace White Paper*, http://www.searchspace.com/files/PDF/nelson_aml_whitepaper.pdf

Fama, E.F. (1970) 'Efficient Capital Markets: A Review of Theory and Empirical Work', *Journal of Finance* 25: 383–417.

FATF (Financial Action Task Force) (2002) *Guidance for Financial Institutions in Detecting Terrorist Financing*, April 24, http://www1.oecd.org/fatf/pdf/GuidFITF01_en.pdf.

Feige, E.L. and Dean, J.W. (2002) 'Dollarisation and Euroisation in Transition Countries: Currency Substitution, Asset Substitution, Network Externalities and Irreversibility', *Paper presented at the Fordham University International Conference on 'Euro and Dollarisation: Forms of Monetary Union in Integrating Regions'*, April 5–6, 2002, New York.

Feldstein, M. (1994) 'Tax Policy and International Capital Flows, *Working Paper No. 3194, NBER*.

Feldstein, M. and Horioka, C. (1980) 'Domestic Savings and International Capital Flows', *Economic Journal* 90, June: 314–29.

FER (Financial Economists Roundtable) (2005) Statement of the Financial Economists Roundtable on Hedge Funds, November, downloaded from: http://www.gsb.stanford.edu/news/headlines/vanhorne_hedgefunds_stmt.shtml.

Financial Services Authority (2004a) *Annual Report*, Financial Services Authority, June.

Financial Services Authority (2004b), *Building Financial Literacy in the UK*, London: FSA.

Fineman, M. (ed.) (2005) *Feminism Confronts Homo Economicus: Gender, Law, and Society*, New York: Cornell University Press.

Fisher, I. (1933) 'The Debt Deflation Theory of the Great Depression', *Econometrica* 1: 227–57.

Flandreau, M. and Clemens, J. (2005) The Ties That Divide: A Network Analysis of the International Monetary System, *CEPR Discussion Paper Series* 5129, July.

Fligstein, N. (1996) 'Markets as Politics: A Political-Cultural Approach to Market Institutions', *American Sociological Review* 61: 656–73.

Fligstein, N. (2001) *The Architecture of Markets*. Princeton, N.J.: Princeton University Press.

Focarelli, D. and Pozzolo, A. (2000) 'The Determinants of Cross-Border Shareholding: An Analysis with Bank-Level Data from OECD Countries'. Paper presented at the Federal Reserve Bank of Chicago Bank Structure Conference, May.

Ford, R. (1990) 'The Cost of Subsiding Industry', *The OECD Observer* Vol. 186, October/November.

Foreign direct investment in the financial sector of emerging market economies (2004) Committee on the Global Financial System (CGFS), Bank of International Settlements, Basel, March 2004.

Foreign direct investment in the financial sector – experiences in Asia, Central and Eastern Europe and Latin America (2005) Committee on the Global Financial System (CGFS), *Working Paper No. 25*, June 2005, Bank of International Settlements, Basle.

Foucault, M. (1991) 'Governmentality', in Burchell, G., Gordon, C. and Miller, P. (eds) *The Foucault Effect: Studies in Governmentality*, Chicago: University of Chicago Press.

Foucault, M. (2003) *Society Must Be Defended*, translated by David Macey, New York: Picador.

Foulke, R.A. (1980) [1931] The commercial paper market, New York: Arno Press.

Friedman, Benjamin M. (2000) 'The role of interest rates in Federal Reserve policy-making', in Kopcke, R.W. and Browne, L.E. (eds) *The Evolution of Monetary Policy and the Federal Reserve System over the Past Thirty Years: A Conference in Honor of Frank E. Morris*, Federal Reserve Bank of Boston.

Friedman, M. (1953) *Essays in Positive Economics*, Chicago: Chicago University Press.

Friedman, M. (1982) *Capitalism and Freedom*, 2nd edn, Chicago: University of Chicago Press.

Froud, J., Johal, S., Haslam, C. and Williams, K. (2001) 'Accumulation under conditions of inequality', *Review of International Political Economy* 8: 66–95.

FSA (Financial Services Authority) (1999) *Annual Report*, Financial Services Authority, June.

FSA (Financial Services Authority) (2002) *Financial Services Practitioner Panel 2002 Survey of the FSA's regulatory performance,* Financial Services Authority, November.

FSA (Financial Services Authority) (2003) *Reducing Money Laundering Risk: Know Your Customer and Anti-Money Laundering Monitoring*, Discussion Paper 22, August. http://www.fsa.gov.uk/pubs/discussion/dp22.pdf.

Fundamentals (2005) 'Mutual Funds and the US Retirement market', 14(4) August 2005.

Fungáčová, Z. (2005) 'Building a Castle on Sand: Effects of Mass Privatization on Capital Market Creation in Transition Economies', *Centre for Economic Research and Graduate Education, Working Paper* No. 256.

Galbraith, J.K. (1967) *The New Industrial State*, New York: New American Library.

Garber, P. (1998) 'Derivatives in International Capital Flow', *NBER Working Paper 6623*, Cambridge Mass.

Garcia, V. (2004) 'Seven Points Financial Services Institutions Should Know about IT Spending for Compliance', *Journal of Financial Regulation and Compliance* 12(4): 330–9.

Gascoigne, C. (2003) 'You can hedge against a drop in the value of your home', *Financial Times*, 8 November.

Gazeta.ru, Russia (10 December 2002) www.gazeta.ru. Accessed 19 October 2004.

Gelpi, R.-M. and Julien-Labruyáere, J. (2000) *The History of Consumer Credit: Doctrines and Practices*, Houndmills, Basingstoke, Hampshire: Macmillan.

Germain, R. (1997) *The International Organization of Credit: States and Global Finance in the World Economy*, Cambridge: Cambridge University Press.

Gill, S. (2005) 'Constitutionalising Capital: EMU and Disciplinary Neo-Liberalism', in Bieler, A. and Morton D.A. (eds) *Social Forces in the Making of the New Europe*, New York: Palgrave.

Gin, J. and Arber, S. (1999) 'Women's Pension Poverty: Prospects and Options for Change', in Walby, S. (ed.) *New Agendas for Women*, New York: St. Martin's Press.

Ginn, J. and Arber, S. (2001) 'Pension Prospects of Minority Ethnic Groups: Inequalities by Gender and Ethnicity', *British Journal of Sociology* 52: 519.

Ginn, J., Street, D. and Arber, S. (eds) (2001) *Women, Work and Pensions: International Issues and Prospects*, Philadelphia: Open University Press.

Gold, M. (2003) *Can DC Plans Pass the Prudence Test?* Available at www.benefitscanada.com.

Gonenç, R. (1990) 'From Subsidies to Structural Adjustment', *The OECD Observer* 186, October/November.

Gore, C. (1996) Methodological Nationalism and the Misunderstanding of East Asian Industrialization, *UNCTAD Discussion Paper No. 111*, January.

Görg, C. and Brand, U. (2000) 'Global environmental politics and competition between nation-states: on the regulation of biological diversity', *Review of International Political Economy* 7(3): 371–98.

Gowan, P. (1999) *The Global Gamble: Washington's Faustian Bid for World Dominance*, London: Verso.

Graham, J. (2005) 'Is Capitalism What We Really Care About? Matters of Concern in Political Economy', *Presentation in Development Seminar*, University of Toronto, November 2005.

Graham, O.L. (1992) *Losing Time: The Industrial Policy Debate*, Harvard University Press.

Granovetter, M. (1985) 'Economic Action and Social Structure: The Problem of Embeddedness', *American Journal of Sociology* 91: 485–510.

Greef, A.O. (1938) *The Commercial Paper House in the United States*, Cambridge: Cambridge University Press.

Green, S. (2000) 'Negotiating with the future: the culture of modern risk in global financial markets', *Environment and Planning D: Society and Space* 18: 77–89.

Greenspan, A. (2002) 'Finance: United States and Global', Speech to the Federal Reserve Board Meeting, April 22, At the Institute of International Finance, New York.

Greenspan, A. (2005a) ' International imbalances', Speech before the Advancing enterprise conference, London, December 2.

Greenspan, A. (2005b) 'Economic Flexibility', Speech to the National association for Business Economics Annual Meetings, Chicago, Illinois, 27 September.

Greider, W. (1987) *Secrets of the Temple: How the Federal Reserve Runs the Country*, New York: Simon and Schuster.

Grossman, G. (1998) 'Subverted Sovereignty: Historic Role of the Soviet Underground', in Cohen, S., Schwartz, A., and Zysman, J. (eds) *The Tunnel at the End of the Light: Privatization, Business Networks, and Economic Transformation in Russia*, Berkeley, CA: International and Area Studies, 24–48.

Gurulé, J. (2002) *Terrorist Financing Rewards Program Press Statement*, November 13. http://www.ustreas.gov/rewards/gurule.html.

Guttman, R. (1994) How *Credit-Money Shapes the Economy*, Armonk, London: M.E. Sharpe.

Haiduk, K., Herr, H., Lintovskaya, T., Parchevskaya, S., Priewe, J. and Tsiku, R. (2004) *The Belarusian Economy At a Crossroads*, Moscow: International Labour Organization/Aveks.

Hall, Peter A. and Soskice, D. (eds) (2001) *Varieties of Capitalism: The Institutional Foundations of Comparative Advantage*, Oxford: Oxford University Press.

Hall, S., Critcher, C., Jefferson, T., Clarke, J. and Robert, B. (1978) *Policing the Crisis: Mugging, the State, and Law and Order*, London: Macmillan.

Hallahan, T.A., Faff, R.W. and McKenzie, M.D. (2004) 'An Empirical Investigation of Personal Financial Risk Tolerance', *Financial Services Review* 13: 57.

Hammond, B. (1957) *Banks and Politics in America. From the Revolution to the Civil War*, Princeton: Princeton University Press.

Hannah-Moffat, Kelly (1999) 'Moral Agent or Actuarial Subject: Risk and Canadian Women's Imprisonment', *Theoretical Criminology* 3: 71.

Harmes, A. (1998) 'Institutional Investors and the Reproduction of Neo-liberalism', *Review of International Political Economy* 5: 92.

Harrington, R. (1987) *Asset and Liability Management by Banks*, Paris: OECD.

Harvey, D. (1990) *The Condition of Postmodernity. An Enquiry into the Origins of Cultural Change*, Cambridge and Oxford: Blackwell.

Harvey, D. (2001) *Spaces of Capital – Towards a Critical Geography*, New York: Routledge.

Hass, R. and Naaborg, I. (2005) 'Foreign Banks in Transition Economies: Small Business Lending and Internal Capital Markets', *De Nederlandsche Bank, Monetary and Economic Policy Division*, Amsterdam.

Hassebrook, C. (2005) 'Transformational Farm Policy: Will It Work?', Speech at Farm Policy and Rural Economy Conference, Washington DC, 24 June.

Havrylyshyn, O. and Beddies, C. (2003) Dollarization in the Former Soviet Union: From Hysteria to Hysteresis, *Comparative Economic Studies*, No. 45: 329–57.

Hayek, F.A. (1980) *The Road to Serfdom (1944)*, Chicago: The University of Chicago Press.

Hedges, J.E. (1938) *Commercial Banking and the Stock Market Before 1863*, Baltimore: Johns Hopkins Press.

Helleiner, E. (1994) *States and the Reemergence of Global Finance: From Bretton Woods to the 1990s*, Ithaca: Cornell University Press.

Henwood, D. (1998) *Wall Street: How it Works and for Whom?*, London: Verso.

Hilferding, R. (1910/1981) *Finance Capital: A study of the Latest Phase of Capitalist Development*, London, Boston: Routledge and Kegan Paul.

Holman, O. (1998) 'Integrating Eastern Europe: EU Expansion and the Double Transformation in Poland, the Czech Republic, and Hungary', *International Journal of Political Economy* 28(2), Summer, 12–43.

Holman, O. (2005) 'The Enlargement of the European Union towards Central and Eastern Europe: The Role of Supranational and Transnational Actors', in Bieler, A. and Morton, D.A. (eds) *Social Forces in the Making of the New Europe*, New York: Palgrave.

Horst, C. and van Hear, N. (2002) 'Counting the Cost: Refugees, Remittances and the "War against Terrorism"', *Forced Migration Review* 14: 32–4.

House of Commons Treasury Select Committee (2004) *Restoring confidence in long-term savings: endowment mortgages*, Session 2003–04, House of Commons Paper 394, London: The Stationery Office.

Huertas, T.F. (1990) 'US multinational banking: history and prospects', in G. Jones (ed.) *Banks as Multinationals*, London/New York: Routledge.

Hull, E.D. and Annand, L. (1987) 'Time to Jump on the Securitization Bandwagon?', *ABA Banking Journal* 79: 137–9.

Hülsemeyer, A. (2000) 'Changing "Political Economies of Scale" and Public Sector Adjustment: Insights from Fiscal Federalism', *Review of International Political Economy* 7(1), Spring: 72–100.

Humphries, J. (2000) 'Rational Economic Families? Economics, the Family and the Economy', in Cook, J., Roberts, J. and Waylen, G. (eds) *Towards a Gendered Political Economy*, New York: St. Martin's Press, Inc.

Hunt, A. (1997) 'Moral panic and moral language in the media', *British Journal of Sociology*, 48: 634–6.

IMF (2000) 'Offshore Financial Centres', *IMF Background Paper*, June 2000, Monetary and Exchange Affairs Department.

IMF (2002) *Coordinated Portfolio Investment Survey Guide*, Second Edition, Washington DC: International Money Fund.

IMF (2002a) *The Statistical Definition of Offshore Financial Centres*, Meeting of the Inter-Agency Task Force on Finance Statistics, May 2–3, 2002, Statistics Department, Washington: IMF.

IMF (2002b) *Statistics on Offshore Financial Centres*, 5th Meeting of the IMF Committee on Balance of Payments Statistics, Canberra Australia, October 21–5, BOPCOM-02/11.

IMF (2004) *Balance of Payments Manual*, Washington DC: International Money Fund.

IMF (2005) *Global Financial Stability Report*, September, Washington, DC: International Monetary Fund.

Ireland, P. (1999) 'Company law and the myth of shareholder ownership', *Modern Law Review* 62: 32–57.

Ireland, P. (2000) 'Defending the rentier: corporate theory and the reprivatisation of the public company', in Parkinson, J., Gamble, A. and Kelly, G. (eds) *The Political Economy of the Company*, Oxford: Hart Publishing: 141–73.

Ize, A. and Parrado, E. (2002) Dollarisation, Monetary Policy and the Pass-Through, *IMF Working Paper*, No. 188, November 2002, Washington, DC: IMF.

Izquierdo, A.J. (2001) 'Reliability at Risk: the Supervision of Financial Models as a Case Study for Reflexive Economic Sociology', *European Societies* 3(1): 69–90.

Izvestia, Russia (20 July 2005) *'Zelenyie' na Sluiszbe FSB'* ['Greenbacks' at the FSB's Service].

James, J.A. (1995) 'The rise and fall of the commercial paper market, 1900–1929', in Bordo, M.D. and Sylla, R. (eds) *Anglo-American Financial Systems. Institutions and Markets in the Twentieth Century*, Burr Ridge/New York: Irwin Professional Publishing.

James, J.A. (1978) *Money and Capital Markets in Postbellum America*, Princeton, N.J.: Princeton University Press.

Johns, A. (1994) 'Not Tax Havens, Havens for Transnational Invisible Trade Enterprise', *Intereconomics* 29: 26–32.

Johnson, H. (1969) 'The Case for Flexible Exchange Rates', Federal Reserve Bank of St. Louis Review, Vol. 51, reprinted in Harry Johnson (1972), *Further Essays in Monetary Economics*, London: Allen and Unwin.

Johnson, P. (1998) *The Government of Money: Monetarism in Germany and the United States*, Ithaca: Cornell University Press.

Jones, C. (1994) *International Business in the Nineteenth Century: The Rise and Fall of a Cosmopolitan Bourgeoisie*, Wheatsheaf: Brighton.

Kabir, L. (2003) *Organizatsiya Ofshornogo Biznesa* [Organisation of Offshore Business], Moscow: Finance and Statistics.

Kager, M. (2002) 'The Banking System in the Accession Countries on the Eve of EU Entry', Department of Economics, Bank of Austria, February 2002.

Kashin, V. (1998) *Nalogovyie Soglasheniya Rossii: Meszdunarodnoe Nalogovoe Planirovanie dlya Predpriyatiy* [International Tax Connections for Russia: International Tax Planning for Companies and Individuals], Moscow: Finance Publishers/ Book-Publishing Association UNITY.

Keen, M. and Marchand, M. (1997) 'Fiscal Competition and the Pattern of Public Spending', *Journal of Public Economics*, No. 66: 33–53.

Kempson, E., Whyley, C., Caskey, J. and Collard, S. (2000) *In or Out? Financial Exclusion: a Literature and Research Review*, London: Financial Services Authority.

Kempson, E., Collard, S. and Moore, N. (2005) *Measuring Financial Capability: an Exploratory Study*, London: Financial Services Authority.

Kester, A. (1995) *Following the Money: US Finance in the World Economy*, Committee on National Statistics, National Academy Press, Washington D.C.

Keynes, J.M. (1925) 'The Economic Consequences of Mr. Churchill' Reprinted (1972) in Moggeridge, D. (ed.) *The Collected Works of J.M. Keynes*, XIII: 207–30, London: Macmillan.

Keynes, J.M. (1936) *The General Theory of Employment, Interest and Money*, London: Macmillan.

Keynes, J.M. (1937) 'The General Theory of Employment', *Quarterly Journal of Economics* 47.

Keynes, J.M. (1943) 'Shaping the Post-War World: The Clearing Union', reprinted (1972) in Moggeridge, D. (ed.) *The Collected Works of J.M. Keynes*, Vol. XXV, Activities 1940–44, Cambridge: Macmillan and Cambridge University Press for the Royal Economic Society.

Knights, D. (1997) 'Governmentality and Financial Services: Welfare Crises and the Financially Self-Disciplined Subject', in Morgan, G. and Knights, D. (eds) *Regulation and Deregulation in European Financial Service*, London: Macmillan Press Ltd.

Kompaniya (1999) No. 12 (60), 5 April, Russia.

Kommersant-Dengi (2001) Russia, No. 29, 25 July, Russia.

Kommersant-Dengi (2005) No. 28, 18 July 2005, Russia.

Komsomolskaya Pravda, 2003, 25 August, 5 and 8, *interview with the Head of the Federal Commission for Equity Market, Mr. Igor Kostikov*, www.kp.ru, Russia.

Konings, M. (2005a) 'Political institutions and economic imperatives: bringing agency back in', *Research in Political Economy*, Vol. 22, New York: JAI Press/Elsevier Science.

Konings, M. (2005b) 'The United States in the postwar global political economy: another look at the Brenner debate', in Coates, D. (ed.) *Varieties of Capitalism, Varieties of Approaches*, New York: Palgrave.

Korporatsiya, Russia (1998), No. 6: 26–7: '*Kalmykia – Territoriya Nalogovyih Lgot*' [Kalmykia is a Territory of Tax Preferences].

Krippner, G.R. (2003) *The fictitious economy: financialization, the state, and contemporary capitalism*, PhD thesis, University of Wisconsin-Madison.

Krugman, P. (1999) 'Labor Pains', *The New York Times Magazine*, 23 May, downloaded from http://web.mit.edu/krugman/www/.

Krugman, P. (2000) *The Return of Depression Economics*, London: Penguin.

Langevoort, D. (2002) 'Taming the Animal Spirits of the Stock Markets: A Behavioral Approach to Securities Regulation', 97 *NW.U.L.Rev*: 135.

Langley, P. (2002) *The Everyday Life of Global Finance*, IPEG paper in Global Political Economy 5, http://www.bisa.ac.uk/groups/ipeg/papers/PaulLangley.pdf.

Langley, P. (2004) 'In the Eye of the "Perfect Storm": The Final Salary Pensions Crisis and Financialisation of Anglo-American Capitalism', *Political Economy* 9: 539.

Lapidus, G. (1999) 'Asymmetrical Federalism and State Breakdown in Russia', *Post-Soviet Affairs* 15(1): 74–82.

Larner, W. (2006) 'Neoliberalism: Policy, Ideology and Governmentality', in de Goede, M. (ed.) *International Political Economy and Poststructural Politics*. London: Palgrave.

Laux, J.K. (2000) 'The Return to Europe: The Future Political Economy of Eastern Europe', in Stubbs, R. and Underhill, G.R.D. (eds) *Political Economy and the Changing Global Order*, Ontario: Oxford University Press.

Lavigne, M. (1999) *The Economics of Transition: from Socialist to Market Economy*, 2nd edn, Palgrave: Houndmills.

Lenin, V.I. (1916/1973) *Imperialism, The Highest Stage of Capitalism*, Peking: Foreign Language Press.

Lerner, F.H. (1990) 'Nonbank Banks: The Credit Card War', *Bankers Monthly*, 107: 34.

Levene, T. (2003) 'Why Rules Won't Wash on Money Laundering', *The Guardian Jobs and Money*, 28 June: 2–3.

Levi, M. (2003) 'Following the Criminal and Terrorist Money Trails', in van Duyne, P.C., von Lampe, K. and Newell, J.L. (eds) *Criminal Finances and Organising Crime in Europe*, Nijmegen: Wolf Legal Publishers.

Levi, M. and Wall, D.S. (2004) 'Technologies, Security, and Privacy in the Post-9/11 European Information Society', *Journal of Law and Society* 31(2): 194–220.

Levine, R. (1996) 'Foreign banks, financial development, and economic growth', in Claude, E.B. (ed.) *International Financial Markets*, Washington DC: AEI Press.

Levine, R. (1999) *Foreign Bank Entry and Capital Control Liberalization: Effects on Growth and Stability*, University of Minnesota, mimeo.

Levine, R. and Zervos, S. (1998) 'Stock Markets, Banks, and Economic Growth', *American Economic Review* 88(3): 537–58.

Levinson, P. (1982) 'The Federal Entrepreneur: The Nation's Implicit Industries' Policy', Washington, D.C.: Urban Institute.

Lewis, J. and Giullari, S. (2005) 'The Adult Worker Model Family, Gender Equality and Care: The Search for New Policy Principles and the Possibilities and Problems of a Capabilities Approach', *Economy and Society* 34: 76.

Lipietz, A. (1982) 'Towards Global Fordism', *New Left Review* I/132: 32–47.

Lipietz, A. (1987) *Mirages and Miracles: The Crises of Global Fordism*, English translation by Macey, D., London: Verso.

Lipsey, R. (1999) 'The Role of Foreign Direct Investment in International Capital Flows', *NBER Working Paper* 7094, April.

LiPuma, E. and Lee, B. (2004) *Financial Derivatives and the Globalization of Risk*, Durham: Duke University Press.

Loungani, P. and Mauro, P. (2000) 'Capital Flight from Russia', *IMF Policy Discussion Paper*, PDP/00/6, Washington, DC: IMF.

Lucas, P. (1994) 'The all-out battle for corporate bucks', *Credit Card Management* 6: 22–8.

Luckhaus, L. (2005) 'After "Deregulation": The Financial System in the 21st Century', Unpublished, on file with author.

Lyon, D. (2003) *Surveillance After September 11*, London: Polity.

MacKenzie, D. (2000) 'Fear in the Markets', *London Review of Books* April 13: 31–2.

MacKenzie, D. (2003) 'Long-Term Capital Management and the Sociology of Arbitrage', *Economy and Society* 32: 349–80.

MacKenzie, D. (2005) 'Opening the Black Boxes of Global Finance', *Review of International Political Economy* 12(4): 555–76.

MacKenzie, D. (2005a) 'How a Superportfolio Emerges: Long-Term Capital Management and the Sociology of Arbitrage', in Cetina, K.K. and Preda, A. (eds) *The Sociology of Financial Markets*, pp. 62–83, Oxford: Oxford University Press.

MacKenzie, D. (2005b) 'Models of Markets: Finance Theory and the Historical Sociology of Arbitrage', *Revue d'Histoire des Sciences* 57: 409–33.

MacKenzie, D. and Millo, Y. (2003) 'Constructing a Market, Performing Theory: the Historical Sociology of a Financial Derivatives Exchange', *American Journal of Sociology* 109: 107–45.

MacKenzie, D. (forthcoming) 'Mathematizing Risk: Models, Arbitrage and Crises', in Hutter, B. and Power, M. (eds) *Organizational Encounters with Risk*, Cambridge: Cambridge University Press.

Maki, D. and Palumbo, M. (2001) Disentangling the Wealth Effect: A Cohort Analysis of the Household Saving in the 1990s, Federal Reserve, Washington.

Mantas (2002) *The Comprehensive Remedy for a Wealth of Financial Industry Challenges*, White Paper, March. http://www.mantas.com/GlobalAssets/ PDF/WhitePapers/mantas_aml_solutions.pdf.

Mantas (2003) 'Money Laundering – Keep it Clean', *Banking Technology*, 30 November. http://www.mantas.com/NewsEvents/News/BankingTechnology113003.html

Markowitz, H.M. (1952) 'Portfolio Selection', *Journal of Finance* 7(1), March: 77–91.

Marx, K. (1973) *Grundrisse*, London: Penguin.

Maurer, B. (2005) 'Due Diligence and "Reasonable Man"', Offshore', *Cultural Anthropology* 20(4): 474–505.

McCarthy, C. (2005) *Speech to the Financial Inclusion Forum*, London, 27 June 2005, http://www.fsa.gov.uk/Pages/Library/Communication/Speeches/2005/0627_cm.shtml.

McFarlane, J. (2003) *Speech to ASIC Stakeholder Forum*, 24 July 2003. Available online: <http://www.anz.com/documents/au/aboutanz/John_McFarlane_speech.pdf> (accessed 07 December 2005).

McKinnon, R. (1973) *Money and Capital in Economic Development*, Washington DC: Brookings.

McKinsey and Co (2006) *Mapping the Global Capital Market 2006*, Second Annual Report, McKinsey Global Institute, McKinsey and Company.

McRobbie A. and Thornton, S. (1995) 'Rethinking "moral panic" for multi-mediated social worlds', *British Journal of Sociology* 46: 559–74.

Menshikov, S. (2004) *Anatomiya Rossiskogo Kapitalisma* [Anatomy of Russian Capitalism], Moscow: International Relations Publishers.

Merchant, K. (2000) 'International Capital Markets', *Financial Times*, 12 July.

Merryl Lunch (2005) EU Enlargement Study, March 2005.

Merton, R.C. (1973) 'Theory of Rational Option Pricing', *Bell Journal of Economics and Management Science* 4: 141–83.

Merton, R.K. (1949) 'The Self-Fulfilling Prophecy', in Merton, *Social Theory and Social Structure*, pp. 179–95, New York: Free Press.

Meulendyke, A.M. (1988) 'A Review of Federal Reserve Policy Targets and Operating Guides in Recent Decades', *Federal Reserve Bank of New York Quarterly Review* 13(3).

Meyercord, A. (1994) 'Recent trends in the profitability of credit card banks', *Federal Reserve Bank of New York Quarterly Review*, 19, Summer/Fall.

Michie, R.C. (1986) 'The London and New York Stock Exchanges, 1859–1914', *Journal of Economic History* 46(1).

Milios, J. (2005) 'European Integration as a Vehicle of Neoliberal Hegemony', in Saad-Filho, A. and Johnston, D. (eds) *Neoliberalism: a Critical Reader*, London: Pluto.

Minns, R. (2001) *The Cold War in Pensions*, London: Verso.

Minsky, H. (1991) 'Financial Crises: Systemic or Idiosyncratic', *Working Paper No. 51*, Jerome Levy Economics Institute, Bard College, April.

Minsky, H. (1993) 'Finance and Stability: The Limits of Capitalism', *Working Paper No. 93*, Jerome Levy Economics Institute, Bard College.

Mintel (1996) *Retirement Planning*, London: Mintel International Group Ltd.

Mitchell, O.S. and Utkus, S.P. (eds) (2004) *Pension Design and Structure. New Lessons from Behavioral Finance*, Oxford: Oxford University Press.

Mittelman, J. (1996) 'The Dynamics of Globalisation', in Mittelman, J. (ed.) *Globalisation: Critical Reflections*, pp. 1–20, Boulder, CO: Westview Press.

Miyazaki, H. (2003) 'The Temporalities of the Market', *American Anthropologist* 105: 255–65.

Montgomerie, J. (2006) 'The Financialisation of the American Credit Card Industry', *Competition and Change*, 10:3, December.

Monthly Review (2001) 'The new economy: myth and reality', *Editorial*, April, 52: 11.

Moran, M. (2003) *The British Regulatory State: High Modernism and Hyper-Innovation*, Oxford: Oxford University Press.

Moreno, R. and Villar, A. (2004) 'The Increased Role of Foreign Bank Entry in Emerging Markets', Bank of International Settlements Paper No. 23.

MORI Research conducted for the Institute of Financial Services (IFS), supplied to the authors by the IFS (2004). Summary available at: http://www.ifslearning.com/news/archive/newsreleases04/mori.htm

Mukhin, A. (2003) *Rossiyaskaya Organizovannaya Prestupnost i Vlast: Istoriya Vzaimootnosheniy* [Russian Organised Crime and the Authority: History of Relationships], Moscow: Centre for Political Information.

Munnell, A.H. and Sundén, A. (2004) *Coming Up Short: The Challenge of 401(k) Plans*, Washington: Brookings Institution Press.

Murphy, R. (2005) *The price of Offshore*, Tax Justice Network briefing paper (3/05). http://www.taxjustice.net/e/press/Price_of_Offshore.pdf.

Myers, M. (1951) 'The investment market after the Civil War', in H.F. Williamson (ed.) *The Growth of the American Economy*, Englewood Cliffs, N.J.: Prentice-Hall.

Myers, M.G. (1931) *The New York Money Market*, New York: Columbia University Press.

Myners, P. (2001) 'Institutional Investment in the United Kingdom: A Review', www.hm-treasury.gov.uk/mediastore/otherfiles/31.pdf.

Naaborj, I., Scholtens, B., Haan, J., Bol, H. and Hass, R. (2004) 'How Important are Foreign Banks in the Financial Development of European Transition Countries', *Journal of Emerging Market Finance* 3(2): 100–23.

National Council on Economic Education (NCEE) (1999) *The Standards in Economics Survey* (conducted by Louis Harris and Associates) New York: National Council on Economic Education.

Navias, M.S. (2002) 'Financial Warfare as a Response to International Terrorism', *The Political Quarterly* 73 (supplement 1): 57–79.

Naylor, R.T. (1987) *Hot Money* (2004 edition) London: Ithaca.

NCFC (National Council of Farmer Cooperatives) (1996) 'How to Start a Cooperative', Cooperative Information Report 7, Washington DC: NCFC.

Nesvetailova, A. (2004) 'The Logic of Neoliberal Finance and Global Financial Fragility: Towards another Great Depression?', *Research in Political Economy* 21: 61–90.

Nitzan, J. and Bichler, S. (2000) Capital Accumulation, in Palan, R. (ed.) *Global Political Economy. Contemporary Theories*, London: Routledge.

Noctor, M., Stoney, S. and Stradling, R. (1992) *Financial Literacy*, a report prepared for the National Westminster Bank, London: NatWest Bank.

Nofsinger, J.R. (2005) *The Psychology of Investing*, 2nd edn, New York: Pearson Prentice Hall.

Nugée, J. (2003) *Addressing Imbalances in Risk for Pension Fund Providers*, State Street Bank.

Nurkse, R. (1944) *International Currency Experience*, Geneva: League of Nations.

O'Brien, R. (1992) *Global Financial Institutions: The End of Geograph*, New York: Council of Foreign Press.

O'Harrow, R. (2005) *No Place to Hide*, New York: Free Press.

O'Malley, P. (1998) *Crime and the Risk Society*, London: Ashgate.

O'Malley, P. (2004) *Risk, Uncertainty and Government*, London: The GlassHouse Press.

O'Neill, P. (2001) 'Remarks Before the Extraordinary Plenary Meeting of the Financial Action Task Force', 29 October. http://www.ustreas.gov/press/releases/po735.htm.

Obstfeld, M. and Rogoff, K. (1995) 'The mirage of fixed exchange rates', *Journal of Economic Perspectives* 9(4): 73–96.

Obstfeld, M. (1998) 'The Global Capital Market: Benefactor or Menace?', *Journal of Economic Perspectives*, Fall 1998.

OECD (1999) *OECD Principles of Corporate Governance*, Paris: OECD.

OECD (2000) *OECD Economic Surveys: The Russian Federation*, Paris: OECD.

OECD (2004) 'OECD's Financial Education Project', *Financial Market Trends* 87 (Paris: OECD) 223–229. Also available online: http://www.oecd.org/dataoecd/28/36/ 33865427.pdf (accessed 07 December 2005).

OECD (2005) *Improving Financial Literacy*, Paris: OECD.

Oomes, N. (2003) 'Network Externalities and Dollarisation Hysteresis: The Case of Russia', *IMF Working Paper*, No. 03/96, Washington, DC: International Monetary Fund.

Overbeek, H. (2000) 'Transnational Historical Materialism: Theories of Transnational Class Formation and World Order', in Palan, R. (ed.) *Global Political Economy: Contemporary Theories*, pp. 168–183, London and New York: Routledge.

Padoa-Schioppa, T. (2004) Member of the Executive Board of the European Central Bank, Speech at Colloquium organised by Groupe Caisse des Dépôts/KfW, Berlin, 22 March 2004. Available Online: http://www.ecb.int/press/key/date/2004/html/ sp040322.en.html

Palan, R. (1998) 'Luring Buffaloes and the game of industrial subsidies: a critique of national competitive policies in the era of the competition state' mandatory changes, *Global Society* 12: 3.

Palan, R. (2003) *The Offshore World: Sovereign Markets, Virtual Places, and Nomad Millionaires*, Ithaca, NY: Cornell UP.

Palan, R. (2006) 'Norms, Sovereignty and the American Empire' in Giesen, K. and Van Der Pijl, K. (eds) *Global Norms for the 21st Century: Political, Science, Philosophy, Law*, Cambridge: Cambridge Scholar Press.

Pijl, K.V.D. (2006) 'A Lockean Europe?', *New Left Review* 37, Jan/February.

Panitch, L. and Gindin, S. (2004) *Global Capitalism & American Empire*, London: The Merlin Press.

Parish, S. (1996) 'Centre Continues to Rail against Legal Separatism', *OMRI Russian Regional Report* 11(3).

Parsons, T. and Smelser, N.J. (1956, 1998) *Economy and Society: A Study in the Integration of Economic and Social Theory*, London: Routledge and Kegan Paul.

Passas, N. (2005) *Informal Value Transfer Systems and Criminal Activities*, Cahier 2005–1, Wetenschappelijk Onderzoek en Documentatiecentrum, Dutch Ministry of Justice, http://www.wodc.nl/images/ca2005-1%20Full%20text_tcm11-74024.pdf.

Paul, D. (2002) 'Re-scaling IPE: Sub-national States and the regulation of the Global Political Economy', *Review of International Political Economy* 9(3): 465–89.

Peck, A. (1985) 'The Economic Role of Traditional Commodity Futures Markets', in Anne Peck (ed.) *Futures Markets: Their Economic Role*, Washington DC: American Enterprise Institute.

Peggs, K. (2000) 'Which Pension?: Women, Risk and Pension Choice', *The Sociological Review* 48(3): 249.

Pensions Commission (2004) *Pensions: Challenges and Choices*, The First Report of the Pensions Commission, London: The Stationery Office.

Pensions Commission (2005) *A New Pension Settlement for the Twenty-First Century*, The Second Report of the Pensions Commission, London: The Stationery Office.

Perold, A. (1999) *Long-Term Capital Management, L.P.* Boston, Mass.: Harvard Business School Publishing.

Persaud, A. (2000) *Sending the Herd off the Cliff Edge: The disturbing interaction between herding and market-sensitive risk management practices*. Winner of the Institute of International Finance's Jacques de Larosiere Awards in Global Finance 2000.

Persaud, A. (2004) *Liquidity Black Holes: Understanding, Measuring and Managing Financial Market Liquidity*, Risk Books.

Peterson, S.V. (2003) *A Critical Rewriting of Global Political Economy*, London: Routledge.

Phillips, S.M. (1996) 'The place of securitization in the financial system: implications for banking and monetary policy', in Kendall, L.T. and Fishman, M.J. (eds) *A Primer on Securitization*, Cambridge: MA/London: MIT Press.

Picciotto, S. (1999) 'Offshore: the State as Legal Fiction', in Hampton, M. and Abbott, J. (eds) *Offshore Finance Centres and Tax Havens: The Rise of Global Capital*, Basingstoke: Macmillan.

Pieth, M. (2002) 'Financing of Terrorism: Following the Money', *European Journal of Law Reform* 4(2): 365–76.

Piketty, T., Saez, E. (2003) 'Income Inequality in the United States, 1913–1998', *The Quarterly Journal of Economics* CXVIII(1): 1–39.

Platt, D. (1980) 'British Portfolio Investment Overseas before 1870: Some Doubts', *The Economic History Review* 33, February: 1–16.

Poole, W. and Rasche, R. (2000) *Perfecting the market's knowledge of monetary policy*, Working Paper 2000-010A, Federal Reserve Bank of St. Louis.

Price, L. (1987) 'Discussion of Contagion Threats in the Interbank Market', in Portes, R. and Swoboda, A. (eds) *Threats to International Financial Stability*, Cambridge University Press: Cambridge.

Pryke, M. and Lee, R. (1995) 'Place your bets: towards an understanding of globalization, socio-financial engineering and competition within a financial centre', *Urban Studies* 32(2): 329–44.

Racocha, P. (2003) 'Joining the EU – Impact on the Financial Sector of New Member States', *National Europe Centre, Working Paper No. 117*.

Radice, H. (1998) 'Globalisation and National Differences', *Competition and Change*, 3(4): 263–91.

Rafferty, M. (2003) 'The Internationalisation of Banking: Portfolio or foreign direct investment? Some implications from the recent merger boom', in Lönnborg, M., Olsson, M., Rafferty, M. and Nalson, I. (eds) *Money and Finance in Transition – Research in Contemporary and Historical Finance*, Sodertorns Hogskola.

Raghavan, C. (2000) 'US Farm Subsidies Favor Large Corporate Farms', prepared by the *Third World Network*, 8 May 2000.

Raven, F. (2005) *Financial Literacy: A Basic Skill for Social Mobility*, EDC Center for Media and Community, 25 May 2005, http://www.digitaldivide.net/articles/view.php?ArticleID=420 (accessed 7 December 2005).

Reid, Julian (2005) 'The Biopolitics of the War on Terror', *Third World Quarterly* 26(2): 237–52.

Reidl, B. (2004) 'Another year at the Federal Trough', Heritage Foundation, Backrounder #1763, 24 May 2004, http://www.heritage.org/Research/Budget/bg1763.cfm (accessed on 6/30/06).

Reininger, T., Schardax, F. and Summer, M. (2001) 'The Financial System in the Czech Republic, Hungary and Poland after a Decade of Transition', Economic Research Centre, *Deutsche Bundesbank working paper 16/01*.

Ricardo, D. (1821) *Principles of Political Economy and Taxation*, London: John Murray.

Rifkin, J. (2000) *The Age of Access. How the Shift form Ownership to Access is Transforming Capitalism*, London, New York: Penguin Books.

Ring, P. (2003) '"Risk" and UK Pension Reform', *Social Policy and Administration* 37: 65.

Rittich, K. (1998) '*Recharacterizing Restructuring: Gender and Distribution in the Legal Structure of Market Reform*', SJD dissertation, Harvard Law School.

Ritzer, G. (1995) *Expressing America: A Critique of the Global Credit Card Society*, Thousand Oaks, California: Pine Forge Press.

Roach, S. (2001) 'Back to Borders', *Financial Times*, 28 September.

Roberts, M. (1995) 'Small Place, Big Money: The Cayman Islands and the International Financial System', *Economic Geography*, Vol. 71, Jul: 237–56.

Rogaly, B., Fisher, T. and Mayo, E. (1999) *Poverty, Social Exclusion and Microfinance in Britain*, Oxford: Oxfam.

Rose, N. (1999) *Powers of Freedom: Reframing Political Thought*, Cambridge: Cambridge University Press.

Ross, C. (2000) 'Federalism and Democratisation in Russia', *Communist and Post-Communist Studies* 33: 403–20.

Ross, S.A. (2001) 'Neoclassical and Alternative Finance', *EFMA Meetings*, keynote address.

Roszkowski, M., Michael, J. and Cordell, D.M. (2004) 'The Comparability of Husbands and Wives of Financial Risk Tolerance', *Journal of Personal Finance* 3(3): 129.

Roy, W.G. (1997) *Socializing Capital. The Rise of the Large Industrial Corporation in America*, Princeton: Princeton University Press.

Rude, C. (2004) 'The Volcker monetary policy shocks: a political-economic analysis', Department of Economics, New School University.

Rude, C. (2005) 'The role of financial discipline in imperial strategy', in Panitch, L. and Leys, C. (eds) *Socialist Register 2005*, London: Merlin Press.

Saber, N. (1999) *Speculative Capital. The Invisible Hand of Global Finance*, London, Edinburgh: Pearson Education.

SAFE (Services Against Financial Exclusion) (November 2005) Toynbee Hall, *Banking the Unbanked: a Snapshot*.

Samoylenko, V. (2004) 'Government Policies for Internal Tax Havens in Russia', *Tax Notes International*, 5 April, 2004, 77–86.

Samuelson, P. (2001) 'Progress and Pitfalls in the State of Modern Finance Theory', *Typescript of talk at Renaissance Technologies*, 24 May, New York: East Setauket.

Sanders, E. (1999) *Roots of reform. Farmers, workers and the American state, 1877–1917*, Chicago/London: Chicago University Press.

Sassen, S. (1991) *The Global City: London, New York, Tokyo*. Princeton: Princeton University Press.

Sassen, S. (1999) 'Embedding the Global in the National: Implications for the Role of the State', in Smith, D.A., Solinger, D.J. and Topik, S.C. (eds) *States and Sovereignty in the Global Economy*, pp. 159–71, London: Routledge.

Schagen, S. and Lines, A. (1996) *Financial Literacy in Adult Life: a Report to the NatWest Group Charitable Trust*, Slough: NFER.

Schmitz, B. (2004) 'What Role do Banks Play in Monetary Policy Transmission in EU New Member Countries?', Centre for European Integration Studies, University of Bonn.

Scholte, J. and Schnable, A. (eds) (2002) *Civil Society and Global Finance*, London: Routledge.

Schor, J. (1999) *The Overspent American: Why We Want What We Don't Need?*, New York: HarperPerennia.

Seabrooke, L. (2001) *US Power in International Finance: The Victory of Dividends*, New York: Palgrave.

Searchspace (2004) 'Searchspace to Demonstrate Fast-Track AML Solution', http://www.searchspace.com/news/showPress.php?id=69.

Semenov, G. (1995) '*Razvitie Svobodnyih Ekonomicheskih I Offshornyih Zon*' [Development of Free Economic and Offshore Zones], Rossiiski Ekonomicheskiy Szurnal [*Russian Economic Journal*], No. 11: 33–44.

Semenov, S. (2003) 'De-Dollarisation in Russia', *Vremya*, 7 August 2003.

Sen, A. (1988) *Ethics and Economics*, Oxford: Blackwell.

Sen, A. (1992) *Inequality Reexamined*, Cambridge, MA: Harvard University Press.

Sen, A. (1999) *Development as Freedom*, New York: Random House.

Seurot, F. (1996) *Les Causes économiques de la Fin de l'Empire Soviétique*, Paris: Presses Universitaires de France.

Shapiro, M.J. (2002) 'Wanted, Dead or Alive', *Theory and Event* 5(4).

Shaw, E.S. (1973) *Financial Deepening in Economic Development*, New York: Oxford.

Shleifer, A. and Treisman, D. (2000) *Without a Map: Political Tactics and Economic Reform in Russia*, Cambridge, MA: The MIT Press.

Shleifer, A. and Vishny, R.W. (1997) 'The Limits of Arbitrage', *Journal of Finance* 52: 35–55.

Shuey, K.M. and O'Rand, A.M. (2004) 'New Risks for Workers: Pensions, Labor Markets, and Gender', *Annual Review of Sociology* 30: 453.

Sikka, P. (2003) 'The Role of Offshore Financial Centres in Globalisation', *Accounting Forum* 27(4): 365–99.

Simensen, I. (2006) 'Emerging market fund inflows soar', *Financial Times*, 2 January/ 1 February 2006.

Simotas, G. and Weisel, J. (1991) 'Credit Card Portfolios on the Auction Block', *Bankers Monthly* 108: 15.

Simpson, B. (2005) 'Exclusive bank card profitability study and annual report', *Credit Card Management* 18: 26–35.

Simpson, T.D. (1992) 'Features of the new financial system in the United States', in Henry Cavanna (ed.) *Financial Innovation*, London/New York: Routledge.

Singh, A. and Weisse, B. (1998) 'Emerging Stock Markets, Corporate Finance, and Economic Growth: Micro and Macroeconomic Perspectives', *World Development* 26(4).

Slovic, P. (1999) 'Trust, Emotion, Sex, Politics, and Science: Surveying the Risk-Assessment Battlefield', *Risk Analysis* 19: 689.

Smith, A. (1776 [2000]) *The Wealth of Nations*, New York: Random House.

Smith, B. (2005) 'OECD's Financial Education Project: Improving Financial Literacy and Capability', Speech for *Canadians and Their Money: A National Symposium on Financial Capability*, Ottawa, 9–10 June 2005. http://policyresearch.gc.ca/doclib/FCAC/Session%205%20Barbara%20Smith.pdf (accessed 12 December 2005).

Soederberg, S. (2005) *The Politics of the New International Financial Architecture: Reimposing Neoliberal Domination in the Global South*, London, New York: Zed Books.

Solnick, S. (1998) *Stealing the State: Control and Collapse in Soviet Institutions*, Cambridge, MA: Harvard University Press.

Sosic, V, and Faulend, M. (2002) 'Dollarisation and the Underground Economy: Accidental Partners?', *Institute of Public Finance Occasional Paper*, No. 15, April 2002.

Sprague, O.M.W. (1910) *History of Crises under the National Banking System*, National Monetary Commission, Government Printing Office, Washington.

Stabile, S.J. (2002) 'The Behavior of Defined Contribution Plan Participants', *New York University Law Review* 77: 71.

Steinherr, A. (1998) *Derivatives: The Wild Beast of Finance*, New York: John Wiley and Sons.

Stern, G.H. and Feldman, R. (2004) *Too Big To Fail: The Hazards of Bank Bailouts*, Brookings Institution Press.

Stoner-Weiss, K. (1997) *Local Heroes: The Political Economy of Russian Regional Governance*, Princeton, NJ: Princeton University Press.

Strange, S. (1997) *Casino Capitalism*, Manchester: Manchester University Press.

Strange, S. (1998) *Mad Money*, Manchester: Manchester University Press.

Strange, Susan (1986) *Casino Capitalism*, London: Basil Blackwell.

Sunstein, C.R. (2000) *Behavioral Law and Economics*, Cambridge: Cambridge University Press.

Svedberg, P. (1978) 'The Portfolio Direct Composition of Private Foreign Investment in 1914 Revisited', *Economic Journal* 88, December, 690–722.

Sylla, R. (2002) 'United States banks and Europe: strategy and attitudes', in Battilossi, S. and Cassis, Y. (eds) *European banks and the American challenge. Competition and cooperation in international banking under Bretton Woods*, Oxford: Oxford University Press.

Szaparáy, G. (2005) 'Development of credit markets in new member states and implications for the transmission of monetary policy', *Paper presented in Finance and Consumption Conference*, IUE, Florence, October, 2005.

Taylor, J.B. (2001) 'Expectations, open market operations, and changes in the federal funds rate', Federal Reserve Bank of St. Louis Review, July/August.

Temple, P. (2001) *Hedge Funds: The Courtesans of Capitalism*, Chichester: John Wiley and Sons.

The Economist (2001) 'Through the Wringer', 12 April 12: 7–12.

The Economist (2005) Global Agenda, the Buttonwood Column: 'Different This Time? Foreigners are again pouring cash into emerging markets. What will happen when they stop?' 23 August 2005.

The Economist, (2002) 'Bubble trouble, and what policymakers should do about it', *Survey of International Finance*, 16 September.

Thompson, E.P. (1963) *The Making of the English Working Class*, London: V. Gollancz.

Tickell, A. (2000) 'Unstable Futures: Creating Risk in International Finance', *Geoforum* 31(1): 87–99.

Tilly, R. (1986) 'German Banking 1850–1914: development assistance for the strong', *Journal of European Economic History* 15: 1.

Toporowski, J. (2005) 'Neoliberalism: The Eastern European Frontier' in Saad-Filho, A. and Johnston, D. (eds) *Neoliberalism: a Critical Reader*, London: Pluto.

TPAC, Technology and Privacy Advisory Committee (March, 2004) *Safeguarding Privacy in the Fight Against Terrorism*.

Tschoegl, A. (2000) 'International Banking Centers, Geography, and Foreign Banks', *Financial Markets, Institutions and Instruments*, January 2000: 1–32.

Tut.by Belarus (17 November 2005), www.tut.by, http://news.tut.by/economics/60199.html. Accessed 19 November 2005.

UN Security Council (2002) *Second report of the Monitoring Group established pursuant to Security Council Resolution 1363 (2001) and extended by resolution 1390 (2002)*, 19 September. http://www.un.org/docs/sc/committees/1267/1050E02.pdf

USDA (1997) 'Co-ops 101: An Introduction to Cooperatives', Cooperative Information Report 55, http://www.rurdev.usda.gov/rbs/pub/cir55/cir55rpt.htm (accessed on 30th June 2006).

USDA (2001) 'Characteristics and Production Costs of US Corn Farms', Prepared by the USDA Economic Research Service, Statistical Bulletin # 974, http://www.ers.usda.gov/publications/sb974-1/sb974-1.pdf (accessed on 6/30/06).

USDA (2002a) 'Agricultural Factbook, 2001–2', Washington DC: GPO.

USDA (2002b) *Agricultural Census*, Washington DC: National Agricultural Statistical Service.

USDA (2005) 'Farmers' Reported Use of Risk Management Strategies', in *Managing Risks in Farming: Concepts, Research and Analysis*, Agricultural Economics Report No. AER774, Washington DC.

USGPO (2003) Transcript of the hearing before the House Subcommittee on General Farm Commodities and Risk Management on the Commodity Futures Modernization Act, US House of Representatives, Committee on Agriculture, Washington DC: USGPO.

Ushakov, D. (2001) 'Ofshornye Zony v Praktike Rossiyskih Nalogoplatelschikov' [Offshore Zones in Practice of Russian Tax-Payers], Moscow: Jurist.

Vaknin, S. (2003) *'Processing the Export Zones'*, 2 October 2003, http://www.buzzle.com/editorials. Accessed 17 February 2005.

Valverde, M. and Mopas, M. (2004) 'Insecurity and the Dream of Targeted Governance', in Larner, W. and Walters, W. (eds) *Global Governmentality: Governing International Spaces*, London: Routledge.

van der Pijl, K. (2006) 'France's European Predicament. From the "No" in the Constitutional Referendum to the Revolt of the *Banlieue*', Forthcoming, *New Left Review*, Jan/Feb 2006.

Van Fenstermaker, J. (1965) *The development of American commercial banking: 1782–1837*, Kent, Ohio: Bureau of Economic and Business Research.

van Munster, R. (2004) 'The War on Terrorism: When the Exception Becomes the Rule', *International Journal for the Semiotics of Law* 17: 141–53.

Veblen, T. (1899) *The Theory of the Leisure Class*, London: The Macmillan Company.

Veblen T. (1924) *Absentee Ownership and Business Enterprise in Recent Times*, London: George Allen and Unwin.

Veblen, T. (1923) *Absentee Ownership and Business Enterprise In Recent Times. The Case of America*, With An Introduction By Robert Leckachman, Boston: Beacon Press.

Veblen, T. (1961) *The Theory of Business Enterprise*, New York: Augustus M. Kelly.

Vedomosti, Russia (22 August 2002) www.vedomosti.ru. Accessed 19 October 2004.

Vergara, O. *et al.* (2001) 'Understanding Limited Resource Farmer's Risk Management Decision Making', Mississippi State University, Department of Agricultural Economics.

Veysey, S. (2002) 'Shift from DB Plans Continuing in the U.K.', *Business Insurance* 36(32).

Viksnins, G. (1980) *Financial Deepening in ASEAN Countries*, Honolulu: University Press of Hawaii.

Volcker, P. and Goyhten, T. (1992) *Changing Frontiers: The World's Money and the Threat to American Leadership*, New York: Times Books.

Volcker, P. (2000) 'Commanding Heights' interview with Paul Volcker on PBS radio, transcript 26 September, downloaded from: http://www.pbs.org/wgbh/commandingheights/shared/minitextlo/int_paulvolcker.html.

Volcker, P. (2002) 'Monetary policy transmission: past and future challenges', Federal Reserve Bank of New York Economic Policy Review, May.

Vosko, L.F. (2000) *Temporary Work: The Gendered Rise of a Precarious Employment Relationship*, Toronto: University of Toronto Press.

Walby, S. (2000) 'The Restructuring of the Gendered Political Economy: Transformations in Women's Employment', in Cook, J., Roberts, J. and Waylen, G. (eds) *Towards a Gendered Political Economy*, New York: St. Martin's Press, Inc.

Walker, R. (1989) 'A Requiem for Corporate Geography: New directions in industrial organization, the production of place and the uneven development', *Geografiska Annaler*, Series B, *Human Geography* 71(1): 43–68.

Warburton, P. (2000) *Debt and Delusion*, Penguin Books.

Warnock, F. and Cleaver, C. (2002) Financial Centres and The Geography of Capital Flows, Board of Governors of the Federal Reserve System, *International Finance Discussion Papers, No. 722*, April.

Warnock, F. and Mason, M. (2000) The Geography of Capital Flows: What We Can Learn From Benchmark Surveys of Foreign Equity Holdings, Board of Governors of the Federal Reserve System, *International Finance Discussion Papers, No. 688*, December.

Warren, T. (2003) 'A Privileged Pole? Diversity in Women's Pay, Pensions and Wealth in Britain', *Gender, Work and Organization* 10: 615.

Washington Post (23 March 1999) *'Russian IMF Loans Routed Through Offshore Company'*, by David Hoffman.

Waylen, G. (2000) 'Gendered Political Economy and Feminist Analysis', in Cook, J., Roberts, J. and Waylen, G. (eds) *Towards a Gendered Political Economy*, New York: St. Martin's Press, Inc.

Wechsler, W.F. (2001) 'Follow the Money', *Foreign Affairs* 80(4): 40–57.

Weinstein, J. (1968) *The Corporate Ideal in the Liberal State, 1900–1918*, Boston: Beacon Press.

West, R.C. (1973) *Banking Reform and the Federal Reserve, 1863–1923*, Ithaca: Cornell University Press.

Westra R., Zuege A. (ed.) (2004) *Value and the World Economy Today. Production, Finance and Globalization*, London, Basingstoke: Palgrave.

Wheelock, D.C. (1989) 'The strategy, effectiveness, and consistency of Federal Reserve monetary policy 1924–1933', *Explorations in Economic History*, 26.

Wheelock, D.C. (1991) *The Strategy and Consistency of Federal Reserve Monetary Policy, 1924–1933*, Cambridge: Cambridge University Press.

White, E.N. (1998) 'Were banks special intermediaries in late nineteenth century America?', Federal Reserve Bank of St. Louis Review, May/June.

White, H.C. (1981) 'Where Do Markets Come From?', *American Journal of Sociology* 87: 517–47.

White, H.C. (2001) *Markets from Networks*. Princeton, N.J.: Princeton University Press.

Whitehouse, E. (2000) *Pension Reform, Financial Literacy and Public Information: a Case Study of the United Kingdom, Social Protection Unit Discussion Paper 0004*, Washington DC: World Bank.

Williams, E.E. (1896) *Made in Germany*, London: Heinemann.

Williams, J. (2000) *Unbending Gender: Why Family and Work Conflict and What to Do About It*, Oxford: Oxford University Press.

Williams, K. (2000) 'From shareholder value to present day capitalism', *Economy and Society* 29: 1–12.

Williamson, H.F. (1951) 'Money and commercial banking', in Williamson, H.F. (ed.) *The Growth of the American Economy*, Englewood Cliffs, N.J.: Prentice-Hall.

Wojnilower, A.M. (1987) 'Financial change in the United States', in De Cecco, M. (ed.) *Changing Money. Financial Innovation in Developed Countries*, Oxford/New York: Basil Blackwell.

Wolters, T. (2000) '"Carry your credit in your pocket": The early history of the credit card at Bank of America and Chase Manhattan', *Enterprise and Society* 1: 315–31.

Worthington, S. (1997) 'Affinity credit card issuers and their relationship with their alumni affinity group partners', *The International Journal of Bank Marketing* 15: 39.

Yao, R. and Hanna, S.D. (2005) 'The Effect of Gender and Marital Status on Financial Risk Tolerance', *Journal of Personal Finance* 4(1): 66.

Young, J. (1971) *The Drugtakers: The Social Meaning of Drug Use,* London: Paladin.

Zanglein, J.E. (2001) 'Investment Without Education: The Disparate Impact on Women and Minorities in Self-Directed Defined Contribution Plans', *Employee Rights* Bailey, *and Employment Policy Journal* 5(1): 223.

Zysman, J. (1983) *Governments, Markets, and Growth. Financial Systems and the Politics of Industrial Change,* Ithaca/London: Cornell University Press.

Index

Abramovich, Roman, 166
Accenture, 199
accounting indicators, in capitalist system
  accounting profession and declared profits, 185–91
  concept of property, 178–81
  profits and subsidies, 183–5
  tax and profits, 181–3
Adult Financial Literacy Advisory Group (AdFLAG), 82
ADVANTA Corporation, 110
Affinity credit cards, 107, 109–10
agricultural sector, 55, see also derivatives
Air Miles card, 109
al-Qaeda, 196, 204
American banking system, see US financial system
American commercial paper market, 154
American Express bank, 103, 110
American Express card, 105–6
American open market system, 8
ANZ survey of 2003, 85–7
Arber, 90
arbitrage, study of
  in hedge fund, 14
  in orthodox finance theory, 18
  as parameter of market efficiency, 15–16
  in spot markets, 14
  'superportfolio', 19
  theory of pricing of derivatives, 14–15
  third feature of, 22–3
ASB era, 186
Asian financial crisis, of 1997, 39
Assassi, Libby, see financial regulation
asset-backed securities (ABS), 107
Association of Consulting Actuaries, 91
'asymmetric federalism', 175
AT&T, 110
9/11 attacks, 193, 195, 200, 202
Aufhauser, 199

Bajtelsmit, 91
Balance of Payments, 39, 41, 45–7
Banca Antonveneta, 121
Bank Americard, 105
bankers' balances, 153
bankers capitalism, 180
Bank for International Settlements (BIS), 13, 42, 142
Bank of America, 106
Bank of England, 13
'banks' Tier 1 capital ratios, 14
Barings Bank, 216
Basle Capital Accord, 196, 216
Bayou Management, 39
BCCI, 216
biopower, 198
Black, Fischer, 15–16, 18
Black-Scholes 'backwards' option pricing model, 16, 18
Blair, Tony, 76–7
Bloomingdale, Alfred, 103
Blunkett, David, 82
bourgeoisie, 134, 139
Breger, Sasha, see derivatives
Bretton Woods Agreement, 29–31, 138, 141, see also gold
Bridgestone Tyre Company, 186
British Airways, 181
British Board of Film Classification, 214
Bromwich, Michael, 178, 185, 190
Bush, George W., 196
business principles, 181
business taxation, 181–2

Cadbury report, 77–8
capabilities gap, see derivative contracts trading, empirical analysis of
capital accumulation, process of, 4
capitalist class, 141
Caribbean UK Crown colony, 13
Carnegie, Andrew, 179
CE3, 122, 124
Central Bank of Russia, 167, 172

Central European Societies, financial
  regulations on, *see also*
  neoliberalism
  European integration, effects of,
    119–22
  foreign ownership and regulations of,
    122–6
  from industrial-led to financial-led
    growth, 115–19
certificate of deposit (CD), 158
Cetina, Knorr, 24
Chase Charge-it Card, 105
Chase Manhattan Bank, 106
Chicago Board of Trade (CBOT), 60
Churchill, Winston, 29
Citigroup, 81
Civil War, 153–4
class patterns, 128, *see also* neoliberalism
Cleaver, 52
Coates, Nick, *see* global finance, patterns
  of; offshore financial centres (OFCs)
Cohen, 76
Commodity Futures Modernisation Act,
  61
Competitive Equality Company Act, 110
consumer optimism, 8
cooperatives, *see* derivative contracts
  trading, empirical analysis of
Coordinated Portfolio Investment
  Survey (CPIS), 39, *see also* global
  finance, patterns of; offshore
  financial centres (OFCs)
corporate income gearing, 14
Coward, Martin, 196
credit cards industry
  formation of universal credit card,
    103–7
  securitisation and profitability of,
    107–11
credit default swaps, 13
credit supply mechanism, 8
crisis, financial crisis, 39
cross-border portfolio investment flows,
  see global finance, patterns of
Cutler, 92–3

'defined benefit' (DB) pension plan, 72,
  89, 97
'defined contribution' (DC) pension
  plan, 72, 89

choice of, 95–100
gendered approach of, 94–5
political economy of, 91–3
risk factors and gender differences of,
  95–100
de Goede, Marieke, 97, 99, *see also*
  financial regulation, and terrorism
deregulation, of finance, *see* financial
  regulation
derivative contracts trading, empirical
  analysis of
  capabilities gap, 66–8
  cooperatives, 65–6
  farmer utilisation of risk management
    strategies, 61
  mini-futures contract, 61–5
  monthly volume for commodity
    futures in Chicago, 64
  open interest on commodity futures,
    65
  standard contract, 61
derivatives, 26, 32–5
  and agricultural sector, 55–8
  Bretton Woods agreement, 29–31
  consequences of trading in, 60–8
  corn and wheat futures trading, 60–8
  dimensions of, 33
  farming in America, 58–60
  and gold standard, 27–9
  implication for small farmers,
    agricultural policy and developing
    countries, 68–9
  as a latent anchor in market, 32–5
  proposition on, 26–7
  shift to floating exchange rates, 31–2
Diners Club Card, 103, 105–6
direct inflation targeting (DIT), 120
direct investors, 40
discount market, 152–3
Dixon, 42
Doha Round, of trade talks, 68
'dollarisation' practices, 167
dot.com boom, 24, 212
Drucker, Peter, 4–5
Duménil, Gérard, 73, *see also*
  neoliberalism

Easton, David, 177
Edkins, Jenny, 196
Efficient Market Hypothesis (EMH), 2

Eichengreen, 28
Employment Act 1946, 141
'enclosed administrative territories', 170
Enron, 78, 183
Environmental Working Group, 59
episodic panic, 78
Equitable Life crisis, 79
Eurodollar markets, 43
Eurofinance markets, 30
Euromarket, 158–61
European Common Agricultural Policy,
    56
European Monetary System, in 1992, 39
European State system, 181
'Executive Order on Terrorist Financing',
    194

Fair and Accurate Credit Transaction Act
    (FACT), 81–2
'fair lending practices', 104
farmers and derivative market, *see*
    derivatives
farming, in America
    distribution pattern of land, sales and
        government payments, 59
    farm size, 59
    small farm finances, 59–60
Federal Open Market Committee
    (FOMC), 159
Federal Reserve Act, 156
Federal Treaties 1992, 173
feminisation, of pensions, *see* 'defined
    benefit' (DB) pension plan; 'defined
    contribution' (DC) pension plan
finance and management, of France and
    US, *see* neoliberalism
Financial Accounting Standards Board
    (FASB), 185
Financial Action Task Force (FATF),
    194–5, 200
financial 'beauty contest', 5, 10
financial capitalism, characteristics of, 7
financial deepening, 56
    salvation by, 57–8
financial illiteracy
    economic panics under
        neoliberalisation with
        responsibility, 75–9
    and intercapability of problems, 81–3
    proposition on surveys of, 83–4
    as weakness of epsodic drivers, 79–83

financial inclusion, 71, 203
financial institutions, 7
financial instruments, 7
financialisation, 2, 3, 9, 72, 73, 89, 100,
    159, 162
financial literacy, 74–5, 79–81
Financial Literacy and Education
    Commission, 82
Financial Passport scheme, 121
financial regulation
    alternative approaches to, 212–14
    emergence of global capitalism, 5
    emergence of technology, 8
    financial capitalism, characteristics of,
        7
    financialisation as pillar of neoliberal
        globalisation, 3–4
    financial transformation on risk
        factors, 6
    fundamental characteristics of
        changed world economy, 4
    Keynesian concept of specialisation,
        6–7
    post-1993 explosion of financial
        operations, 5–6
    process of capital accumulation, 4
    protecting financial consumers,
        214–15
    supervision of financial institution,
        208–12
    systemic risks in, 215–17
financial regulation, and terrorism
    financial citizenship and account
        usage, 202–4
    regulation and risk, 196–9
    terrorist finance, 194–5
    transaction monitoring, 199–202
Financial Reporting Standard 18 on
    Accounting Policies, 187
financial scandals, 2
Financial Services Action Plan (FSAP),
    120–1
Financial Services Authority, 71, 76
Financial Stability Review, parameters of
    arbitrage, 14–16
    long term capital management, 16–20
Financial Times, 58
First USA, 110
'flight-to-quality' concept, 19
floating exchange rates, 31–2
Ford, 109, 183

Fordism, 5, 7, 92, 103–6
Ford Motor Company, 110
Foreign Direct Investment (FDIs), 40, 122, 184
foreign exchange reserves, of China and South Korea, 13
Foucault, Michel, 198–9
French Regulation School, 114
Friedman, Milton, 57
Froud, Julie, *see* financial illiteracy
fundamental value, concept of, 32–3

Garcia, Virginia, 201
Gates, Bill, 180
'gendered political economy', 90–1
General Electric, 109
General Electric Capital Corporation, 110
General Farm Commodities and Risk Management committee, 61–2
General Motors, 9, 109, 216
general panic, 78
generic 'farmer', *see* derivatives
G7 government bonds, 13
Ginn, 90
Glass-Steagall Act, 104
global capital accumulation, 25, 36
global finance, patterns of
  emergence of OFCs, 41–7
  foreign investment and finance, measurement of, 40–1
  geographic network analysis of portfolio capital flows, 47–51
global financial sphere
  in the late 19th century, 26–7
  mathematic models in, 5–6
  post-1973, 5
  under post-Fordism, 5
  potential of e-commerce, 6, 8
  in the 1980s, 31–2
  'security blanket' in, 9
  in the 21st century, 26–7
global financial stability, 30
global financial stock, growth of, 4
global hegemony, of the US dollar, 31–2
globalisation, 23–4, 36, 38, *see also* arbitrage, study of
global microstructure, notion of, 24
global positioning system (GPS), 26–7, 34

gold, 14, 26, *see also* Bretton Woods Agreement
  standard of the late 19th century, 27–9, 35
Gold Card, 105
golden age, of financial markets, 3–4
Goldsmith, Jim, 186
Gonenç, 184
Gramm, Phil, 195
Grand Cayman's hedge funds, 14, 17
'Granovetterian' sociology, 20, 22
Great Depression era, 104, 128, 131, 141, 143
Greenspan, Alan, 212
Greenwich reference, 26
Growth and Stability Pact, 120–1, 125
Gulf Wars, 16

Haiduk, Kirill, *see* USSR off-shorisation, political economy of,
hedge funds, 38, *see also* arbitrage, study of; long term capital management
heightened financial instability, 1
Herstatt Bank, 208
Hilferding, Rudolf, 141
Holiday Inn motels, 104
hurricanes, in the US, 13
hybrid class, 134

illiquidity, 20, 63, 153
IMF Balance of Payments Manual, 40–1
'impertinent obstructions', 57
implied volatilities, *see* long term capital management
implied volatility, 16
index option, 18
innovation (financial innovation), 1, 2, 4, 9, 11, 159, 161
Institute of Financial Services (IFS), 86
'intangible property', principle of, 179
Intel, 184
Interbank Card Association, 106
Internal Revenue Service (IRS), 130
International Accounting Standards Committee's Framework for the Preparation and Presentation of Financial Statements, 187–8
International Counter-Money Laundering and Financial Anti-Terrorism Act, 194

International Direct Investment (IDI),
    40
International Financial Reporting
    Standards (IFRS), 189
International Monetary Fund, 142, 166
international political economy (IPE),
    25
    literature, on finance, 2
International Portfolio Investment (IPI),
    39
investor euphoria, 8
Italian Banca Nazionale del Lavoro, 121
Italian Central Bank, 121

Jianakoplos, 91
Johnson, Harry, 31–2
JWM partners risk model, 23

Kansas City Board of Trade (KCBOT), 60
Kempson, 81
Keynes
    and gold standard, 29
    idea of speculation, 6–7
    Keynesian compromise, *see*
        neoliberalism
    Keynesian consumer market, 111
    Keynesian demand management and
        full employment policies, 104
    Keynesianism, 29–30
    Keynesian macroeconomics, 137
Konings, Martijn, *see* US financial system
KPMG, 181

Laden, Osama bin, 200
Latin American elections, 13
Leaver, Adam, *see* financial illiteracy
leisure class, 134
Lenin, 141
Levittown, 104
Lévy, Dominique, 73, *see also*
    neoliberalism
LIBOR, 34
'life cycle' model, of pension provision,
    94
liquidity, 28, 62–3, 69, 114, 125, 153,
    154, 156, 158, 159, 164, 211, 217
'lock in' neoliberal policy, 120
long term capital management, 16–20,
    212
    crisis of, 19–20
    and globalisation, *see* globalisation

history of, 17
impact volatilities, 16–18
and mathematical models, 21
Pace standard accounts of, 17
risk model of, 18
and stock options, 18–19
and understanding of arbitrage, 20
LTCM, *see* long term capital
    management

Mackenzie, Donald, *see* arbitrage, study
    of; long term capital management
Madonna, 110
mainstream economists, 5
managerial class, 134
Mantas, 200–1
Markowitz's portfolio theory, 6
Marx, Karl, 131, 133, 141, 146, 177
MasterCard, *see* MasterCharge card
MasterCharge card, 105–6
MBNA, 110
McCarthy, Callum, 203
McCarthyism, 143
McDonalds, 104
McFarlane, John, 80, 85
McNamara, Frank, 103
McRobbie, 76
Meriwether, John, 17, 19, 21
Merrill Lynch study, 123
Merton, Robert C., 15, 17
Merton, Robert K., 20
Microsoft, 180, 182
Mid American Commodity Exchange
    (MidAm), 62
mini-futures contract, *see* derivative
    contracts trading, empirical analysis
    of
Minneapolis Grain Exchange (MGE), 60
Mintel survey 1996, 84
Mitchell, 96
Miyojin, Shigeru, 21
monetarism, theory of, 33, *see also* US
    financial system
money, 26
money laundering, 43, 193, 194–5, 196,
    200–1, 203, 204, 205
MoneyMinded program, 83
'money stock', concept of, 160
'monopoly capital', 180
Montgomerie, Johnna, *see* credit cards
    industry

Mopas, Michael, 199
MORI, 86–7
mugging, concept of, 76
Multinational Corporations (MNCs), 102, 107, 109
Munster, Rens van, 199
Murphy, Richard, 182, *see also* accounting indicators, in capitalist system
Myners report, 91–2

Nasdaq index, 34
National Bank Acts, 154
National Bank of Hungary, 125
national central banks, in the early 20th century, 28
National Council of Farmer Cooperatives (NCFC), 66
National Council on Economic Education (NCEE), 85
neoclassical finance, 16
neoliberal compromise, 134–5
neoliberalism, 31, *see also* Central European Societies, financial regulations on
capital income under, 128–30
and class domination in US, 133–5, 145–6
class patterns and struggle, 140–4
vs earlier Keynesian compromise, 136–40
earning power under, 130–1
economic panics under, 75–9
income and social patterns in France, 135–6, 145
income vs class structure, 131–3
interpretation of, 141
role of labour flexibility in, 34–5
neoliberal policies, 113
Nesvetailova, Anastasia, *see* financial regulation
New York Money Trust, 156
Nixon, 32
noise trading, 15
non-bank financial institutions (NBFIs), 50
non-bank private sector, 13
Nugée, John, *see* financial regulation

occupational pension plans
DC pension plans, *see* DC pension plans
gendered approach, 90–1

OECD book, 74, 83–4
OECD countries, 114, 184, 194
OECD economies, 52
OECD norms, 182
OECD policy, on the prevention of harmful tax competition, 195
OECD's *Principles*, 77
OECD study, 79–80
'off-balance sheet' transactions, 7, 42
offshore financial centres (OFCs), 38
definition of, 45–7
history of, 42–5
hub analysis of, in international capital flows, 49
intra-OFC total assets, 51
O'Harrow, Robert, 196
options, 14–15
Black-Scholes pricing model of, 16, 18
five-year index, 18
index, 18
long expiry, 18
O'Rand, 91
over the counter' transactions, 7
ownership society, 97

Palan, Ronen, *see* accounting indicators, in capitalist system
Parmalat, 9, 183
Parsonian notion, of 'the economy', 16, 22
patents, 179
peak earning years, 94
Peck, 58
pensions, feminisation of, 89
perfect market, 15
permanent optimism, of investors, 114
Persaud, Avinash, *see* financial regulation
'perverse' price mechanism, 178
physical economy, 5
Pin-Fat, Véronique, 196
popularisiation of finance
financial illiteracy, 74
pensions, feminisation of, 89
consumer credit industry, after deregulation, 89
portfolio investment, 40
post-Bretton Woods financial revolution, of world economy, 2–5

post-World War II phenomena of
    internationalisation, by
    multinationals, 40
Presley, Elvis, 110
privatisation of risk, 56, 57, 69
'product benefits card', 109
professional entrepreneur, 6
professional investor, 6
Programme commun de gouvernement of
    1972, 137
promissory notes, 154
Prudential, 81
    Financial Literacy Project of, 82–3
public indignation, 78

Rafferty, Mike, *see* global finance,
    patterns of; offshore financial
    centres (OFCs)
Raviv, Or, *see* Central European
    Societies, financial regulations on
'real bills' doctrine, 157
Reid, Julian, 201
repo, 21
(risk) gender and, 95–100
risk perceptions, 99
risk tolerance, 98
Rolls Royce, 186
Royal Dutch/Shell group, 21, 24
ruling classes, 134
Russian banks, 19
Russia's off-shorisation, political
    economy of
    American Express survey of, 169
    dimension of capital mobility, 167–9
    distribution of foreign investment in
        Russia, 168
    OECD report, 174–5
    and post-Soviet state transformation,
        172–6
    rise and decline of domestic offshore
        in Russia, 120–2

Salomon group, 17, 21
Samuelson, Paul, 23
'satellite cities', *see* ZATO
Scholes, Myron, 15–18
Schumpeterian creative destruction, 6
Searchspace technology, 201
Sears Reobuck, 110
securities investment, 6
securitisation, 7–8, 107–11, 158

effect on Balance of Payments, 45–6
security transfer station, 39
Services Against Financial Exclusion
    (SAFE), 203
short sell, 15, 21
short-term bills of exchange, 152
Shuey, 91
Singapore dollar bonds, 34
Slovic, 99
small and medium enterprises (SMEs),
    123–4
Smith, Nick, 62
Snyder, Ralph, 103
social agendas, 28
social exclusion, 71, 80–1
social-liberal society, 139
Solomon Brothers Bank, 108
special purpose vehicles (SPVs), 39
S&P 500 index, 16, 18
'spot' markets, 14
Standard Accounting Practice, 12, 186
standard contract, *see* derivative
    contracts trading, empirical analysis
    of
Steinherr, Alfred, 56, 58
stockmarket crash 1987, 16
structural liquidity surplus, state of, 125
swapping, 21
swap spreads, 24
systemic risk, 8, 9, 114, 150, 207, 209,
    213, 214, 215–17

Terrorist Financing Rewards Program, 200
Thatcher, Margaret, 76
*The ACCA/BAA Distinguished Academic
    1999 Lecture*, 178
The Guardian, 202
theoretical pricing, 14
Third Money Laundering Directive, 195
Thornton, 76
Tickell, Adam, 60
'toll-free telephone number', 82
trademark, 179
Transportation Security Administration
    (TSA), 198
TravelPlus airline card, 109
Turkish government bonds, 13

UK Financial Services Authority (FSA),
    196, 203, 208
UK Pensions Commission reports, 80

UN Security Council Resolution 1373, 194
UN Security Council Resolution 1377, 194
USA Patriot Act, 194, 201
US Commission on Consumer Finance, 107
USDA Agricultural Census data, 59, 67
USDA Value Added Producer Grant Program, 66
US Federal Reserve, 32, 39, 43, 81, 127, 140, 142, 155–8, 160–1, 163–4, 212, *see also* US financial system
US financial system, *see also* neoliberalism
  contradictions of, during post-World War II period, 158–60
  Federal Reserve System, 155–7
  foundation of, 152–5
  monetarium and, 160–3
  new forms of Federal Reserve Control, 163–4
US laws, 107, 112
US Steel Trust, 179
US Technology and Privacy Advisory Committee (TPAC), 202
US-VISIT programme, 199
Utkus, 96

'value-at-risk' price model, 17–18
Valverde, Mariana, 199

Veblen, 180, 187
Vietnam War, 30, 43
Vodafone, 189
Volcker, Paul, 32, 142, 160
Volcker shock of 1979–82, 31–2, 37, 161–3

Waine, 92–3
Walby, 90
Walker, Slater, 186
Warnock, 52
Warren, 94
Washington consensus, 95
'wealth effect', 114
Western economy, 17
Wharton Business School, 85
Wigan, Duncan, *see* financial regulation
Williams, Karel, *see* financial illiteracy
Wood River Capital Management, 39
World Bank, 142
WorldCom, 78
World War II, 104, 128, 131, 133, 143, 158–60
Wyatt, Watson, 91

ZATO, 170, 173
zero-coupon yields, 13
Zhang, Wei, *see* financial illiteracy